QUILT TREASURES

QUILT TREASURES

THE QUILTERS' GUILD HERITAGE SEARCH

PHOTOGRAPHS BY DAVID CRIPPS

The
Quilters' Guild

Published by The Quilters' Guild of the British Isles in 2010.
First published in 1995 by Deirdre McDonald Books, London.

The Quilters' Guild of the British Isles
St Anthony's Hall, Peasholme Green
York YO1 7PW

Registered Charity Number 1067361
Company Registration 344 7631

ISBN 978-0-9564789-0-0

Printed and bound by Montgomery Litho Group, Glasgow

Frontispiece: This quilt was made to celebrate Queen Victoria's Jubilee in 1887.
202cm x 204 cm (6 ft 7 in x 6 ft 8 in).

CONTENTS

ACKNOWLEDGEMENTS

The British Quilt Heritage Project was initially made possible through a generous donation by a Guild member, the late Angela Brocklebank. Other financial help of varying types was subsequently given by the Radcliffe Trust, the Broderers Charity Trust, the Save & Prosper Trust, the Welsh Arts Council, Highlands & Islands Enterprise, Ross & Cromarty Enterprise, Polaroid Ltd and Fiskars UK Ltd. The Quilters' Guild wishes to record its deep appreciation for the generosity of all these donors.

Without the support of its members, many of whom gave prizes for raffles or undertook individual fund-raising projects, The Quilters' Guild documentation programme would have been impossible. Thanks and special recognition must go to all those Guild co-ordinators and representatives who organized local venues and staffing, dealt with the media, sold raffle tickets and helped with the queues. The project would not have succeeded without the enthusiastic support of these organizers and their helpers – none of whom flinched from the kitchen work and dispensing countless cups of coffee, or the sheer physical labour of dealing with a perpetual stream of bags and bundles of quilts moving through the examination and photographic processes.

Many textile specialists lent a helping hand during the course of the Project, as did collectors Jen Jones and Ron Simpson. The Guild is grateful for their involvement as well as the contribution by David Cripps and his assistant, Paul Westbrook, who demonstrated patience and good humour in equal measure throughout the three-year programme. Their special skills and visual expertise added an important dimension to the Project's success.

Since it was first published in 1995, *Quilt Treasures* has proved an invaluable reference for those interested in the unique character of British quilts. The book has an international audience and, in addition to stimulating further research, it has provided inspiration for those practitioners of the craft who want to know more about their heritage. The Guild, an educational charity, has had many requests for the book to be reprinted. In undertaking this task, it would especially like to record its thanks to six of the seven original authors and to QGBI Enterprises.

PREFACE

THE BRITISH QUILT Heritage Project, launched by The Quilters' Guild in 1990, had two important aims. Recording the special historic character and artistic skills of Britain's quiltmakers and the social and economic conditions in which they worked was of prime importance. The secondary aim was to raise public awareness and appreciation of this particular aspect of textile heritage and also to educate families to cherish and take proper care of quilts in their possession. The Guild, an educational charity, organized and raised money for this research programme.

The documentation phase of the Project opened in Chester in October 1990 and finished in Carmarthen in November 1993. During that three-year period, 3,967 items – quilts (finished and unfinished), small domestic articles and quilted and patchwork clothing – were brought to twenty-nine different documentation-day venues in England, Wales and Scotland. In addition, a small team went to the Isle of Man to record quilts there and several private collections were seen and noted, making a total of 4,183 items. Every member of the public who participated in the Project was given a copy of *Quilt Care in the Home*, a booklet published by The Quilters' Guild Heritage Committee.

In undertaking such a massive programme of documentation, the Guild decided it would aim its research at patchwork and quilting made prior to 1960, since that date marked a resurgence of the craft. It was also made clear that the Project would encompass not only patchwork and wholecloth quilts made in the UK but also fragments, costume and other small items showing these techniques. As expected, a number of quilts turned up that had been made in North America (and other places) – also 'quilts' which were knitted, crocheted, or of the woven Marcella variety, and the thick, satin-covered comforters that were popular from the 1930s to the 1960s.

Prior to the outset of the Project, careful consideration was given not only to the kind of question that would be put to quilt owners regarding family history and the quiltmaker but also to the technical information that would be required. Documentation forms that had been used on a number of American projects were consulted: however, it soon became apparent that many of the questions they asked were not relevant to the British tradition. Through a wide process of consultation with quilt historians in the UK and abroad, two different lines of questioning and examination evolved: the first concerned social history, attempting to put the quiltmaker in the context of her (or his) environment, work and economic and social life; the second was technical. Examiners were asked to record both quilting and patchwork patterns, sewing techniques, embellishments, fabrics, methods of construction, size, colour, filling and finishing. In retrospect, additional technical questions could have been asked (e.g. thread colour, which grew in importance as more wholecloth quilts were examined), but then the parameters had to be defined.

The attempt to record social history proved disappointing, since a large number of quilts brought for recording had no known provenance. In only a few cases was the name of the maker known. The more usual comments were: 'I found this in a trunk/attic/my mother's house when I was clearing it out'; or 'I bought this in an auction sale/market/antique shop and I don't know where it came from'. Even in cases where quilts had been handed down in the family, there was generally only a vague idea of their exact origins and usually some confusion about whether the quilts had been made by, say, a grandmother or great-grandmother. Some people who had been quite emphatic in providing specific dates were proved wrong as a result of technical examination of the fabrics.

The Quilters' Guild is structured into eighteen regions in the UK, and initially it was hoped to hold at least two documentation days in each region. For various reasons (financial and staffing) this did not always work out. Northern Ireland was left out of the project altogether because of the documentation work already carried on there by the Ulster Folk & Transport Museum in Holywood, while Scotland, because of the distances involved, required four documentation days.

Local Guild members (usually regional co-ordinators or representatives) took on the job of finding venues, establishing media relations, organizing coffee for members of the public and lunch for the workers, not to mention staffing arrangements. In addition to the regular documentation team, it often required up to thirty people to make a documentation day operate smoothly.

For some years prior to the Project, a Guild member, the late Sybil Lewis, had been compiling a directory of heritage quilts, showing where they were to be found in Britain. This directory proved valuable as the Project got under way, in that it became possible to approach known owners and invite them to bring their quilts for recording. Museum collections, with one or two exceptions, were generally not included because it was felt that these quilts were already in the public domain.

The complex job of planning and working out the logistics of the documentation days – liaising with local Guild organizers, finding accommodation and often making travel and other arrangements and moving equipment – was shouldered by Jean Roberts, Project Co-ordinator. Jean also undertook the daunting task of collecting all the completed forms and, with the help of Caroline Louden, putting the data into the special computer which had been purchased for the Project.

At the beginning of the Project an important decision was taken about photography. Polaroid shots were used to help with initial identification, but rather than take record snapshots and have to recall quilts for professional photography it was decided that the Project would use the services of a professional photographer from the outset. Fortunately this job was taken on by David Cripps, MBE, who has a special affinity for photographing textiles, and occasionally David's assistant, Paul Westbrook. Although not every single quilt was photographed by David (lack of time and poor definition made it too difficult to photograph the bulk of the wholecloth quilts, so other methods of recording patterns were adopted), the majority of items brought to the documentation days were visually recorded.

In addition to the services of David Cripps, the Project was most fortunate in securing the help of Deryn O'Connor, retired principal lecturer in printed textiles at Farnham College, Surrey. The role that Deryn and Tina Fenwick Smith, then curator of the Guild's Averil Colby Fabric Collection, played cannot be overstressed: their knowledge and ability to date eighteenth- and nineteenth-century

DOCUMENTATION
DAYS

*Numbers in brackets refer to items
brought to venues*

• Inverness
(135)

• Paisley
(144)
• Edinburgh
(107)

• Kelso
(129)

• Chester-le-Street
(66)

• Penrith
(146)
• Bowes
(270)

• Isle of Man
(74)

Preston • • Halifax
(88)   (102)

• Chester
(135)

• Nottingham
(265)

• Harleston
(157)

• Shrewsbury
(93)
• Knowle
(96)

• Swavesey
(192)

• Carmarthen
(192)
• Hereford
(95)

• Chelmsford
(114)

• Grove
(137)
• London (118)

• Pontypridd
(228)

• Portishead (67)
• Dulwich (183)

• Saltford
(44)
• Basingstoke
(165)
• East Grinstead
(148)

• Exeter
(118)
• Dorchester
(147)

• Truro
(86)

printed fabric gave the British Quilt Heritage Project a unique advantage.

The aforementioned and regular members of the documentation team (those who travelled to most venues) included the Guild's then Heritage officer, Janet Rae, who worked in a supervisory role; then curator of the Guild's Heritage Quilt Collection, Dinah Travis; Margaret Tucker, who had special knowledge of textile conservation; and Pauline Adams and Bridget Long, who took on the specific remit of looking at wholecloth quilts and quilting patterns. One of the Guild's founder members and quilt collectors, the late Angela Brocklebank, took part frequently as an examiner, and other textile specialists contributed their expertise as the Project progressed. These included author Dorothy Osler, a former Guild Heritage Officer with special knowledge of North Country quilting; Clare Rose, a freelance textile historian and author; Mary Brooks, then textile conservator at York Castle Museum; Rosemary Blackett Ord, who has special knowledge of chintz quilts, and Christine Stevens, from the Department of Farming, Crafts & Cultural Life, the Welsh Folk Museum, St Fagans.

Documentation days, as they progressed, often became likened to the textile version of an antiques roadshow. There was a major difference: as an educational charity, the Guild was unable to become involved in making valuations and some members of the public found this disappointing. Generally, however, public reaction to the Project and the co-operation with it was overwhelming. With an average number of 137 quilts being brought to each venue, it was impossible to avoid queuing and people proved extremely patient. When the documentation day was held at Bowes Museum in Barnard Castle, Co. Durham, the turnout – of 270 – was so large that, regrettably, people had to be turned away although additional examiners had been drafted in for the day.

Such was the general interest in the Project that many members of the public who had brought quilts got caught up with the enthusiasm of it all and stayed and stayed and stayed. The process of examination, in which owners were invited to participate, together with the very act of hanging the quilts for photographs, provided a special kind of quilt show that many found hard to resist. The woman in Chester who asked a Guild helper to phone her husband and tell him to 'make his own lunch' because she wasn't going to hurry home was not unusual: people who thought they could speed through the examination process generally took delays in good humour, and through interest, decided that they weren't in such a hurry after all. Such attitudes, interest and co-operation made the British Quilt Heritage Project an enormous public success, and helped fulfil all of the Guild's initial aims and objectives.

MOVING ON

Since *Quilt Treasures* first appeared in 1995, research into British quiltmaking heritage has moved on dramatically. The Quilters' Guild of the British Isles, always at the forefront of new development, has continued to lead the way in its support of heritage activities, education and exhibitions.

The Guild is an educational charity and in 1998 it formed the British Quilt Study Group (BQSG) to encourage more specific research into quilt history. The BQSG programme of activities includes a yearly seminar. The research papers presented are published each year in *Quilt Studies* and the subject matter is varied, ranging from fabrics to the Turkey Red dyeing industry, technical methods of working, social and family histories relating to specific quilts, and historic trends.

Research into the quilting tradition has meant the publication of more books, the development of on-line discussion groups and even the inclusion of quilt studies into academic programmes. Additionally, individual museums, including the Bowes Museum in the North of England; the Musee des Traditions et Arts Normands in France; the Dutch Open Air Museum at Arnhem in the Netherlands; the Museum of European Cultures, National Museum in Berlin, Germany; the new International Quilt Study Center and Museum in Lincoln, Nebraska, USA; and the Victoria & Albert Museum in London have stimulated interest with major exhibitions of historic quilts and international symposiums. And the recording of quilts in private ownership has continued to spread. This activity, which originated in the United States, in recent years has been taken up by individual historians and other guilds in European countries and Australia.

Quilt history research is as much about the makers as the quilts. Often the human interest stories bring a few surprises. In amending this new edition, for example, the authors were delighted to learn that the Gilfach Goch Quilting Group in Porth, under threat 15 years ago (see page 144), has been revitalised and its membership increased to twelve! The one incident that seems to have interrupted the weekly quilting bees was a lorry backing into their hall! The group, now in a new hall, has three quilting frames permanently on the go and Mrs Lorraine Bryant, once the organiser and chief marker of traditional Welsh designs, still 'mentors' the meetings – at age 94!

One side effect of the British Quilt Heritage Project was the growth of the Guild's own quilt collection, either through donation or purchase. Begun in the early 1980s when quilts were collected to provide a reference for study, the Guild now owns the largest quilt collection in the UK.

The Collection focuses exclusively on quilts made in Britain and includes some notable items: the '1718 Silk Patchwork Coverlet', the oldest known dated patchwork; items made by influential mid-20th century quiltmakers, authors and teachers; a group of important nineteenth century silk and velvet pieced bed coverings, including a unique quilt made to commemorate Queen Victoria's Golden Jubilee (see frontispiece); a pair of signed and dated mid-nineteenth century coverlets that contain religious phrases and biblical quotations; a rare late 18th century Broderie Perse coverlet; and the Averil Colby fabric collection of printed and woven fabrics from the late 18th century through to the mid 20th century.

In its 29th year, the Guild took another major step forward by relocating its registered Heritage Collection and its national headquarters from Halifax, Yorkshire to St Anthony's Hall in York. Previously, access to its Collection was mainly through loans to major British museums and other institutions abroad. The largest ever loan of over 40 pieces went to Tokyo in 2006, where it was seen by 250,000 people.

St Anthony's Hall is one of York's famous medieval guildhalls and its renovation by York Conservation Trust has provided the Guild with exceptional spaces for exhibitions, educational activities and research facilities. Revenue grants from the Heritage Lottery Fund and financial support from the Arts Council for the opening exhibition, helped fund the enterprise. The Quilt Museum and Gallery is officially 'Accredited' by the Museums Libraries and Archives Council (MLA) for meeting national standards in its operation, the services it provides to visitors and the way it looks after its collections. A challenging exhibition schedule that shares heritage quilts with the general public and also shows new textile work, plus a lively education programme for people of all ages, makes St Anthony's Hall one of York's most exciting new venues.

Below left: The '1718 Silk Patchwork Coverlet' is one of the Guild's most treasured textiles. The coverlet has a unique mix of patchwork blocks and images, all pieced over papers. The initials EH and the date are included in the piecing.

Below right: St Anthony's Hall, York, home of the Quilt Museum and Gallery and national headquarters of The Quilters' Guild of the British Isles.

Fig. 1.1. 1915 tea cosy created from silk cigarette cards. See reverse and detail on page 11.

Fig. 1.2. Detail of Land Army quilt. See page 14.

CHAPTER 1

WHY MAKE A QUILT?

Janet Rae

DURING THE PAST three hundred years, quiltmaking, as a craft, has been practised with skill ranging from the superb to the indifferent on a variety of good and poor cloths and for many different reasons.

Not all men and women who have undertaken to make a quilt have shown artistic talent or even an appreciation of colour. Indeed two hundred years ago, in some circles, such notions would probably have caused dismay, if not merriment. Where nowadays many quiltmakers approach their work with purely artistic motives, such objectives would have been quite foreign in a society where the main concerns were very practical: food, clothing and warmth.

If talking about patchwork design, then the British tradition once considered to be primarily mosaic (of the type described in Chap. 3) holds a few surprises: block patchwork with simple geometric forms was undertaken in Britain long before the American influence crossed the ocean. More importantly, from the late eighteenth century, British quiltmakers were working the unique frame layout described in Chapter 2. The wholecloth quilt, another British tradition, also developed its own special character - practicality may have been a guiding force but there was no shortage of artistic input in terms of pattern.

To ask why a particular quilt was made opens many other intriguing avenues of enquiry. Poverty was often the motivating factor behind the making of utilitarian bed covers, which were put together with odd scraps and worn remnants and filled with whatever happened to be to hand. However, some items such as the nineteenth-century Broderie Perse coverlets were meant to be decorative, while other quilts were made as gifts, in the name of friendship, for competitions, to raise money, or to demonstrate political or religious affiliations. Furthermore, to many men and women, particularly in the North of England, quiltmaking was a source of income – they plied the needle as a means of putting food on the table.

Quiltmaking also has a celebratory context in Britain – birth and marriage. During the British Quilt Heritage Project only a small number of cot quilts – forty-six – were offered for examination, but this is only to be expected with an item requiring such frequent washing. Death, the third great human event, was not definitely identified as a reason for making a quilt, although one mystery quilt from Caithness appeared which perhaps would have fitted into this category: made in all-over hexagons dating from about 1870, it had a white rosette centre with the words 'In Remembrance' appliquéd in black and the initial 'M' in the centre. This centrepiece, however, was a replacement and no explanation could be given about the quilt by the present owner. A Suffolk-puff quilt with a central cross raised similar speculation about the intentions of the maker, but, again, no detail was available. (Research in America has identified many different types of mourning or 'memory' quilts.)

The British Quilt Heritage Project threw up quilts that had been made for a variety of reasons, but one of the most common explanations offered was that the quilt was for a 'bottom drawer' or wedding. Over 300 quilts were designated thus. Many of these attributions, however, were speculative – which is perhaps indicative of the general romance often attached to the craft. Dealing with family 'legend' also contributed to confusion, as in the case of an Essex family with a Turkey Red and white quilt of squares embroidered with names, initials, places and simple designs. Family legend said that it was either a wedding present or had been made as a fund-raiser for the local church. There were few family names on the quilt, however, but quite a large number from the Great Yeldham area, so the fund-raising option was the likelier of the two;

and, in any event, the quilt was very much in the genre of those discussed in Chapter 8. The original owner, Mrs Herbert Brown of Chipping Ongar, was probably the raffle winner. She used the quilt to cover and protect a large mirror during bombing raids in World War II, one of the interesting bits of information that was offered as 'an aside'.

A commemorative wedding quilt that includes fabric from brides' dresses is shown on page 147. Another quilt with wedding associations was that made by Edith Blenkin in 1930 and used only as a display cloth for presents at family weddings. Mrs Blenkin came from a family of lead miners in Weardale and her husband, Henry, was a cashier at Shildon Wagonworks (he also made his wife's quilt frames). Mrs Blenkin was a keen member of the New Shildon Women's Institute and, during World War I when her husband was in the Services, she held his job until his return. Her quilt in cream cotton sateen was laid out in medallion fashion with three borders. The quilted patterns included a chequerboard of circles with single knots in the middle; two feather borders with roses at the corners and a border of circles, also with corner roses.

Some family stories about quilts were very romantic. One such concerned Bonnie Prince Charlie. The quilt, made in silks, velvet and brocade, with pieced hexagons, squares and triangles, set in a frame layout, allegedly included a panel that had come from his waistcoat. Indeed the panel was of some interest, being embellished with laid and couched threads, including some gold thread. The rest of the fabrics were very much from the 1850-1900 period, however, and no documentary evidence was available to back up the Prince Charlie association.

Several Northumberland quilts examined during the course of the Project also carried reference to Joe the Quilter, one of quilting's greatest legends. Joe was a professional quilter in Northumberland who was murdered in 1826, allegedly for the money he was believed to have earned from his profession. He was aged seventy-six at the time and the crime was particularly violent, but no one was ever caught. His cottage in the village of Warden was pulled down in 1872 and he remains to this day one of the area's most captivating legends. Attributing quilts with certainty to this professional maker is, however, very difficult, if not impossible. Although several quilts were described as possibly made by Joe the Quilter, there was no evidence to support this belief.

Patchwork as a Substitute

Quilts by another legendary figure in quilting, born almost seventy-five years after Joe's death, were thankfully more easy to identify. Averil Colby (1900-1983) is well known to quilt historians for her

Fig. 1.3. Averil Colby's love of gardening was a major influence in her work.

books on patchwork and quilting. She is equally identified with that most English of patchwork shapes, the hexagon, and one of her pieces of work was recorded (see fig.3.8, p.43).

Miss Colby's passion for patchwork bears some consideration, especially when discussing reasons why people made quilts. Born in Yorkshire and educated at Cheltenham Ladies' College, Averil Colby studied horticulture at Studley Agricultural College in Warwickshire. For some years after finishing her studies, she ran a forty-acre smallholding in Somerset with a friend. When the two women 'fell out', Miss Colby moved to live with her mother in Devon, the two finally going to live in Liss in Hampshire. It was at this particular stage of her life, and while she was missing her beloved garden, that she decided to join a local branch of the Women's Institute and took part in making a quilt. She found

Fig. 1.4. Silk, velvet and brocade were used by a Scottish Women's Rural Institute group to make this elaborate table cover during World War I.
100 cm x 163 cm (3 ft 4 in x 5 ft 4 in).

it a very satisfying replacement for her gardening activities.

> ... being deprived of her outdoor activities there was no doubt great satisfaction was derived in making her garden bloom via patchwork. Wreaths, rosettes, swags, trails etc. of flowers, all executed in hexagons, are the hallmark of Miss Colby's patchwork.[1]

Miss Colby later returned to Somerset and resumed her career as a gardener. Aside from a spell in the Land Army during World War II, she spent the rest of her life in the Old Court House, a house dating from the seventeenth century.

She was nearly sixty when she took up her writing career after being approached by the firm of Batsford, who asked her to write a book on patchwork. That book, published in 1958, was followed by four more: *Samplers* in 1964; *Patchwork Quilts* in 1965; *Quilting* in 1972; and *Pincushions* in 1975. The books in themselves made her something of an authority on the craft but added to that was her practical involvement. For a time she was associated with Miss Muriel Rose, who ran a small shop, off Sloane Street in London, called the Little Gallery. The Gallery promoted the work of leading craftspeople and Miss Rose played a major role in re-establishing patchwork and quilting in Wales. One of the major commissions she took at this time was an order from Claridge's Hotel for quilted bed covers to use in their new Art Deco wing.

It is generally accepted that Miss Colby helped Miss Rose as a designer, a fact which often causes some confusion: the meticulous hexagon quilts bearing the Colby 'look' were often stitched by others, but to Miss Colby's designs. Certainly Miss Colby had help when samples were required for her books – there would naturally have been a limit to the amount of work she was able to carry out, especially with her other commitments. One of these commitments was an active role in the Federation of Women's Institutes: from 1956 to 1961 she was chairman of the national organization's Handicrafts Committee.

Miss Colby had very definite ideas about quiltmaking. She believed in hand sewing, as opposed to machine sewing, and she believed that quilts should be used. She also thought patchwork an excellent method of teaching plain sewing and considered that there were two things a patchworker should never do: '(1) use unsuitable materials or use materials in an unsuitable way; (2) sew badly'.[2] She was a fanatical forager of fabrics: the floral ones she accumulated were used to special advantage in her hexagon garden patchwork, where bouquets or beds of flowers were specially assembled out of many different floral prints.

A Reason to Socialize

Many modern quiltmakers would endorse Miss Colby's love of textiles as a reason for making quilts. But, of course, patchwork and quilting can also be very sociable activities and many quilts made by groups surfaced during the British Quilt Heritage Project. In addition to the group quilts discussed in Chapter 8, many of which were made to raise money, reference should be made to the Women's Institute (WI) quilts, made as presentations, including the one shown on page 38 and the table cover made in Angus for

Fig. 1.5. Cotton dressmaking and shirting samples from the 1930s.

Queen Elizabeth The Queen Mother during World War I. Glamis Castle, where The Queen Mother (then Lady Elizabeth Bowes Lyon) resided, was turned into a convalescent home during the War and Lady Elizabeth did as much as she was able to help the patients there. The table cover, made by the local branch of the Scottish Women's Rural Institutes, was a gift to Lady Elizabeth, who in turn handed it back to be raffled in aid of a wartime cause. The present owner inherited it from the raffle winner. It has an unusual design – a pieced twelve-petal dahlia in metallic brocades, silks and velvets (see fig.1.4, p.6).

Competitions, another reason for quiltmaking, also were mentioned during the Project. The Eisteddfodau, the traditional music, literature and fine-arts festivals held in Wales, were cited several times. 'She was an Eisteddfod winner' was a frequent comment. Eisteddfodau were held at both local and national level and no distinction was made in the documentation programme between these categories so far as quiltmaking was concerned. A glimpse at just one national Eisteddfod programme, however, gives a flavour of the event with regard to quilting: at the height of the effort by the Rural Industries Bureau to revive the craft, in 1928, a prize of £1 10s was awarded to someone from the Rhondda Valley who had entered a quilt in the General Domestic Craft category of the National Eisteddfod. The quilt is described as being for a double bed and hand-sewn, but regrettably no other details are given.

The majority of quilts claiming an Eisteddfod connection that were brought for examination were not identified as entries or prize winners – nor were they necessarily, as might have been expected, in the tradition of Welsh wholecloth quilting. A quilt made by Margaret Williams (see p.140) of Gwaun-cae-Gurwen, South Wales, in 1930 was a cut-and-fold Turkey Red on white appliqué; while a quilt made by Edith Mary Hodgkiss, of Llangynidr, Powys, a frequent winner of prizes for embroidery, was created in a pieced frame design, with a pinwheel centre in blue and red. This frame quilt by Edith Hodgkiss, nee Pugh, together with a second wholecloth quilt, was believed to have been made before her marriage in 1919. Edith worked as a housekeeper/cook before she married and it is thought that the second quilt with its elaborate quilting design was made for her bottom drawer.

Fabric Led

Some quilts that were documented were 'fabric led' in that they were made of fabric samples. If resourcefulness is part of your nature, then how else would you make effective use of small rectangles of cloth? Men's suiting samples were particularly predominant in this category and many warm quilts were made of these pieces, often put together with decorative embroidery stitches (see fig.3.4, p.38). Use was made too of cotton shirting and dressmaking samples – particularly of the colourful type shown in figure 1.5 on page 7.

The captivating printed panels of children's pictures also inspired a quilt in the nineteenth century. Circus, farmyard, sport and winter scenes are a few of the topics portrayed in the thirty-two different panels. Each panel is titled. 'The Toy Man' is shown in figure 1.6 on page 10; others include 'Snowballing the Bully', 'My New Boat' and 'Tip us a Copper, Won't You?' The quilt was reported to have belonged to the family of the vicar of Buckland in Surrey.

The variety of fabrics used for quilts offered some surprises: two quilts were created out of pink corset material! The first, made in the 1930s, had been purchased in a charity shop. Fashioned in a crazy pattern, and decorated with green embroidery featherstitch, it contains pieces of plain pink satin which have been turned in different directions, thus changing the reflection of light on the fabric (see fig.1.7 p.11). The second corset quilt, made about the same time, was composed of elongated hexagons set in rows. It had been stitched by an elderly lady whose friend worked in a Spirella factory in Wrexham and contained many different pink corset fabrics. Spirella agents worked from home, having been trained by the firm to measure and fit clients. Like others in the same business, they took orders for a variety of different types of foundation garments that were made of silk, satin rayon, satin-backed crepe and satin batiste. The predominant colours were white, tea-rose pink and peach and the garments were boned with spiral steel.

Yet another example of small pieces of cloth being put to economic use could be found in the many tea cosies and cushions presented for documentation. Many of these had been made in the tradition of crazy patchwork and used luxury fabrics such as silk and velvet. Of the sixteen tea cosies recorded, perhaps the most interesting was one made in 1915 containing printed silks which had been issued by the British cigarette manufacturers Godfrey Phillips. The firm, which put these silk pictures in cigarette packets between 1911 and 1925, issued over 100 different series depicting a variety of subjects. The tea cosy pictured in figure 1.8 on page 11 was obviously made by a collector of the different silks, for it contains pictures from different series: flowers, portraits of famous people, footballers etc. Godfrey Phillips was not the only firm to put silk 'cards' in cigarette packets: J. Wix, manufacturers of Kensitas, produced its series of flower silks between 1934 and 1935 and a range of British Empire flag and national flag silks the year before that.

THE TOY MAN

Fig. 1.6. Printed panels depicting many different scenes were used to create a quilt for a Surrey family. C. 1850-70. 160 cm x 246 cm (5 ft 3 in x 8 ft).

Costume, Quilts and Wartime

Some of the reasons offered for making quilts, especially those using recycled fabrics, also applied to pieces of costume examined during the Project. Although there were not many examples, costume was seen often enough to give an indication of the uses of patchwork and quilting techniques during different periods of fashion. The 1930s quilted housecoats and bedjackets, discussed in Chapter 5, were quite at variance with the elegant 'undress' of the eighteenth century and with the 'make do' housecoats produced during the War.

Contrary to hopes and expectations, very few quilted nineteenth-century petticoats – especially important for warmth but also relevant to fashion – were brought for documentation (see, however, an eighteenth-century example on p.71). And a quilted christening cape, made by a Durham midwife in 1883 for her own son, had been created from purchased quilted fabric and trimmed with four tassels. The maker was a member of the local Methodist

Fig. 1.7. Scraps of pink satin from a corset factory were used to make this crazy quilt in the 1930s. The quilt was backed with Argentinian sugar sacks.
160 cm x 183 cm (5 ft 2 in x 6 ft).

Fig. 1.8. A 1915 tea cosy made of silk cigarette 'cards', believed to be printed by Godfrey Phillips. See also detail.

Chapel quilting club, a club whose members exercised their skills to raise money for the Chapel. Other items, including two waistcoats and two skirts, had foreign origins. One waistcoat, believed to have Eastern European origins, had no provenance, while the second, in orange and white (Robbing Peter to Pay Paul pattern), was made from a recycled old quilt and had been purchased in a quilt shop in San Francisco.

Probably the most poignant items of patchwork and quilting presented for documentation were those associated with war. The Red Cross quilts that came in charity bundles from Canada during World War II are described in Chapter 7. A map of the battlefields, printed after the invasion of Belgium in 1914, ended up as the centrepiece of another quilt, made by Mary Jane Morgan-Richards in Wales. The map (see fig.1.9), originally printed in the *Manchester Guardian*, had been reproduced on cream cotton for sale to the public and Mary Jane used it, together with furnishing cottons, to piece a quilt with eight frames (see fig.1.10).

In addition to these were the examples of patchwork clothing which had been made as a result of the wartime rationing of clothing. Many people were pushed into recycling, and dressing gowns sewn in a crazy pattern were a favourite. Magazines of the time helped to promote this useful pastime, according to one former secretary in the Women's Auxiliary Air Force (WAAF) who taught herself crazy patchwork after seeing an illustration in a magazine. She managed to find a paper pattern for a housecoat and cut the pieces from butter muslin. Then she applied pieces of cotton, silk, crepe, rayon, georgette and seersucker with herringbone stitch. She began working on her garment in 1941 and took it with her as she was moved about the country with the WAAF, finally finishing it with an old blackout-curtain lining in 1945. It had never been worn.

Two other crazy patchwork dressing gowns were lined with parachute silk. Both had been made in 1946 by a farmer's wife for her daughter to take to boarding school: one dressing gown was for the daughter and the other for the daughter's doll. Machined with pieces of cotton, silk, velvet, linen, rayon and wool, the gowns were made without any decorative embroidery stitching.

Among some of the most interesting examples of wartime recycling were two pairs of crazy patchwork slippers that had been brought to the Truro documentation day. The shoes had been made in 1942 for a 'make do and mend' demonstration by a Launceston teacher. Created from recycled velvet fabrics, the slippers had soles of plaited wool coat material and were lined in black. The lacing holes of the slippers had been piped and the 'laces' were handmade cord with tassels.

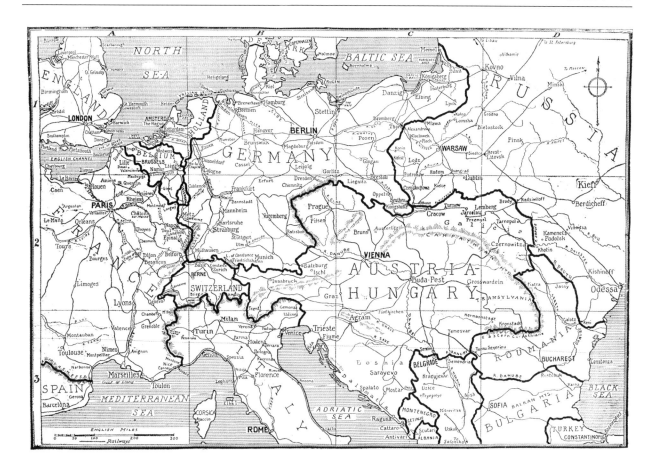

Fig. 1.9. A map of the World War I land campaign, originally published on 7 August 1914 in the *Manchester Guardian*, was subsequently printed on cotton. One quiltmaker at least used the map as the centrepiece of a quilt, see below. (© *The British Library Board*)

Fig. 1.10. Frames of floral furnishing fabrics, all heavily quilted, were used to emphasize the map.
197 cm x 215 cm (6 ft 7 in x 7 ft 4 in).

Another memorable example of World War II work was a wholecloth quilt commemorating the work of the Land Army (see fig.1.11). It was made by Elizabeth Hamilton in 1946-7 as part of a post-diploma course at Edinburgh College of Art – a course which had been interrupted by the war. Elizabeth, who opted to join the Land Army rather than one of the other services, was given some initial training at an agricultural college before being sent to a farm near Perth, where she had to finish the morning milking by 6.30 a.m. and where she worked a fourteen-hour day during harvest. Life on the second farm to which she was assigned – a hill farm near Ballinluig – was slightly less onerous but she still undertook almost all of the duties previously assigned to the men. These included (when the ground was frozen and could not be worked) felling trees for firewood and dragging the larch and pine logs out of the forest, with the help of a horse. Elizabeth worked as a Land Girl for five years and ultimately became a teacher of art. But the quilt she made reflects the many different types of activities she was engaged in during the war. The quilting patterns (her own design) include the Land Army insignia and the farm work she undertook, ranging from driving a tractor to feeding the chickens.

Fig. 1.11. *Opposite.* Detail of Land Army commemorative quilt made by Elizabeth Hamilton after World War II.
199 cm x 232 cm (6 ft 6 in x 7 ft 7 in).

Fig. 2.1. *Right:* Detail of frame quilt from Cornwall. See p. 30.

Below: Fig. 2.2. Centre panel of double-sided early nineteenth century quilt. See p. 34.

Fig. 2.3. *Above:* Detail of silk patchwork quilt made by Mary Jane Scott. See p. 22.

CHAPTER 2

IN THE FRAME

Janet Rae

ONE CAN ONLY speculate about the design influences at work when, in the last century, quiltmakers such as the four Thornton sisters of Mirfield, Yorkshire, sat down with their sewing. The sisters were obviously fond of patchwork, yet why did they decide to use the same layout for all of their quilts – frames or borders around a central square?

Each of the four quilts attributed to this family (and fortunately all have survived in pristine condition) was painstakingly created: three of the quilts have printed oval panels as centres, with up to ten pieced frames, while the fourth has a dahlia-style centre with leaves (see fig.2.4, p.18). Two of the Thornton quilts are almost identical in their use of framed piecing patterns, the chief difference being the printed panel centres: one panel was manufactured in 1805 and the other in 1810. That quiltmaking, of whatever description, was a customary pursuit in the family is known from family records dating from 1798, when a 'twilting frame' was mentioned in an inventory of goods belonging to Joseph Thornton, Quarry Place, Mirfield, Yorkshire. These items were made over to his son, Peter, when he took on his father's business of innkeeping. Peter was the father of Hannah (1798-1872); Elizabeth (1799-1864); Susannah (1806-66); and Margaret (1812-75), who were the makers of the quilts which passed down in the family and were eventually discovered in an attic by the present owner.

Layout Identification

In the early documentation days of the Project, quilts like those of the Thornton sisters – created by the placing of patched frames uniformly around a square centre – appeared often enough to call for some type of description or generic classification. They were quite unlike the American version of a 'medallion' quilt – one usually designed with a turned square (or square-on-point) centre and repeating blocks – or, for that matter, the all-over single-pattern British mosaic quilt with (or without) a centre. In addition to the frame method of construction, the one other identifying feature was that the centre square was usually sited straight-on, as opposed to being turned on point to become a diamond. Given these distinguishing characteristics, the word 'frame' was adopted to describe this uniquely British method of assembling a pieced quilt.

Frame patchwork quilts were brought to documentation days in almost every part of the country, though they were more numerous in southern England. Most could have been classed as scrap quilts, since they often contained many hundreds of different pieces of dress fabric. Some were quite elaborate in terms of piecing and appliqué and probably only used for 'best'. Others, clearly for utilitarian use, had been put together in a great hurry. They appeared as both coverlets and as completed three-layer quilts with quite elaborate quilting patterns.

About 15 per cent of the pieced quilts presented for documentation fell within the 'frame' category. The majority of these had been made in the last half of the nineteenth century, although a surprising number were sewn in the first thirty years of the twentieth century, indicating the continued popularity of this particular patchwork layout.

The earliest frame quilt examined – one bearing a date – was a simple and crudely pieced example made in 1796 by Ann Cartwrite of Staffordshire, when she was aged twenty-two (see fig. 2.5, p.19). The inscription on the quilt reads:

LIVE TO LOVE

FAITH HOPE AND CHARITY, LOVE JOY AND PEACE

ANN CARTWRITE CRESSWELL (STAFFS)

DUTY FEAR AND LOVE, WE OWE TO GOD ABOVE

ANN CARTWRITE IN THE YEAR 1796

Fig. 2.4. One of four frame quilts made by the Thornton sisters of Mirfield, Yorkshire. It was probably made between 1840 and 1860. 244 cm square (8 ft square).

Ann married farmer John Fielding on 9 July 1807 and the quilt is believed to have been made as part of her trousseau. The fabrics have been recycled from old clothing with browns and beiges predominating and there is no filling: the backing is made of cream cotton and the quilting executed in a diagonal grid. The composition of the pieced side is simple and the borders irregular: the centre is made of alternate light and dark squares surrounded by frames (five on two sides and six on the other two). These include strips of dark fabric with a lighter corner square, while patchwork of crude squares and rectangles placed haphazardly make up other frames. The quilt is finished with a wide printed outer border with dark squares as corners.

Another simple frame quilt dating from the same period was recorded during the Truro documentation day, which presented opportunity for detailed study of the fabrics. The centre of this quilt was composed of sixty-four squares, including some squares composed of triangles; there was a light strip frame around the centre and the remainder of the quilt was a mix of squares and triangles put together haphazardly. Most of the block-printed fabrics dated from between 1780 and 1800, although some were made as late as 1805. Unlike Ann's quilt, however, this example displayed considerable quilting, all of which had been executed to fit in the frame layout.

Although many of the frame quilts did have quite a documentary history in that the names and occupations of the makers were known, no clues relevant to design influences were ever discovered during the Project. All, it would appear, were made in the usual domestic circumstances of the time (in poor and wealthy households alike). The Project, however, did record one frame quilt that had been made professionally in Wales. It had come from a Brecon shop which was being cleared in 1950. The storeroom

Fig. 2.5. Ann Cartwrite of Staffordshire made this simple frame quilt in 1796, when she was twenty-two years of age. 216 cm x 250 cm (7 ft 1 in x 8 ft 2 in).

inventory revealed a 100-year-old wool, silk and brocade frame quilt still bearing a label, 'to be collected'. It had been made a century before by an outworker employed by Jones the Draper, The Struet, Brecon.

One possible reason for the popularity of the frame layout might be guessed from the Thornton quilts: during the first decade of the nineteenth century there was a great vogue for printed commemorative and floral panels. These would have provided a natural starting point for any budding quiltmaker. Using the panels as a centre, the maker could then build the quilt outwards by adding pieced rows until the cover was the required size. Certainly the Thorntons were not the only quiltmakers to use the printed panel as a focal point – other frame quilts were recorded in the Project, including a quilt made by Eleonar Hunter of Ulverstoll, Lancashire, in 1828. Its printed centre – a Tree of Life – was surrounded by six borders pieced of triangles, squares-on-point, and Flying Geese.

The explanation for the use of frames may also lie in economy and a wish to use up even the smallest piece of fabric left over from dressmaking; or because piecing in strips (as opposed to blocks) was an easy way of working. You could, after all, sit with (and easily transport) a small workbasket and make limitless numbers of patchwork strips – against the day when you had enough strips to put together a whole quilt. Certainly this would have explained the disregard for the positioning of light and dark colours and a general lack of planning so evident in some of the more simple frame quilts.

Neither can one discount the outside design influences of the Victorian period when there was a penchant for using ornamental borders. The industrial revolution, in the nineteenth century, and the classical revival drew on design sources from many different countries – China, India, Greece and Persia, to name but a few. The ornamental border became an important part of domestic design, featuring not only in mosaic-tiled floors, dados and wood marquetry but also in clothing such as woven shawls.

Chiefly Cotton

The vast majority of those frame quilts and coverlets brought for documentation were made of cotton. One exception, brought to the Grove documentation day, had been purchased for 10p in a jumble sale in 1973 and was made of silk. Many of the papers used for piecing had been left in, and they included newspaper cuttings dated 1860, advertising farm animals and agricultural implements. Another frame quilt of silk, velvet and satin was brought to Harleston documentation day. Made by Mary Jane Scott between 1850 and 1900, it includes frames of diamonds set as Baby Blocks and squares-on-point. It has a centre of diamonds and yellow strip frames which give real emphasis to the layout (see fig.2.6, p.22).

Wool frame quilts also appeared, though less frequently: a quilt made in 1880 by a young girl apprenticed to a tailor and dressmaker in Monmouth had been pieced with a mix of cotton, wool and shoddy worked in triangles, octagons, hexagons, squares and rectangles. Another very simple example of a frame quilt, made of tweed suiting samples, was brought to Bowes Museum when a documentation day was held there. The centre was made of squares composed of two triangles embellished with feather stitching.

An example of the traditional Welsh frame quilt in wool – with its simple construction and strong contrasting plain colours so reminiscent of the American Amish quilts – was also recorded during the Project. Dating from the second half of the nineteenth century, it has a centre of four triangles (see fig.2.7, p.22).

In terms of fabric, perhaps the most spectacular frame quilt was one brought to East Grinstead (see fig. 2.8, p.23). Although it does not have as many frames as other examples, its inclusion of many different fabrics – cotton, silk, rayon, satin and crepe – gives it a jewel-like appearance. It was made in about 1930 by Miss Ina Macrae, who lived at Great Dunmow and Colchester, Essex, and she used recycled clothing as well as haberdashery samples to make first a padded dahlia centre (the amount of padding indicates that she may well have intended to make only a cushion) and then frames of varying patchwork patterns: Brick Wall, hexagons and Nine Patch squares-on-point are all included.

Little If Any Planning
Contemporary quiltmakers who undertake the pieced frame design are challenged at the outset by the mathematics of the exercise. Elaborate planning is required in the use of colour and in the correct sizing of each frame – otherwise one ends up with irregular pieces or poorly turned corners. It was obvious from even the most elaborate of the frame quilts examined in the Project that opportunities were often missed for effective placing of colour and that the majority of the quiltmakers had problems of skill when it came to precision piecing. Additionally, although most quilts were worked from a centre square, the finished measurements of the quilt were often distorted out of true rather than precisely square – a result that cannot always be attributed to the ravages of washing. These factors contribute to the theory that the frame layout was more dictated by the ease of working in patchwork strips than by any other factor. Even the Thornton quilt on page 18, for all its visual impact, has its technical imperfections.

Fig. 2.6. Jewel-like silk patchwork is given extra emphasis by the use of yellow frames. Made by Mary Jane Scott of Northumberland in the latter part of the nineteenth century. 228 cm x 236 cm (7 ft 5 in x 7 ft 8 in).

Fig. 2.7. A wool frame quilt from Wales made in the early twentieth century. 183 cm x 207 cm (6 ft x 6 ft 9 in). *(Photo: Dinah Travis.)*

Fig. 2.8. A complex frame quilt of the 1930s containing cotton, silk, rayon, satin and crepe. Its padded centre indicates the maker probably only intended to make a cushion. 199 cm x 219 cm (6 ft 6 in x 7 ft 2 in).

Fig. 2.9. The centre of this frame quilt, made in Blackwood in the later nineteenth century, was made with two squares-on-point, forming a rectangle. 180 cm x 204 cm (5 ft 10 in x 6 ft 8 in).

Fig. 2.10. A George III commemorative panel was used as the centre for a frame quilt made in Cumbria in the early nineteenth century. 205 cm x 247 cm (6 ft 8 in x 8 ft 1 in).

Almost (but not quite) an exception to this poor planning in assembly was a quilt from the late nineteenth century brought to the Pontypridd documentation day (see fig.2.9, p.23). Made for a 'bottom drawer', it is unusual in that the centre is formed of two squares-on-point surrounded by squares. With a rectangular centre, the finished quilt measures 180 cm x 204 cm (5 ft 10in x 6 ft 8 in). This particular quilt shows evidence of planning and forethought: the centre and first four frames (including the Flying Geese frame) are well executed. The fifth pieced frame, however, presents some visual confusion because of the placement of light and dark triangles. Was this deliberate? One favourite piece of quilt folklore says that deliberate mistakes were often introduced into quiltmaking because 'only God is perfect'.

Nineteenth-century Education

Because of the mathematical precision required in the assembly of frame quilts and the state of women's education in the nineteenth century, it was of little surprise that the majority brought for inspection were flawed in some way – even though they were worked with papers. There were obvious difficulties in working out measurements, especially when it came to the corners.

The four Thornton sisters may well have had more than a passing knowledge of maths, however, since boatbuilding was one of the family occupations, together with innkeeping. But even they didn't always get it right at the corners. Another frame quilt which may have been influenced by a precision craft was that brought to the Penrith day (see fig.2.10, p.23). Made in the early 1800s near Carlisle, and passed down through the family, it was reported to have had a connection with a joiner's workshop. The centre, a printed George III commemorative panel, is surrounded by five borders: strip frames alternate with pieced frames made of triangles and squares. There are some star blocks incorporated and, most unusual, the outside patterned fabric frame has mitred corners. This feature was rare among the frame quilts examined.

The quilt with the most frames around a centre – fifteen – was believed to have been made in Hornby Castle, Yorkshire, in the early 1800s (see fig.2.11, p.26) and was brought to the Swavesey documentation day. Probably the most complex frame quilt to be examined, it has alternating frames of fabric strips combined with frames of patchwork patterns that include elongated diamonds, hexagons, four-patch squares-on-point and triangles.

In contrast were the simple utilitarian frame quilts where strips of fabric were stitched round a centre square. Quilts could be fashioned very quickly in this style, since pieced patterns were not included and very few fabrics were required. Sometimes, when the quiltmaker was obviously intent on economy and using everything to hand (while at the same time refusing the challenge of elaborate piecing), scrap squares and rectangles were simply run together around the centre square.

A pleasing example of this approach was found in a quilt rescued off the back of a cow in a Devon field. It had been made of household scraps, both wool and cotton, by a Mrs Philips in about 1880. Mrs Philips was a farmer's wife who lived near Honiton and her sewing skills, learned both from her mother and through her own efforts, were quite basic: the quilt she created has a rather distorted star centre surrounded by ten frames which initially were laid out to provide a light/dark contrast (see fig.2.12, p.26). An old quilt was used for the wadding of this particular hand-sewn cover and it has an all-over diamond quilting pattern.

Another quilt that could be said to fit into the utilitarian category was brought to the Inverness documentation day. Dating from about 1900, it had a centre created of squares composed of two, three or four triangles, all of which were arranged in haphazard fashion. It had seven frames top and bottom and six on either side: one, composed of strips, had four-patch square corners, while another, composed of non-uniform rectangles, had pieced pinwheel corners. Some attention had been given to the positioning of strong colours within the frames.

Another utilitarian and simple frame quilt was that made by a Mrs Redfearn and Mrs Raine, who ran a post office in Eggleston, Co. Durham. Dating from the second half of the nineteenth century, it had a printed panel for a centre and five frames, all of them strips with squares in the corner. Self-coloured, floral and geometric fabrics had all been used and some attention paid to the quilting: patterns used included a variation of the wave, the tulip or bell, shallow ripple and eight-petal flower.

A Variety of Patterns

Squares-on-point, pieced squares and triangles were among the most commonly used patchwork pieces for frame quilts. Of the pieced squares, two or four triangles making a square were most common although there were four- and nine-patch squares on some examples. Corners of frames were often simple square blocks, although one quilt made on a Welsh farm in about 1825 had corners of the Broken Dishes pattern. This particular quilt had a Mariner's Compass centre and rather crude quarter sections of a compass in the corners of the outside border.

One very unusual patchwork quilt appeared in a frame coverlet brought to Preston (see p.27). It has no known provenance, but very precise piecing from a technical viewpoint. Made of furnishing

Fig. 2.11. One of the most complex examples of a quilt made with the frame layout was sewn in Hornby Castle, Yorkshire in the early 1800s. 215 cm square (7 ft square).

Fig. 2.12. Simpler examples of frame quilts often used large and irregular strips and rectangles. Made about 1880 in Devon and rescued from the back of a cow. 175 cm square (5 ft 9 in square).

Opposite: Fig. 2.13. Complex frame quilt featuring squares, octagons, elongated hexagons and various stars.
284 cm x 324 cm (9 ft 4 in x 10 ft 8 in).

fabrics dating from between 1795 and 1805, the coverlet contains squares and octagons with stars in the middle. It has at some point been damaged or altered – its badly fitting outer corners are not in keeping with the quality of the centre.

Pieced triangles set as squares were used often, although curiously many quiltmakers failed the imagination test when it came to placing the finished squares. The concept of dividing a square into two or four triangles – and using contrasting light and dark fabrics – was followed in most cases but many failed to see that squares pieced of two light and two dark triangles could be placed to give the effect of a band of squares-on-point. Pieced squares were often made into a frame in a hit-or-miss manner. Triangles were infrequently used in a sawtooth form, although one early-nineteenth-century example featured a sawtooth frame with a narrow white insert between each triangular piece.

Sawtooth as an outline was used in two quilts brought to the Truro documentation day. In both cases, the sawtooth was done in Turkey Red, it was used to emphasize the centre square or focal point and the sawtooth corners had been successfully turned. The quilt, made by a Mrs Honey in about 1900, in addition features graduating Turkey Red squares radiating outwards from the centre to the corners (see fig.2.14, p.31). Mrs Honey's quilt has a pinwheel centre and ten frames along the side with eleven at top and bottom. It has been hand-quilted in a variety of patterns, each following the individual frame. The top and bottom frames are executed in a running feather pattern.

Red sawtooth or zigzag as an emphasis turned up again in a quilt brought to the Exeter documentation day. It had been made in either Devon or Cornwall between 1800 and 1850. Primarily of floral prints with a printed panel centre, it had one unique frame – unique when compared with the pieced patterns found in others. Two rows of alternating light and dark print triangles had been put together in an Ocean Wave pattern; the overall effect of this design was only slightly let down by the corners of plain squares in a non-complementary print.

Hexagons Little Used

It is easy to understand why the hexagon pattern was seldom used in the creation of a frame quilt, though it did appear in appliqué form or as a centre. Its six sides would have made it more difficult to piece into a frame. One quilt made in the last half of the nineteenth century, brought to the Nottingham documentation day, featured a centre of hexagons set in an elongated hexagon on a white ground appliquéd with pinwheels and Broderie Perse birds. It had seven frames on the sides and nine at top and bottom to give it length: some were appliquéd with pinwheels and others fashioned of bladed windmills.

Another curious frame coverlet with hexagons, which turned up in Surrey, had a large centre of hexagons laid out as white rosettes in a Grandmother's Flower Garden pattern. Because of the date of the fabrics, it is believed that the centre was perhaps pieced in about 1820 (although one fabric used dated back to 1790), then put away and picked up again as much as thirty or forty years later, at which time it was supplemented with fabrics of that date. It is believed to have been made (or at least started) by a Mary Moore, who was born in England in 1804. The finished coverlet was traditionally handed down to the eldest of the Moore family and in 1901 it went with its owners to Glendale, California, but returned some years later.

The Moore coverlet has nine frames: four of these are made up of squares pieced from four triangles and placed so that light and dark fabrics contrast: one frame is Windmill; three are pieced white triangles alternating with printed triangles; and one frame is made of white hexagons with a chain of patterned hexagon rosettes running along the middle.

The Log Cabin pattern appeared in only one instance and this in a quilt in which blocks have been set to form frames around a square-on-point centre. Made by women of the Wickett family of Cornwall, in the early twentieth century, the quilt contains all self-coloured fabrics in red, grey, mauve, black and beige wool, silk and velvet, all of which combine to give the finished article very strong definition (see p.46 in Chap.3).

One frame quilt, which was discovered in a suitcase under a bed, included a frame with a T-block patch as well as examples of piecing that included Flying Geese with Windmill corners. Made by a farmer's wife in Eskdale, it included several plain sashed frames and an all-over quilting pattern of clamshell.

Use of Appliqué

Clamshells as appliqué appeared on an early-nineteenth-century frame quilt brought to Dorchester (see fig.2.16, p.30). This quilt, which was made in east Cornwall, with chintz and cotton dating from 1800 to 1830, features pieced or appliquéd frames alternating with strips. One frame is made of applied clamshells with squares set in the corners; other frames include squares-on-point and triangles. The use of appliqué in frame quilts was moderate and often appeared as a form of embellishment in a corner. Sometimes the technique was used to produce the central focal point.

The quilt made by the Thornton sisters (see p.18) has an applied centre and eleven frames, some of these frames acting as sashing between pieced lines of triangles and squares-on-point.

Fig. 2.14. Turkey Red cotton was used for emphasis in a quilt made by a Mrs Honey in 1900.
212 cm x 248 cm (6 ft 11 in x 8 ft 1 in).

Fig. 2.15. Sarah Holdcroft of Manchester showed great appliqué and patchwork skills in her 1870s quilt.
255 cm square (8 ft 4 in square).

Opposite: Fig. 2.16. Detail of the centre of a Cornish quilt shows clamshells used in an unusual cable pattern.
217 cm x 248 cm (7 ft 1 in x 8 ft 1 in).

A coverlet brought to the Grove documentation day had a centre with applied flowers and hexagon rosettes, while some of the corners of the individual frames were applied with hearts and circles. Printed panels were incorporated into the outside border of this quilt, which was made about 1840 – possibly for a wedding.

A fourteen-year-old girl, Ann James of Aberelwyn, Glandwr, Whitland, believed to have made her frame quilt in about 1825, used a mixture of appliquéd rosettes and shapes, including hearts, fixed with herringbone stitch, for the centre. The pieced frames incorporated squares-on-point, triangles made into squares and strips of fabric.

Another coverlet, of unknown origin, had a 53-cm (21-in) square-on-point centre featuring a block of roller-printed fabric with floral stripes and birds and butterflies. Surrounding this, in the triangular corners, were appliquéd fern leaves in highly glazed cotton. This coverlet, dating from the first half of the nineteenth century, was brought to the Exeter documentation day. Its outer two frames were simply strips of fabric but some of the inner frames showed more investment of time: one contained squares of sashed linen with applied squares-on-point and corners with applied hearts. Both the sashing and the squares were of a fern-leaf fabric. A Prussian blue striped fabric separated this from the next frame, which again had sashed linen blocks, this time applied with hearts and an applied square in the corner. The third frame to be applied also had squares-on-point, this time of a larger size.

A very labour-intensive example of appliqué combined with piecing was found in a quilt made in about 1870 by Sarah Holdcroft of Manchester. Many of the cotton fabrics used date from an earlier time – between 1820 and 1860 – and the quilt has an amazing array of rosettes, leaves, hearts and other shapes (see fig.2.15, p.31).

Another dramatic use of appliqué was that used on a frame quilt by Jemima Finchett of Chester, a professional dressmaker who worked in the early twentieth century. Both she and her husband were Welsh – he was head gardener at Trevallan Hall, Rossett. Taking a red, white and blue colour theme (the red a Paisley print), she applied folded cut-out shapes to plain white frames, some five frames in all. Three of the frames are printed strips.

Embroidery and canvas work also appeared as focal centres in frame quilts, though the Project only turned up a few examples.

Needlepoint wool on canvas was used as the starting point for quiltmaker Ann Gammin of Bratton Fleming, North Devon in about 1860. Most of the skill and time were obviously invested in the centre in this instance – the frames were simple constructions of patterned strips of fabric alternating with frames of squares and triangles, all now badly faded.

Similar concentration on the centre was demonstrated by a farmer's wife, Mrs Braithwaite of Helton, near Penrith. Her quilt had a centre of hand-spun linen embroidered in wools and only four frames, including an outside border with eight-point stars in the corners.

Again, an embroidered centre signed in blue cross-stitch by 'Margaret Pickering Aged 14 Years 1818' was used in a quilt with only two frames and an incomplete third. None of the frames was pieced and it is apparent that the quilt was used as a suitable vehicle for Margaret's practice piece of embroidery.

Two in One

It was not uncommon during the course of the documentation programme to discover old quilts used as filling for new quilts. One surprise, however, was the discovery of a number of double-sided quilts, with both sides constructed in a frame layout. Some of these were quite utilitarian and crude in appearance. One brought to Pontypridd and made by a Mrs Mary Evans was filled with a blanket: Mrs Evans apparently was well known for putting together two or three worn blankets and covering them with patchwork. The centre of one side was a square of shawl fabric with eight frames: the other side had ten borders along each side and twelve at top and bottom. Irregular rectangles, squares and triangles had been used for the frames and strips of fabric.

A two-sided frame quilt brought to the Truro documentation day had many of the same fabrics used on both sides. One side, however, began with a square-on-point, while the other was a square set straight-on. One unusual use of appliqué emerged on both sides: squares had been turned on point and applied with crosses. Believed to date from the beginning of the twentieth century, the quilt had a wide variety of patterned fabrics and some frames were constructed with reference to the use of light and dark colours.

A very labour-intensive double-sided frame quilt was brought to the Grove documentation day. Nothing is known about the social history of the quilt but the fabrics indicate that it was made in the first half of the nineteenth century. There is interesting applied work on one side, including an applied cable chain. One frame is made of diamonds with four corners of applied flowers; another frame has applied leaf shapes and hexagon rosettes with corners of applied leaves; another is made of pieced triangles with corners of applied triangles, etc. – up to eight frames in total (see fig.2.17, p.34).

The reverse side of this quite amazing quilt has a centre of hexagon rosettes and a series of frames which feature piecing and appliqué. There are four patched squares, star blocks and two pieced chevron borders (see fig.2.18, p.35)

Fig. 2.17. The front of this early-nineteenth-century quilt has applied flowers, leaves, rosettes and an unusual chain around the centre. It has a total of eight frames but nothing is known of its maker.

Fig. 2.18. The reverse of the double-sided frame demonstrates an equal investment of time but more emphasis on patchwork than appliqué.
290 cm x 294 cm (9 ft 6 in x 9 ft 7 in).

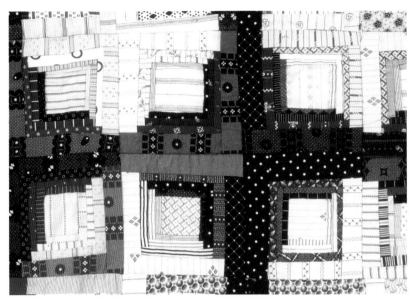

Fig. 3.1. *Top left:* Detail of a small quilt made by Averil Colby in 1960.

Fig. 3.2. Detail of unfinished floral quilt with paper templates remaining. see fig. 3.7 on page 42.

Fig. 3.3. *Top right:* Log Cabin quilt from the Isle of Man. See page 47.

CHAPTER 3

PATTERNS IN ABUNDANCE

Dinah Travis

THE INDIVIDUALITY of the British quiltmaker was well illustrated in many patchwork patterns which were recorded during the documentation phase of the Project. As anticipated, a large number of the pieced quilts recorded showed the use of allover pattern in which geometric shapes joined to form a mosaic layout. This approach to patchwork, a contrast to the practice popular today of working in blocks of pattern, was seen in all areas of Britain. The mosaic style of layout, often known as 'English Patchwork', was generally considered to be the fundamental British style. The documentation programme, however, proved this assumption to be incorrect. Patchwork patterns not only appeared in the mosaic-style layout but also in the frame (see Chap.2) and block-style layouts. Generally the patterns were simple in concept; for example, in the form of the hexagon rosettes from the mosaic quilts, eight-pointed stars in single colours from the block quilts and borders of rectangles, triangles and squares in the frame quilts.

Mosaic

The simplest of the all-over patterned quilts is one showing a mosaic of rectangles made from tailors' woollen fabric samples or some other readily available fabrics. A number of these simple mosaic quilts were seen in the Project. That samples had been used in quilts was evident from numbers printed on the pieces or from regularly spaced holes that indicated they had once been fixed into a sample book. In this type of quilt the pieces were sewn together with a basic running stitch or, after 1860, a simple machine stitch. Figure 3.4 on page 38 shows an example from Penrith with samples in a wide range of woollen tweeds cut in rectangles. This quilt was probably made for the purely functional purpose of keeping the cold out and for a minimal cost.

The mosaic-style pattern developed more complex designs with the availability of different fabrics and the use of spare time in sewing them together by the lady of society. In constructing the more intricately pieced mosaic-patchwork quilts the patchworker cut out fabric shapes, tacked them round paper shapes and then oversewed the pieces to form an interlinking mosaic. The most common geometric shapes of these tessellating patterns were hexagons, diamonds, octagons with squares, squares, rectangles and triangles in various sizes. Quilts where square shapes predominated were very popular and 439 of these were recorded. As anticipated, the most popular geometric shape, however, was the hexagon. All-over hexagon patterns accounted for 365 quilts and a further 222 featured single or double rosette hexagon patterns. Illustrated in figure 3.5 on pages 38-9 is a detail of a small quilt of precious silk fabrics showing a centre of hexagon rosettes on a black silk ground surrounded by a border of diamonds with a fringe edging. A coloured twisted cord has been applied along the dividing line of the hexagons and the diamonds and a yellow Russian braid applied over the joins of the diamonds. The quilt is unique, with the centre of each hexagon rosette showing a delicately painted flower, and it may have been a cover for a small table or some other precious object. It was found in an attic cupboard after the death of the owner's grandmother.

The Project revealed a number of quilts with a combination of varying geometric shapes in an all-over intricate pattern, such as one from South Wales in which the shapes joined together to form an all-over pattern of tessellating Maltese crosses. The arrangement of different fabrics within a tessellation can make many pattern variations depending where the dark and light tones and contrasting coloured fabrics are placed. Examples found in the Project included hexagons in plain and printed fabrics tessellating in single, double or elongated rosettes dating from the early 1800s;

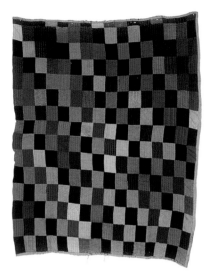

Fig. 3.4. Simple mosaic quilt made from rectangles of woollen tweed samples from the Penrith area.
158 cm x 193 cm (5 ft 2 in x 6 ft 3 in).

Fig. 3.5. Quilt of pieced rosettes made by the Women's Institute group from Sway, Hampshire, in 1926.
145 cm x 244 cm (4 ft 9 in x 8 ft).

three diamonds in silks and velvet of a dark, medium and light colour building up into a hexagon to give the impression of a three-dimensional child's building block from the Victorian era; diamonds cut from working men's shirting materials of the early 1900s to make an all-over pattern or six diamonds grouped into a tessellation of six-pointed stars; and plain Turkey Red and plain white cotton hexagons arranged in stripes. This last quilt, dating from the Edwardian era, was a very stark and formal arrangement of hexagons made and used by a working-class family for their

home. Similar quilts, which were heard about during the Project in the Isle of Man, turned up in the guesthouses at the beginning of the twentieth century. Octagons with squares, squares and rectangles have all been seen in similar situations in both rich silks and velvets; and everyday cottons.

Mosaic patterns sometimes have more defined layouts. A typical quilt may combine a centre of triangles, surrounded by diamonds formed into building blocks and edged by a border of diamonds which have been arranged to form hexagons of six-pointed stars.

Fig. 3.6. Detail of a silk quilt showing hexagon rosettes with painted centres on a black ground surrounded by a border of diamonds and corner blocks of pieced six-pointed stars.
110 cm x 164 cm (3 ft 7 in x 5 ft 4 in).

These shapes may be separated by a narrow border or run into one another. The pieces would generally be assembled into the quilt top in the same way that a frame quilt is built up with the central section sewn first and then borders added gradually to piece the quilt frame by frame.

Mosaic pieced quilts with a central medallion were not uncommon. For example, one from Dorchester had a medallion consisting of alternating red and white concentric diamonds surrounded by a mosaic of small diamonds of everyday cotton fabrics dating from about 1900. The quilt edge echoed the red of the centre with a red binding. Illustrated in figure 3.5 on page 38 is a quilt from Sway pieced by the local Women's Institute for a raffle in 1926. It was made from an all-over mosaic of rosettes. The central seven rosettes are of exactly the same colour, making a central medallion stand out from the rest. Each rosette has a central hexagon surrounded alternately with squares and triangles. The reverse of the quilt has an added decorative interest in the form of a massive pieced bow. Other layouts include those where the different pieces are arranged in strips from the top to the bottom of the quilt and where the quilt has been divided up into regular shapes with the mosaic pieces formally arranged within these larger shapes – a layout similar to that of a rug or carpet.

The unfinished quilt in figure 3.7 on page 42 from the Judkyn-Pratt Collection in Bath shows great draughtsmanship in the planning and skill in the construction of the patchwork. The fabrics date the quilt as being from the end of the eighteenth century. The design of a vase of flowers on a mat surrounded by trails of flowers,

Opposite: 1. Simple block patterns found on British quilts during the Project's documentation programme. They are all based on simple divisions of a square. Some of them have curved seams.

2. Block patterns found on both British and American quilts of the 1930s during the Project's documentation programme. Their names are Shoo Fly, Ohio Star, Bear's Paw, Dresden Plate, Windmill, Square within a Square, Maple Leaf and Fans.

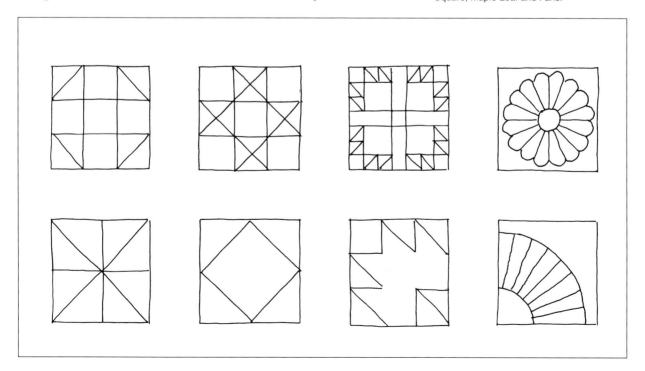

Fig. 3.7. An unfinished pieced quilt with the paper templates remaining in the reverse of the patchwork made in the late eighteenth century.
233 cm x 283 cm (7 ft 8 in x 9 ft 3 in).

Fig. 3.8. A detail of fig. 3.7 with the papers in the reverse of the quilt showing clearly the use of balance marks to ensure accurate piecing.

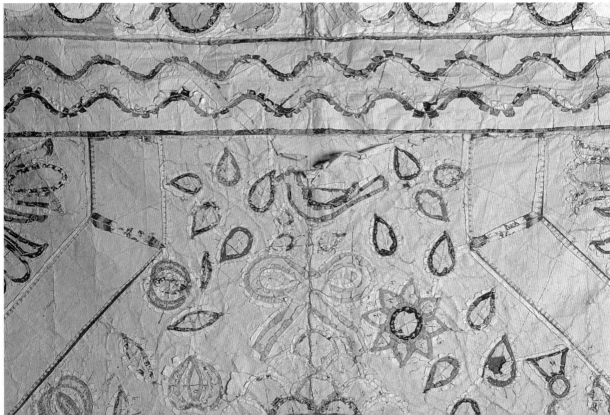

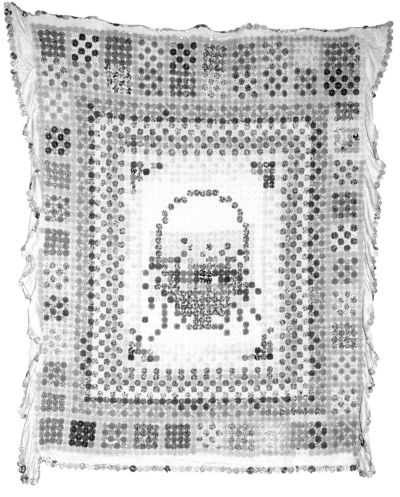

Top: Fig. 3.9. A detail of a small quilt of gathered patches made by Averil Colby in 1960.
58 cm x 76 cm (1 ft 10 in x 2 ft 5 in).

Above: Fig. 3.10. A typical simple Welsh block quilt made in coarse woollen fabrics with thirty red and black blocks arranged on their point alternately with plain black squares surrounded by alternating black and red plain borders.
165 cm x 201 cm (5 ft 4 in x 6 ft 7 in).

Left: Fig. 3.11. A quilt made from Suffolk puffs (Yo-yo) arranged in the shape of a basket of flowers bordered with rows of coloured puffs, blocks of puffs and a frilled edge finished with more puffs.
158 cm x 186 cm (5 ft 2 in x 6 ft 1 in).

borders and a series of medallions appears like one for applied patchwork with some surface embroidery. The patterns are still in the back of the quilt held secure with linen tacking thread and it can be seen that the pieces were oversewn together over paper templates. The complex design was drawn to actual size on paper and then cut up to use as templates for the fabric pieces. The balance marks (see fig.3.8, p.42) on the papers can clearly be seen in the detailed photograph of the reverse of the quilt. This quilt may have been pieced in Wiltshire where it was purchased in 1960.

Some unusual quilts made from other types of tessellating pieces were also seen during the Project. A lovely piece of white linen with a bobble-fringe edging that was brought to Portishead was made from gathered hexagons. These quilts with gathered patches are difficult to date but, according to Averil Colby in her book *Quilting*, they were popular in the middle of the nineteenth century. The hexagons in the quilts where this technique has been used varied in size from 2½ centimetres to 8 centimetres (1 inch to 3 inches). Individual patches were constructed by sewing together two different-sized hexagons. The larger hexagon was gathered to fit the smaller one, the two joined with stuffing laid centrally between. Then they were stab-quilted to take up the bulk of the fabric. The pieces were joined together into a quilt by oversewing them together in the usual way. The example illustrated in figure 3.9 on page 43 is a detail of a small quilt made by Averil Colby, dated 1960, in which single white rosettes with red centres have flat red diamonds and triangles placed between to complete a formal tessellation. As well as in the Colby book, further examples of this form of patchwork can be seen in *Traditional Quilting* by Mavis Fitzrandolph.

Suffolk-puff quilts were found in Paisley, Preston, Basingstoke and Edinburgh. Individual puffed pieces are made from a circle of fabric with the edge gathered up, flattened and then oversewn together to make a flexible and soft quilt. One example from Scotland dates from World War II and the streaks of colour in the quilt show how the maker used fabrics as and when they were available. Another Suffolk-puff quilt from Preston was constructed with pieces forming a large central cross with wide borders; a quilt from Basingstoke (see fig.3.11 p.43) has Suffolk puffs arranged in the shape of a basket of flowers bordered with rows of coloured puffs, blocks of puffs and a frilled edge finished with more puffs. The fabrics may have been sugar-sack cottons. It was probably made in Canada in 1927 and is believed to have been made to celebrate a wedding and was then brought to Britain with the family. It demonstrates how a technique travels from one continent to another. The Suffolk-puff technique is not thought to be British in origin and was probably learned from women's magazines of the 1930s, though there is a Suffolk-puff coverlet in The Quilters' Guild Heritage Collection with fabrics dating from about thirty years earlier than this. The Suffolk puff has a completely different name in the United States: there it is called Yo-yo.

Block

Another widely used formation is a square that is divided up into smaller shapes making a pattern unit: these units are sometimes alone at strategic points in a quilt such as in the centre or repeated on the corners of a frame quilt. In other quilts the square is repeated regularly, sometimes with a border between the squares. These squares are commonly known as 'blocks' and the borders as 'sashing'. It is generally believed that the pieced block-pattern quilts are American in origin.

There must be some doubt about this assumption because during the Project pieced blocks dating from before the influence of the American block quilt were found all around Britain, particularly at the documentation days in Wales and in private Welsh collections. The British block patterns are simple in form and as a rule are constructed by placing the shapes together face to face and joining them with a running stitch along the seam line. The triangles and the diamonds of the Windmill pattern and the eight-pointed star are typical examples of these patterns. They were often found in the central square and the corners of the borders of a typical frame quilt or repeated with sashing. Many of these simple blocks were seen both in Scotland and in Wales and were reminiscent of the Amish style of quilt from America in their simplicity and the use of the plain-coloured woollen fabrics. Does this show that this style of quilt was taken to America by settlers from Wales or Scotland as well as from other European countries? Illustrated in figure 3.10 on page 43 is a simple but quite striking Welsh wool quilt with thirty red and black squares-on-point alternating with plain black squares surrounded by alternating black and red plain borders. This is a typical block design found in British quilts where the block is based on a three-by-three division of a square.

The familiar pattern of baskets was seen on several quilts, particularly in red and white fabrics, as illustrated by the red and white baskets quilt on page 55 that was documented in London. The sixteen baskets make a pleasing border to a centre of other techniques. The owners of the quilt said it was made especially for visitors by the women of their farming family in the district of Mourne, Northern Ireland. Another similar quilt came to the day at Penrith. Four red baskets are bordered by chevrons and a final border of large triangles divided up like the body of a basket in this quilt.

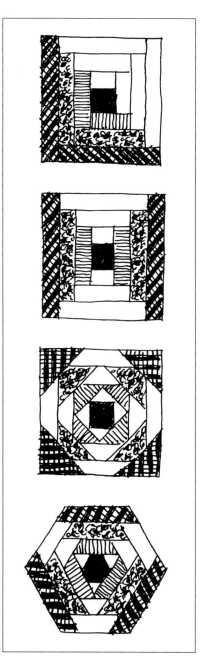

3. Various units of Log Cabin showing the basic 'Log Cabin' block, the 'Court House Steps' block, a 'Pineapple' block and a hexagonal block.

Fig. 3.12. Worked in blocks and pieced over papers, this coverlet displays a high degree of technical skill on the part of the maker. The border doubles back on itself as a wide binding. Made by Isabella Oliver in Kidderminster between 1835 and 1840. 185 cm x 217 cm (6 ft x 7 ft 12 in).

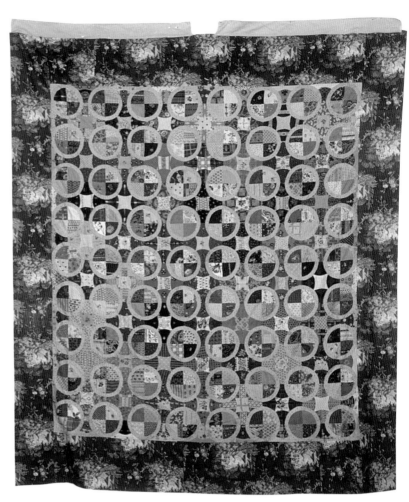

Fig. 3.13. A Log Cabin quilt showing an imaginative use of the basic arrangement of the blocks so that with a clever arrangement of colour the layout gives the impression of a frame quilt. 225 cm x 236 cm (7 ft 3 in x 7 ft 9 in).

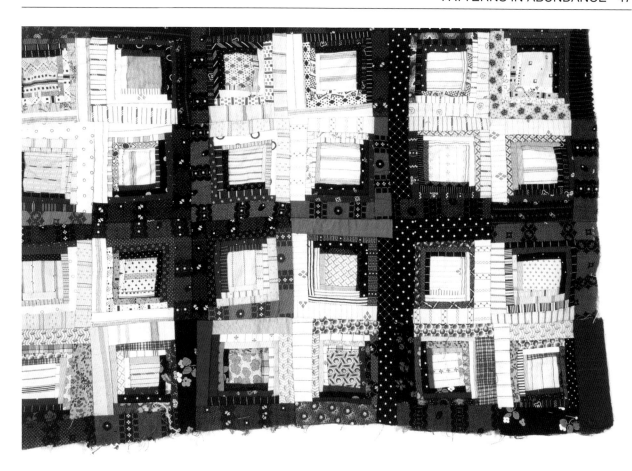

Fig. 3.14. A detail of a Log Cabin quilt from the Isle of Man showing a basic layout using both woven and printed fabrics.
143 cm x 184 cm (4 ft 8 in x 6 ft).

Above: Fig. 3.15. A variation of a Log Cabin pattern called 'Pineapple' where the strips are positioned round the square and the contrasting strips go round at an angle on the corners.
163 cm x 205 cm (5 ft 4 in x 6 ft 8 in).

Left: Fig. 3.16. This quilt from Edinburgh made in approximately 1880 shows straight furrows set round a central square.
164 cm x 194 cm (5 ft 4 in x 6 ft 4 in).

The block pattern known as Irish Chain was seen both in Liverpool and Penrith, both well known for their Irish connections. Applied tulips within the chain pattern, similar to those in the Irish Patchwork Exhibition of 1980 in Somerset House, London, were also examined as were American Irish Chain quilts dating from the 1930s. Illustrated on page 55 is a detail of a quilt with a single Irish Chain pattern in red on white surrounding a medallion of various other techniques made in 1886 by a farmer's wife.

An unusual pattern appeared in a finely-executed coverlet made in Kidderminster by Isabella Oliver between 1835 and 1840. The name for the pattern used in the coverlet is not known (see fig.3.12, p.46). The dominant quartered circles are surrounded by another circle, which is also worked in quarters, both of these shapes being worked in the corner of each square. The coverlet, which has never been washed, was pieced in English fashion, on papers. The design itself demanded a high degree of skill – the oversewing of each piece is very fine.

Many repeated block quilts with definite American or Canadian connections dating from the 1930s and the World War II period were viewed and it is these, together with the decline of the cotton trade in the British Isles and the import of the prints from the USA, that have influenced the British quiltmakers of today. The American blocks that most commonly appeared were Shoo Fly, Dresden Plate, Ohio Star, Bear's Paw and Fans.

Log Cabin

The Log Cabin pattern, held by many people also to be American, appeared all over Britain, particularly in Scotland, the North of England and the Isle of Man. The simplest of these quilts from the Isle of Man is said to have been based on the measurements of the maker's hand and appears similar to those of the Scandinavian countries. All were made from coarse woven woollen fabrics and cotton shirtings of the working-class community. In Edinburgh the Log Cabin quilts examined on documentation day were finely made in silks and velvets and generally more sophisticated.

The Log Cabin pattern is a combination of units like a repeated block pattern but without any sashing. The unit is either repeated uniformly or turned to make a variety of different layout patterns. These layouts can be strong in their design as a result of using contrasting fabrics. (Each unit is made from strips of fabric sewn round a central square, with the dark fabrics on two adjacent sides and the light fabrics on the other two.) The strips were often sewn on to a backing square of fabric which in many cases became the back of the quilt showing all the stitching and the joining of the units. There were many examples where the blocks were arranged so that their dark sides were together and formed a square-on-point of dark fabric alternating with a contrasting light one. The British have adopted the American name for this: Sunshine and Shadows.

The detail illustrated in figure 3.14 on page 47 of the Log Cabin quilt from the Isle of Man shows this basic layout using mostly blue, red and white cotton fabrics with some browns, both woven and printed. The quilt was made by a member of the Thomson family in about 1900.

The Log Cabin quilt illustrated in figure 3.13 on page 46 from Chelmsford shows an imaginative use of the basic arrangement of the blocks along with a clever arrangement of colour that together give the impression of a frame quilt. This quilt was made in about 1900 by the women of the Wickett family from Cornwall.

Another common layout is one where the contrasting fabrics are arranged in diagonal lines reminiscent of the furrows of a ploughed field. The quilt shown in figure 3.16 on page 47, made by Grace Mungall of Edinburgh in approximately 1880, shows straight furrows placed diagonally round a central square of four dark corners. Other Log Cabin variations were made with a slightly different block where the contrasting coloured strips of fabric were sewn round opposite sides of a hexagon; yet another had strips positioned round the square and contrasting strips at an angle round the corners: this is called 'Pineapple' (see fig.3.15, p.47) because it makes shapes that resemble the fruit. Also a variation was seen where the fabric strips have been sewn on opposite sides of the square and then the contrasting ones on the other two sides. This variation is called 'Court House Steps', probably because the design shows a stepping line where the strips meet at the corners of the block.

Crazy

The crazy patchwork patterns appear chiefly on the ornate quilts from around the late nineteenth and early twentieth centuries and then appear again on the Canadian Red Cross quilts of World War II. Odd-shaped pieces of fabric were tacked on to a backing fabric and secured in place with a fancy stitch where the pieces overlapped. The leftover scraps of dark, rich dress silks, ribbons and velvets together with yellow embroidery outlining the pieces in the Victorian quilts both large and small made a sumptuous-looking covering for various pieces of household furniture in contrast to the Red Cross quilts which were utilitarian in appearance and purpose. Often the crazy-shaped pieces seemed to have been arranged within a square: this is because the patchwork was usually constructed in batches of manageable-sized squares which were then joined to the main body of the quilt rather than by adding very small pieces to this unwieldy larger piece of the whole quilt.

Fig. 4.1. A detail from a frame-style quilt showing the use of buttonhole stitch to apply a motif to the background. Also the design of the print shows buttonhole stitch. 250 cm x 270 cm (8 ft 2 in x 8 ft 10 in).

CHAPTER 4

APPLIQUÉ, EMBELLISHMENTS AND EMBROIDERY
Dinah Travis

Fig. 4.2. A detail from a Tree of Life designed quilt from Bermuda showing the use of the Broderie Perse technique with hemstitch applying the bird to the background.
173 cm x 181 cm (5 ft 8 in x 5 ft 11 in).

APPLIQUÉ IS THE MOST creative of all the patchwork and quilting techniques. It allows complete freedom of expression, having no limitations of shape – other than that of the quilt itself – in which the design has to conform. Many styles of appliqué designed quilts, both simple and complex, were seen during the Project. About one-quarter of the patched quilts examined were found to have appliqué on them. A proportion of these were made up from a base fabric with applied shapes, and the others had applied shapes combined with pieced patchwork.

The earliest among the appliqué quilts, dating from between about 1775 and 1860, often had specific motifs such as a bird or flowers cut from a print and then applied to a plain backing cloth

Fig. 4.3. A good example of an appliqué quilt made in 1810 which has objects randomly arranged within a beautiful, flowing thistle border.
234 cm x 260 cm (7 ft 8 in x 8 ft 6 in).

with a buttonhole (see fig.4.1) or herringbone stitch (see fig.4.5, p.54) covering the raw edges of the cut fabric. Alternatively they were sewn down using a simple hemming stitch with the edge of the shape turned under. These shapes sometimes made a unit on their own, or were combined with others to make a composite picture such as a tree. In many cases the appliqué formed the central motif for a coverlet or quilt, with borders made from various other applied shapes or a combination of applied and pieced shapes. This technique of applying the printed cut-out shapes is called 'Broderie Perse'. Illustrated in figure 4.2 is the detail from a coverlet showing a magnificent bird on a branch of a tree that has been assembled from various prints. This coverlet was made in Bermuda by the wife of a shipping-fleet owner and is typical of this style of quilt, with a Tree of Life in the centre surrounded by two or three borders with a trail of foliage, baskets of flowers or animals and insects. The Broderie Perse appliqué is composed of prints from seven different fabrics.

Some of the appliqué quilts examined in the Project abounded with the shapes of simple household items such as a churn, a house, a teapot, vases or baskets packed with flowers or fruit and even a hand and a cow telling the story of everyday life. Figure 4.3 is a very good example of such a quilt, made by Miss Alice Lonsdale in 1810, which has objects randomly arranged within a beautiful, flowing thistle border. You will be able to guess at the story of her life from the objects that she has chosen to apply on the quilt. The items depicted are numerous and, in some cases, quite detailed. The motifs include a wineglass, teapot, saucepan, apron, globe, candlestick, anchor, bird, music and music case and chest of drawers.

The quilt illustrated in figure 4.4 on page 54 (a detail of which can be seen in chapter 9 'Reading A Quilt' in figure 9.25, on page 207) was made by Mrs Jane Richards of Rippingale, Lincolnshire, in 1829. The maker's sister was a dressmaker and probably provided most of the fabrics used in the quilt. Jane Richards, the maker, married a farm labourer and had eight children. The quilt was passed to the eldest daughter and has come down the family through the female line ever since. The quilt has more than two hundred small squares, each of which is applied with an everyday item; the diagonal corners are also applied with very small and neat herringbone stitch. Today, herringbone stitch has been forgotten as a stitch for appliqué. It is much more flexible and less heavy than buttonhole stitch, which makes a solid and often distracting outline to a shape. The larger central square of the Richards quilt shows a red manor house, similar in style to those seen in embroidered samplers of the eighteenth century, surrounded by a church, a windmill, farm animals, birds and a fish, milkmaids, vases of flowers and a heart. This tells the story of the farming life of the Richards family during the nineteenth century.

The red manor house appeared as a motif in the centre of several documented quilts. The detail illustrated in figure 4.5 on page 54 is from a quilt that emigrated with the maker from Gloucestershire to South Africa and back. The house is surrounded by a grid, in the squares of which are applied numerous pots of flowers, animals, etc., perhaps to remind the family of home.

Figures

People appeared as appliqué in many quilts and some of the most amusing examples must be those on a quilt made in about 1900 by Mrs Barratt, a missionary's wife in India. The detail illustrated in figure 4.6 on page 54 shows that some of the figures are oriental and the others are ladies with umbrellas. They are mingled with neatly sitting cats, standing birds, kites and parasols. Could this perhaps have been made by a group of people being taught basic sewing skills? Mrs Barratt, who was originally from Norwich, spent most of her life in India.

Random Shapes

Other types of appliqué quilts included those with shapes cut randomly from a basic print and applied on panels. The panels were joined with narrow strips of contrasting print giving a formality to the freely cut shapes. One of these quilts, from Chester, had simple shapes, but the quilter from Nottingham who made a similar cover (see fig.4.7, p.55) had been more selective in how she cut the fabric and considered the prints for their subject matter, although she arranged the pieces in a random way. This quilt was made by Catherine Scott, an accomplished needlewoman and aunt of HRH Princess Alice, Duchess of Gloucester. Miss Scott gave the quilt to her companion.

Fold and Cut

Another style that occurred in a number of the more simply designed appliqué quilts was the fold-and-cut motif, created from fabric in the same manner as a child might fold and cut a paper snowflake pattern. These fold-and-cut patterns are also used in the quilts from Hawaii. The British patterns are much smaller than the Hawaiian ones, and they were often arranged in a repeated block layout or placed symmetrically round a larger shape. Basic geometric shapes and simple shapes such as hearts were also used in these quilts and the colours were often Turkey Red on white. A simple red cut-out applied pattern can be seen in the centre of the quilt in figure 4.8 on page 55 that was brought to Bowes Museum in Barnard Castle, Co. Durham, and also in the red and white basket quilt in figure 4.9 brought to the London documentation session. Again there are hearts in this quilt and this could be a symbol of marriage. Many curved red and white patterns were seen, one of which was the Prince of Wales feathers simply arranged radiating from the centre of the quilt. The soldier's quilt with the Prince of Wales feathers illustrated in Chapter 8 (see fig.8.1, p.170) shows another appliqué technique: small punched circles from the cut for uniform buttonholes were applied to form the three feathers. Each circle was held in place by one stitch, a technique similar to the one used when embellishing with sequins.

Red and Green Appliqué

A pattern of red and green flower blocks on a white backing was another of the simpler applied designs documented; broad flowers and leaves appeared in the form of a cross or a bunch of three flowers with four or nine blocks set within a trailing vine border. There were also borders of swags and of thistles. These were often unlined coverlets and mostly from the north-east of England; there are examples of this style in the Beamish Museum. Some of these

Above: Fig. 4.4. The red manor house was seen in the centre of several quilts. In this detail the house is surrounded by a grid, in the squares of which are applied numerous pots of flowers, animals, etc.
245 cm x 255 cm (8 ft x 8 ft 4 in).

Right: Fig. 4.5. A quilt with over two hundred small squares, each of which features an everyday item and diagonal corners. Very small and neat herringbone stitch was used to apply the shapes to the background.
231 cm x 263 cm (7 ft 7 in x 8 ft 8 in).

Below: Fig. 4.6. A quilt made by a missionary's wife in India. Some of the figures are oriental and the others are ladies with umbrellas, both mixed up with neatly sitting cats, standing birds, kites and parasols.
149 cm x 175 cm (4 ft 11 in x 5 ft 9 in).

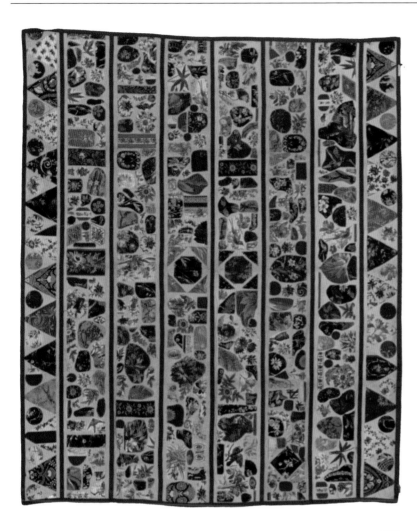

Left: Fig. 4.7. Eight panels of randomly applied shapes divided up with narrow Turkey Red sashing strips over the joins. 181 cm x 214 cm (5 ft 11 in x 7 ft).

Above: Fig. 4.8. A detail from a quilt showing a red cut-out pattern centre surrounded by simple vases of tulips and an Irish chain pattern.
254 cm square (8 ft 4 in square).

Below left: Fig. 4.10. This quilt portraying four vases of lilies with a swag border supported by hearts was made in Northumberland in 1910 by a teacher who had spent her early childhood in America.
202 cm x 205 cm (6 ft 7 in x 6 ft 8 in).

Below: Fig. 4.9. A cut-out pattern centre surrounded by smaller cut-out patterns and hearts with a wide border of baskets all in Turkey Red.
186 cm x 188 cm (6 ft 1 in x 6 ft 2 in).

quilts had family connections with America, where the same style of applied patterns was popular. The quilt with four vases of lilies illustrated in figure 4.10 on page 55 was made between 1910 and 1914 by Anna Marcella Lewis, a teacher from Northumberland, who had spent her early childhood in America. Perhaps the small red hearts between the vases and holding the swags round the border suggest that the quilt was made for her wedding.

1930s Appliqué

Blocks with applied crinoline ladies, butterflies, horse-chestnut leaves and the familiar Sunbonnet Sue pattern were seen on quilts that were brought over to Britain from Canada or America. These were made in the mauve, pink, green and yellow fabrics so popular in the 1930s when the North American influence was probably at its strongest. Many were made from kits or patterns that were printed in the magazines of the period. Egypt was yet another source of applied work dating from the opening of the Tutankhamun tomb in 1922 to the present day (see p.167).

Embellishments and Adornments

As well as the traditional appliqué techniques the Project revealed many forms of applied and embroidered embellishments, from heavily adorned Victorian quilts sparkling with sequins and beads to red and white chequered signature quilts. Richly decorated quilts were seen all over the country but the affluent society of the Victorian era in Edinburgh, London and Dorchester produced more than anywhere else. Some of these quilts were made to commemorate a special occasion.

Crazy patchwork, the most prolific example of embellishment and embroidered work, was brought to documentation sessions in all areas of Britain. Nearly two hundred such quilts were recorded. They ranged from specimens with very simple embroidery stitches round the edges of the patches, often in yellow, to quilts with so much embellishment that it was difficult to see the detail of the fabrics.

The first quilt of this type to be viewed by the Project appeared in Chester and the sparkle of the sequins, beads and buttons on the velvets and silks caught every eye. The illustration (see fig.4.11, p.58) of the whole quilt shows nine blocks surrounded by a narrow border. There is also a wide border of three more blocks of crazy patchwork on each side, with corner blocks of eight-pointed stars covered with sprigs of embroidery massed with beads and sequins of different shapes, a central button and gold braid couched down round the star (see detail in fig.4.13, p.59). All the pieces are edged with an embroidery stitch in many variations. Extra interest is provided by applied shapes such as the butterfly seen in figure 4.12 on page 58. An image of Queen Victoria's head and the Golden Jubilee date of 1887 are also included. The family who own this quilt lived originally in Chapel-en-le-Frith, Derbyshire, and then moved to Ireland.

A crazy quilt of a similar age (see fig.4.14, p.59) is believed to have come from Southport and was made by Alice Wall for a married sister in 1885. It has an even larger variety of decorative stitches. Buttonhole, feather and cross-stitch, a spider's web, Olympic rings, flags, cup and saucer, beetles, a robin and other symbols combine to make a highly ornate cover.

Another piece of crazy patchwork (see detail in fig.4.16, p.62) thought to have been divided up between the family shows other decorative additions in the form of ribbon embroidery and applied flocked leaves and pansies together with ribbons showing two portraits of military gentlemen.

Jubilee Quilt

The ornate and colourful quilt in the frontispiece seen in Barnard Castle, made to celebrate the Golden Jubilee anniversary of Queen Victoria's succession to the throne, was sewn for a family in lieu of rent. It shows a rich combination of velvets and silks in dahlia-shaped flower heads on an embroidered Log Cabin base surrounded finally with an elaborate embroidered border of pieced fans. The embroidery incorporates many different stitches and details of figures of the period on the fans – including policemen, soldiers, fashionable ladies and children playing with toys as well as realistic sprays of flowers (see detail in fig.4.17 on pp. 62-3). It is a truly unique quilt.

Embroidery

Embroidery was present on a great number of the quilts brought for documentation. Cross-stitch was used to record a name and date (see p.136), as seen in samplers of the nineteenth century, to record the signatures of people who had made a donation to a project, and also to picture naturalistic flowers. Over six hundred signatures are lettered on a quilt shown in figure 4.15 on page 60 made by the Red Cross for the World War I effort to raise funds and to keep up the morale of the people. It is made up from forty-nine applied red cut-out flower shapes with names embroidered in white stem stitch on the eight petals of each flower. Lord Kitchener's is one of the names.

The unfinished quilt top in figure 4.18 on page 63 made by Evelyn Jones in 1880 is composed of pieced rectangles of dark woollen flannel fabrics in a simple frame arrangement and embellished richly with embroidered flowers in coloured wool. The

Above: Fig. 4.11. An ornately decorated crazy patchwork quilt with stars and a fan.
162 cm square (5 ft 4 in square).

Right: Fig. 4.12. Detail of fig.4.11 showing the crazy shapes applied with embroidery stitches and an applied butterfly.

Opposite top: Fig. 4.13. Detail of fig.4.11 showing one of the six-pointed stars adorned with sequins, beads, a button and an outlining couched thread.

Opposite: Fig. 4.14. Detail of a crazy quilt set in blocks within a border showing embroidery stitches with numerous variations and several different motifs.
162 cm x 164 cm (5 ft 4 in x 5 ft 5 in).

Mary C. Fallas

Mabel S Fallas

Margaret E Duncan

...a Fallas

Jean Fallas

Knox

Alderson

Hamilton

Kitchener

Asquith

Queen Mary

King George

Commander...

Roberts

Jellicoe

Beatty

French

Grey

Charlie Bate

W. J. McClune

Mrs...

flowers are particularly beautiful, showing a botanist's attention to detail and character.

A number of coverlets with blocks of very naturalistic flowers dating from the turn of the century were documented. Their popularity was probably attributable to the manufacture of the iron-on transfer from about 1875 by William Briggs Co. and the ease of their use. Some of these blocks in quilts and coverlets were joined together with lace sashing. Another unusual coverlet in Chester was one made with alternate lace and white embroidered blocks; handmade, machine-made and crocheted laces were all recorded. Also documented were a number of other quilts that were augmented with lace edging, including one coverlet made from printed religious texts, and a Victorian crazy quilt.

The oldest embroidered quilt (see Chap.5, fig.5.6, p.70) came to the Shrewsbury day. The date 1695 is embroidered within one of the leaves of a motif. The motifs represented in the designs are exotic trees, flowers and birds worked in chain stitch; they appear in graduated shades of colour on a background of crisscross back-stitch quilting and are arranged all over the quilt. The illustrated detail shows one of these motifs with part of the narrow border.

An early eighteenth-century quilt with similar chain-stitch embroidery from the Needlework Development Scheme came to the Paisley day. It had the same type of exotic flowers in chain stitch with shaded colours but these motifs were regularly arranged within the central square of the quilt. The Needlework Development Scheme to promote greater interest in embroidery and design was started in Scotland in 1934. Initially organized through the four Scottish art schools, the Scheme focused on collecting foreign and British embroideries which could be used for exhibition and as teaching aids. Except for a five-year period during World War II, the Scheme continued until 1961, by which time it had amassed 3,500 embroideries. The embroideries were subsequently dispersed to various museums and educational institutions.

The popular revival in the 1930s of the Jacobean style of design was also in evidence in the wool-embroidered coverlets that were recorded. Also seen were embroidered coverlets with beautiful scenes of water, birds and irises. These came to Britain in the 1920s from China, along with many other imported embroidered items. One of these appeared in Dorchester. Other embroidered coverlets came from India and some from America. The increase in travel by more and more people from the beginning of the twentieth century to and from both the Americas and the Eastern countries must have influenced the outlook and approach to the designing of quilts today.

Opposite: Fig. 4.15. Detail of signature quilt with over six hundred names recorded. It was made to raise funds for the World War I effort and to keep up the morale of the people. There are forty-eight flower-shaped cut-outs.
214 cm square (7 ft square).

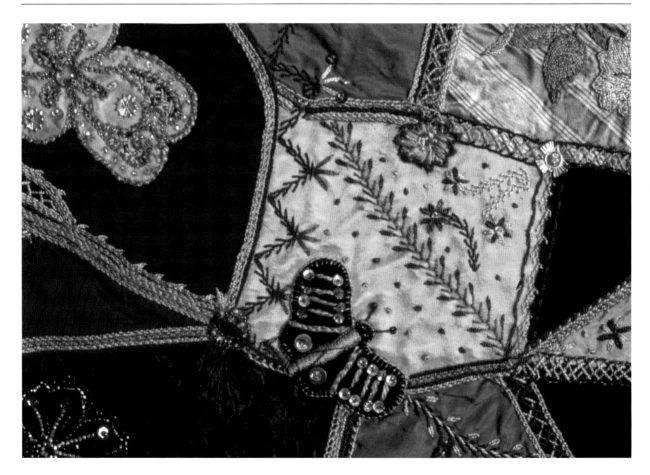

Fig. 4.16. This piece of crazy patchwork that was divided up between the family has many decorative additions in the form of ribbon embroidery and applied flocked leaves and pansies.
93 cm x 145 cm (3 ft 1 in x 4 ft 9 in).

Fig. 4.17. Detail of quilt made to celebrate Queen Victoria's Golden Jubilee in 1887 showing the decorative piecing of stars, fans and small Log Cabin squares, all covered with detailed embroidery.
(See also frontispiece.)

Fig. 4.18 . Unfinished quilt, dated 1880, made from woollen tweeds and realistic flower embroidery.
156 cm x 171 cm (5 ft 1 in x 5 ft 7 in).

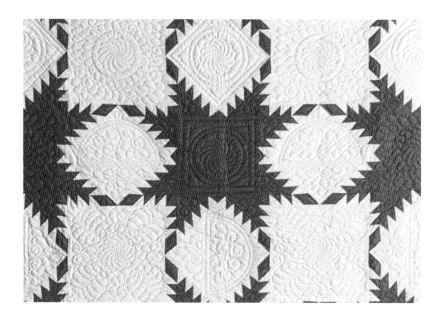

Fig. 5.1. Detail of Feathered Star quilt shown on p.111.

Fig. 5.2. Detail of cotton sateen strippy quilt shown on p.95.

CHAPTER 5

TRADITIONS OF QUILTING

Pauline Adams & Bridget Long

IN 1937, ELIZABETH HAKE wrote in her preface to *English Quilting Old and New…*

> quilting as a home industry may have been universal in England up to fifty years ago. If a survey of each county could be made within the next few years, it is reasonably certain that some remarkable evidence to support this theory would be forth-coming from the last remaining traces of this fascinating art.

Nearly sixty years after Mrs Hake wrote those words, a period interrupted by war and austerity, by changing fashion and customs and by a resurgence in patchwork and quilting emanating from America, the survey has at last been done. It did not show quilting traditions for all counties as she had confidently expected, but it did bring forward a wealth of fine and always interesting examples of traditional quilting.

Quilting is the process by which the three layers of a quilt are simultaneously joined and decorated. The three layers are like a sandwich, consisting of a top (which may be plain or print, patchwork or appliqué), a wadding (known as 'batting' in America) and a backing fabric on the reverse. Some quilts have no wadding, being 'flat quilted' through top and backing only, which serves again as decoration and to hold the layers together. There are two other techniques of quilting which appeared in Britain early on – stuffed quilting, where the stitched pattern shapes were filled with stuffing from the back, creating areas of high relief; and corded quilting, where the top and back fabrics were stitched in a pattern of channels and cotton cord or wool yarn was inserted from the back, creating lines of high relief. Some quilts were simply and quickly 'knotted' or 'tied' through the three layers. A 'wholecloth' quilt is one where a single fabric (joined if necessary) has been used for the quilt top. The quilting stitch is a running stitch through the three layers of the quilt sandwich. Its decorative effect comes from the dimpled shadows made by the many stitches which went to make up the sewing of each pattern.

The authors suspect that for the most part 'better' rather than 'ragged remnant' quilts were brought for documentation. They also think it likely that utility quilts tended to become very worn and were thrown out (wholecloth quilts being less valued, perhaps, than patchwork quilts), while those quilts perceived as 'masterpieces' would be cherished and thus survive. In this way, the data assembled from the many quilted items seen during the Project's documentation sessions represent, at best, a sample of surviving quilts rather than the proportions of different types actually made in Britain or brought here from overseas. The data relates only to those quilts examined during the Project. If conclusions can be drawn, ideas clarified and queries raised as a result of this research, then that must be all to the good.

EARLY QUILTS

Two examples of quilting from the seventeenth century were recorded and they proved to be the oldest quilts seen during the entire Project. The two were from either end of the century and appeared vastly different in style and technique.

The magnificent full-sized quilt demonstrating a sophisticated design in stuffed quilting (see fig. 5.3, p.66), thought to have been made early in the 1600s, was seen at Truro in Cornwall. The design has a large central rectangle surrounded by a wide border. The rectangle contains a circle showing a ship at sea bordered by a rim containing pictures of hounds and four male heads set north, south, east and west of the ship. The remainder of the rectangle has

Fig. 5.3. Stuffed silk quilt, possibly Indo-
Portuguese work, early seventeenth century.
223 cm x 256 cm (7 ft 4 in x 8 ft 5 in).

Fig. 5.4. Detail of fig.5.3 showing hunting scene.

military/hunting scenes below (see fig.5.4) and two examples of a double-headed eagle above. The borders contain hunting scenes with horses, stags, hounds, unicorns, gryphons and armed men dressed in wide breeches, doublets and helmets. The border is edged on both sides by a narrow twisted rope pattern. An extra linen backing has been added at some stage to the quilt and the design resewn.

This quilt shows a number of design characteristics typical of Indo-Portuguese work and its layout is remarkably similar to one described by Averil Colby.[1] Quite how a quilt of this origin ended up in the south-west of England is not known, but possibly, bearing in mind the seafaring activities of many Cornish men, it was brought back after a long sea voyage.

The second quilt from the seventeenth century, dated 1695 in the embroidery, is of a style which continued well into the eighteenth century. Its main interest is the chain-stitch embroidery (see fig.5.6 on p. 70). The background quilting is of diagonal lines that create a simple diamond pattern.

The earlier quilt is stuffed with cotton while the wadding used in the later quilt is wool. The use of different fillings emphasizes the style contrast of these two quilts.

EIGHTEENTH-CENTURY QUILTING

Any item made before the 1800s was greeted with some excitement during the Project. It was a privilege to examine examples of quilted or pieced household textiles that had managed to survive more than two centuries of general domestic wear and tear. Although the Project recorded comparatively few items made before 1800, those that were seen gave a good impression of the varied styles and techniques to be expected from this period.

Nineteen quilted items from the eighteenth century were examined. They separated naturally into four different types - clothing; functional plain quilting; decorative wadded quilting; and corded, with associated quilting.

Clothing

The oldest item of clothing was a striking green silk 'undress' made in about 1720. A loose garment with no fastening at the front, it was used for informal wear in the style of a modern housecoat. Coarsely woven linen bands were added to the inside back and front at a later date to draw the undress in and fashion a makeshift fastening in front, perhaps for modesty's sake. The body of the garment was quilted in an all-over diamond pattern, with a border containing a flowing vine design of flowers and leaves around the hem and up the front edge to the roll-back collar. This undress had a sophisticated design and showed evidence of competent workmanship. It was obviously intended for a lady of some means and demonstrates how fashionable quilted clothing was during this century. The wadding in the undress would provide warmth, but it is suggested that protection from cold was not the only reason behind the construction of such a garment.

The item of clothing most associated with eighteenth-century quilting is the petticoat. Quilted petticoats originated as functional warm garments, but, with the evolution of the dress style which allowed the skirts to open in the front to reveal a show garment underneath, ornately quilted petticoats became fashionable.

Two very similar quilted petticoats were recorded, both of which are made of silk, have glazed wool backings and are filled with wool wadding. The 'show' area of the petticoats is decorated in a wide undulating pattern containing simple stylized flower motifs (see fig.5.5) with widely spaced infilling of smaller wave motifs and zigzag lines. Both petticoats have comparatively simple decorative motifs and are of a type that was designed, made and sold 'off-the-peg' in quilt workshops.

A third petticoat, examined at Edinburgh, had a far more sophisticated look (see fig.5.7, p. 71). The petticoat of pink silk was worn by Janet Andrew when she married John McEwan at

Opposite: Fig. 5.5. Diagram of eighteenth-century floral motifs from silk petticoats. Scale 1:44.

Fig. 5.6. Detail of an embroidered motif from a quilt made in 1695 also showing the back-stitch quilting.
168 cm x 189 cm (5 ft 6 in x 6 ft 2 in).

Greenock, Strathclyde, in 1762. The complex quilting pattern covers the bottom 53 centimetres (21 in) of the petticoat and is repeated three times around the hem. It consists of an ornate floral bouquet with tulips and exotic flowers, together with other stylized floral and cloud motifs, above a narrow diamond and clamshell border. The quilting design appears to have been worked on the front and back pieces of the petticoat before it was made up so that the pattern does not quite match at the neatened side seams. The design of this petticoat is much finer with closer spacing to the quilting lines and far smaller quilting motifs. Even the background diamond pattern at the top has a spacing of only 1.25 centimetres (½ in).

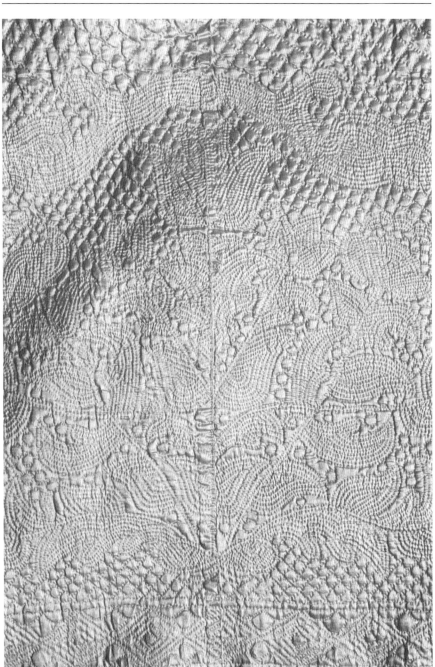

It is clear that a number of professional quilters operated in London during this period. They made quilted garments and sold quilted material and fabric marked with quilting designs for making up at home.[2] It is known that Janet Andrew visited London in 1759 when she stayed with her mother's relations and saw both the funeral of George II and the coronation procession of George III. It is possible that the petticoat that she wore for her wedding was obtained in London from a professional petticoat maker. Similarly, it can be speculated that the 1720 undress was professionally made, since the family history has it that it was made by the Huguenots in Canterbury, Kent.

Fig. 5.7. Quilted silk petticoat made for Scottish wedding in 1762, length 84 cm (2 ft 9 in), circumference 268 cm (8 ft 10 in). Detail features formalized bouquet of flowers with diamond background.

Functional Quilting

Quilting which merely held the fabric layers of a bed cover together was common. It was worked in an all-over layout such as diamonds or zigzag line waves as a functional pattern with no thought given to decorative effect. It either anchored the top and back fabric as flat quilting or it enclosed wadding.

The frame quilt dated 1796 (see fig.2.5 on p.19) and a detail of a plate-printed cotton (see fig.9.12 on p.198) feature such all-over quilting. An early eighteenth-century embroidered quilt seen at Chester had a background of flat diamond quilting spaced 1 centimetre (2/5 in). The fabric in this example was quilted before it was embroidered.

Decorative Wadded Quilting

Wadded quilts of this period had some status as fashionable textiles intended for the households of the rich. Ornate quilting designs were seen in association with embroidery but the complex layouts and a variety of quilting motifs were also combined to create striking wholecloth quilts.

The layouts of the quilts were in the formalized central motif with delineated borders style or 'framed'. They seem to have been confidently drafted with good proportions of scale, suggesting that this style of layout was well established by this period. The frame layout, it is suggested, had probably evolved over time, with the influence from the layouts of embroidered textiles and imported Indian fabrics proving to be highly significant.

A quilt recorded at Paisley has a top of linen decorated in the centre with crewelwork flowers (see fig.5.9, p.74). The embroidered area has been cut and rejoined and a plain linen border added in order to create a piece large enough for a quilted bed cover. Its central circle motif has rims and a complex infilling of flowers.

Two other examples had a large central circular motif containing flowers, but in each case the circle was surrounded by four large triangles creating a star effect. One was a seventeenth-century Chinese silk embroidered bed cover, featuring flowers, leaves, birds and butterflies, which was later quilted on wool wadding. The other example was a wholecloth quilt of silk quilted on wool. Remarkably, although the owner acquired these quilts from different sources, they had such similar layouts and combinations of motifs it is conceivable that they were designed or worked by the same hand.

Corded Quilting

Corded quilting, a decorative technique related to embroidery, was very popular during the eighteenth century. It is possible that the technique has its roots in the Middle East, where it evolved as a

Fig. 5.8. Detail of back and hem of cream corded cotton coat, Damascus/Turkish nineteenth century.

method which gave texture, firmness and body to the item without creating a thick warm layer typical of wadded quilting. The method was also well known in Italy. It must be remembered, however, that the Italian city states had very strong trading links with the Middle East for centuries.

The Eastern link can be demonstrated by the 'Turkish Coat'. Three examples of this coat style were documented, of which two are probably from the nineteenth century and one from the twentieth century. All three display the same shape with square set-in sleeves, an A-line cut to the body, with a wider border around the hem and front edges and side slits instead of pockets. The entire coat is covered in corded quilting in a zigzag with simple floral-motif design (see fig.5.8).

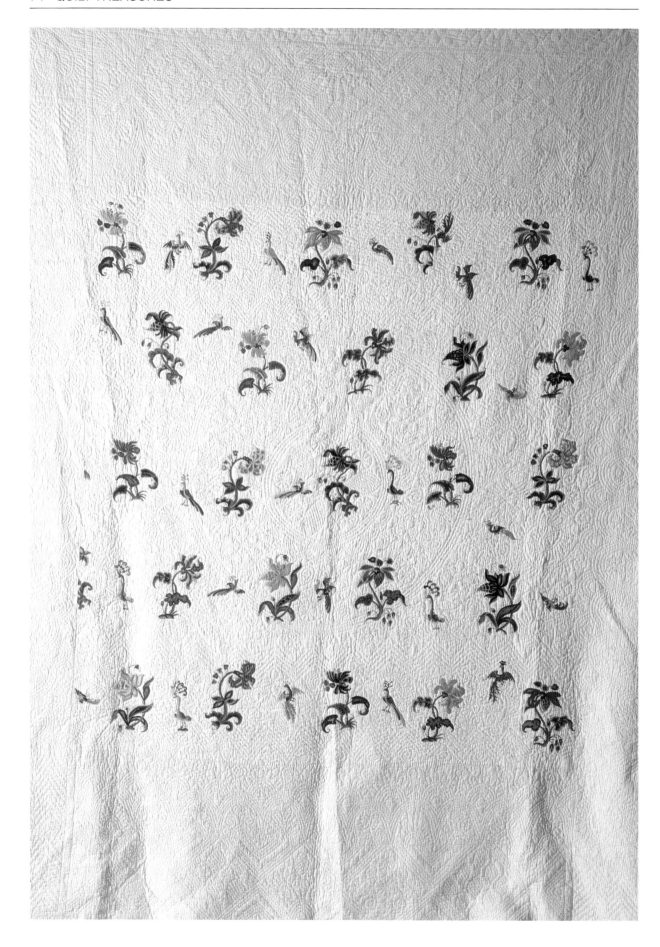

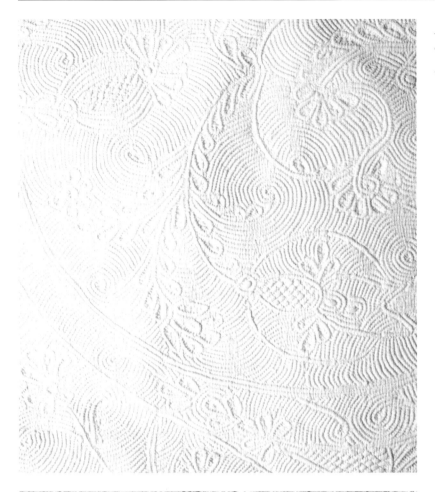

Fig. 5.10. Detail of early-eighteenth-century fragment of corded quilting, featuring all-over pattern of meandering flower and leaf sprays with line infill. Probably French. 95 cm x 401 cm (3 ft 1 in x 13 ft 2 in).

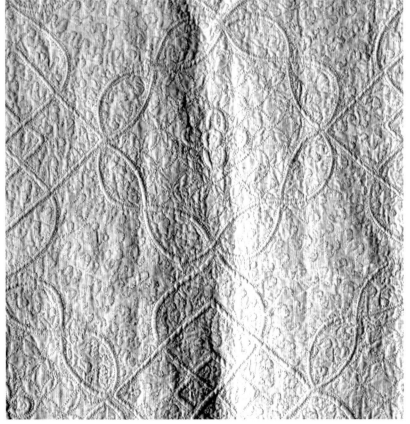

Fig. 5.11. Detail of early-eighteenth-century linen fragment featuring corded and flat quilting. Diaper pattern with wineglass and meander infill.
41 cm x 64 cm (16 in x 2 ft 1 in).

Opposite: Fig. 5.9. Early-eighteenth-century linen quilt embellished with embroidery. Whole quilt, except for part of both side borders, features large centre circle containing floral motifs, and borders of arches, squares and flowers.
210 cm x 227 cm (6 ft 11 in x 7 ft 5 in).

The coat has its origins in the Ottoman Empire, particularly in cities such as Damascus.[3] The coats were intended to be worn as loose informal over-garments on occasions such as social gatherings at the bath house. The coats continued to be made into the twentieth century and could well have been brought back to Britain as souvenirs of visits to the area.

Three items of eighteenth-century corded quilting were seen. Two fragments from the early 1700s were obviously cut down from larger items. One piece from south-west England was used, until fairly recently, as an altar cloth in a Roman Catholic church (see fig.5.10, p.75). The placing of the design motifs suggests that it was part of a larger piece and, since it was over 401 centimetres (13 ft) long, it was likely originally to have been a bed cover. This example is fully corded,[4] with both the floral and leaf motifs and the background made up of rows of cords.

A small linen fragment recorded in Swavesey features an all-over interlaced diaper pattern reminiscent of strap work (see fig.5.11, p.75). This piece is notable for flat quilting in the uncorded areas in a wineglass and a meander (vermicular) pattern.

A large bed cover from Edinburgh features corded quilting in an ornate frame layout (see fig.5.12, p.78). The quilt contains corded motifs with the larger uncorded areas infilled with random flat quilting stitches called 'stipple' quilting. The centre square of the quilt encloses a large complex pattern interpreted as plumes and scrolls incorporating intertwined initials and topped with a coronet. This motif is repeated in each corner of the centre square, with tulips, leaves and hearts along each side. A wide border containing a pot with a variety of flowers has a pineapple motif in the corners and is enclosed between two narrow floral borders (see fig.5.20, p.86).

The three corded items documented are examples of a typical eighteenth-century labour-intensive decorative technique intended for people of wealth. The popularity of cording does not seem to have continued widely into the nineteenth century. A corded quilt was recorded which is dated 1807, but it appeared to have Indian connections: some corded and stuffed ribbon fragments seen in Kelso are thought to have been made in India in the second half of this century, to be sold by the length for insertion.

There was a revival of corded quilting in the twentieth century and a number of corded cushions from the 1920s and 1930s, including some made from kits, were seen. More notably, a wedding dress and jacket made from silk grosgrain in 1954 featured a unique corded pattern on the skirt, bodice and jacket collar. The dress was made in two weeks by the bride's aunt, who came over from the Netherlands for the wedding.

Eighteenth-century Patterns

The majority of the patterns on the quilted items were of either a stylized or a naturalistic floral type. This was not entirely unexpected, since many designs from other sources at this time were flower-based. The eighteenth-century quilter was inspired by the look of the exotic flowers seen on imported Chinese and Indian textiles and was surrounded too by home-based flower shapes such as tulips, lilies and dianthus, the flowers seen in European-influenced domestic items.

Common infill patterns such as clamshell, wineglass and spiral were noted. Zigzag wave or square-on-point and triangular motifs occurred as infill or enclosing other motifs. A border pattern which in much later quilts would be called Welsh Trail was found on two decorative wadded quilts.

QUILTING 1800-1850

The period embracing the first half of the nineteenth century has been defined as the 'high point' of traditional quilting in Britain and certainly some remarkable quilts of this time have survived the ensuing years. However, only nine examples of wholecloth quilts that could be confidently attributed to this period were seen during the Project. Thus most of the quilting examined accompanied patchwork. Study of nineteenth-century quilting was aided by the fabrics used in piecing which provide clues for the dating of the quilts. In addition, a noteworthy group of pieced quilts of the period were found to have labels giving dates and, in many cases, the maker's name or initials.

With very few exceptions, all quilts of this period were of the wadded, rather than the corded or flat quilted, type. It has been suggested that no corded quilt made later than the end of the eighteenth century has survived. However, a cotton quilt examined in Edinburgh, displaying a pattern of corded and stuffed leaves, stems, fruits and flowers on a flat unwadded background, had a date in the cording of 1807, bringing it close to the survival limit. The family history of this quilt suggests that it was made in Bangalore, India. The quilt certainly remained there until 1888, when it was sent home to Edinburgh to the then owner's mother.

A number of other quilts were flat quilted, making them more akin to unlined coverlets of the period. These included a group of three quilts that belonged to Dr and Mrs Lomas of Allonby, Cumbria, and were likely to have been made in the period 1820-35.

The simplest examples of quilting were mosaic patchwork quilts where repeating shapes such as hexagons or diamonds were outlined approximately half a centimetre (¼ in) from the seam lines. Such outlining was employed purely as a method of

Fig. 5.12. Corner of centre square of eighteenth-century linen bed cover featuring corded and flat quilting. Ornate corded pattern of monogram, coronet and plumes. The narrow crossing borders continue to the edges of the quilt. Large background areas infilled with stipple quilting and cording. Probably French. 248 cm x 264 cm (8 ft 2 in x 8 ft 10 in).

anchoring the three layers of the quilt, without thought being given to the decorative effect.

Quilting in a basic all-over pattern such as clamshell or wineglass was seen on many quilts, particularly on ones from south-west England. A straight line wave was also frequently used as an all-over quilting pattern. The highest percentage of recorded quilts showing this style originated from the Isle of Man or Cumbria, demonstrating a strong regional influence. A detail of a printed cotton depicting Richard Cobden (English economist and politician, the 'Apostle of Free Trade'), from the top of a wholecloth quilt, shows an example of all-over diamond quilting (see Chap.9, fig.9.16, p.202).

It is easy to imagine that pieced quilts that are quilted in an outline or all-over pattern were made to give the patchwork side precedence as the quilt top. It is, however, far harder to make assumptions about the top layer when considering quilts with both attractive piecing and quilting designs. Again, it has been suggested that the plain side of the pieced quilt, showing quilting designs to their best advantage, was a continuation of the eighteenth-century wholecloth tradition and that it would have been on display with the pieced side underneath. Some quilts were studied that showed poor-quality fabric on the plain side; it is unlikely that these would have been for show.

Many early-nineteenth-century pieced quilts have intricate designs and outstanding fabrics, sometimes including special purchases such as the printed medallion panels. It is difficult to imagine that such patchwork would take second place to the plain quilted side. A quilt from north Devon dated 1834 has a centre panel commemorating Wellington's victory at Waterloo surrounded by triangles pieced in Birds in Air and Broken Dishes patterns (see fig.9.22 on p.207). The plain side of the quilt is made of white linen showing a register mark and the manufacturer's trade stamp – Edward Shannon of Coleraine – while the quilting is fairly naive in scale and layout. The patchwork was obviously the 'show side'.

Layouts

The majority of quilting layouts seen from this period were of the frame or border style. These quilt layouts were influenced by textiles such as Indian cotton chintzes and embroidered and quilted coverlets from the previous century. The strong central pattern surrounded by delineated borders was a look that had evolved as a fashion in textiles from the most expensive through to the everyday domestic variety over this period.

A quilt documented at Inverness (see figs.5.15 and 5.17 on pp.82-3) demonstrates a typical frame layout of this period. The quilt is notable for the very effective close quilting in the central square, where the spacing of the diamond background infill is 1 centimetre (2/5 in) wide. The distinctive central six-petal floral motif, repeated in the four central corners, shows a remarkable similarity to the motif seen in *English Quilting* by Elizabeth Hake. It features the same small flower in each petal and only lacks the stippling at the flower centre to be identical – it is infilled with close lines instead. A large curved area on each edge of the central square, filled with stipple quilting which highlights some oval and triangular unquilted areas, was seen in both quilts. One can only speculate on the possibility of a link between the two quilts.

The frame layout of this period looked similar wherever the quilts were examined and examples were seen in Scotland, north-east and north-west England, the south-west, Wales and the Welsh borders. Close analysis and measurement of a group of selected quilts firmly dated within this period reveal that the formula for an effective layout was often one-third of the quilt length for the central rectangle or square and two-thirds for the borders. All quilts had borders strongly delineated by straight lines dividing the patterns.

Frequently, the motif at the centre of the layout was a large circle or 'wheel'; and a quarter circle, often incorporating the same design as the centre circle, was used as a fan motif in the corners of the centre shape.

Fig. 5.13. Diagram of quarter of the quilting layout of pieced frame quilt made by Ann Morse in Whitland, Dyfed, in about 1820-5. 203 cm x 218 cm (6 ft 8 in x 7 ft 2 in).

Fig. 5.14. Diagram of quarter of the quilting layout of Windmill block patchwork quilt, made by a Yorkshire girl named Mary between 1845 and 1850. 238 cm x 261 cm (7 ft 10 in x 8 ft 7 in).

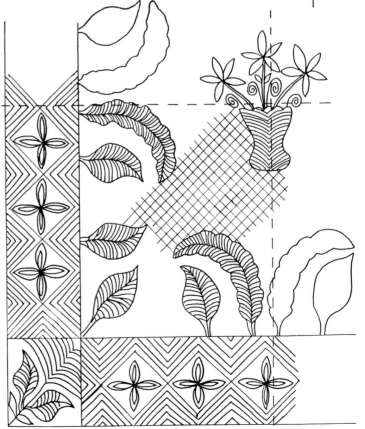

The quilt from Devon in figure 5.16 on page 82 has at its centre a large circle with three narrow rims of cable, ribbon and spiral waves. The circle contains a basket with sunflower and spiral flowers. A fan with crosshatch infill and ribbed rim appears in the corners of the central square.

The Project demonstrated that during the period between 1800 and 1850 a general simplification of the frame/border layout came about. Quilts made in the very first years of the nineteenth century do seem to be far more intricate in terms of both the layouts and the quantity and distribution of the selected quilting patterns. In some earlier examples, it was noted that the delineation of wide pattern borders was achieved by the use of very narrow borders that contained simple patterns such as dogtooth, chain or ribbon. The designs within the borders themselves were more likely to be complex combinations of motifs, often freehand drawn, whereas later they tended to be just simple repeats of single patterns.

During this period the fashion for quilting moved out of the rich houses and quilting was more widely practised in modest homes. It is possible that the simplification of the quilted frame layout demonstrates this loss of interest shown by ladies of leisure and means and reveals the development of quilting into a more country-based domestic occupation. Women without the experience or time to draft complicated quilting layouts or the skill to draw complex freehand patterns would tend to utilize simpler motifs that would repeat effectively.

A cotton quilt made in Mathry, Dyfed, in the early 1800s demonstrates the earlier intricate frame layout (see fig.5.18, p.83). It has an unusual open centre infilled with very fine diamonds, and strong tulip motifs in each corner of the centre square.

Two quilting layouts illustrate the change in the frame style during the first half of the nineteenth century. The first, a pieced frame quilt, was made by Ann Morse in Whitland, Dyfed, between 1820 and 1825 and the style of the frame layout can only be described as 'hectic'. The second quilt has a Windmill pattern pieced top and a far simpler quilt layout. The quilt was sewn in Yorkshire by a seventeen-year-old girl called Mary while she was ill in bed and it was likely to have been made between 1845 and 1850 (see figs.5.13 and 5.14).

No true strippy quilt with both pieced strippy top and matching strippy quilting layout was seen from this period. A quilted strippy layout was viewed, however, on one of the three quilts from the Lomas family of Allonby, Cumbria. This pieced frame quilt contains cotton fabrics from the 1815 period (see fig.9.5 p.190) and is quilted in six strips. Four strips contain infill patterns of clamshell and wineglass, while the other two strips have floral vines with a

Fig. 5.15. Pieced cotton quilt with printed central panel, made in early nineteenth century.
216 cm x 383 cm (7 ft 1 in x 12 ft 7 in).

Fig. 5.16. Centre of reverse of pieced frame cotton quilt, made in Devon in early nineteenth century. Featuring circular motif enclosing flower basket, and four corner fans. Note curved-diamond/clamshell infill pattern.
262 cm x 272 cm (8 ft 7 in x 8 ft 11 in).

Fig. 5.17. Back of pieced quilt shown in fig. 5.15, linen, wadded with wool. Quilted in frame style with floral motifs and very fine diamond and stipple quilting in the centre. Borders of wineglass, running fern and wave, with flower and spiral infill. Original outer-side borders removed.

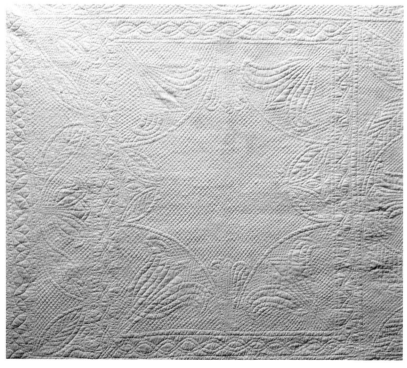

Fig. 5.18. Centre of early-ninteenth-century cotton wholecloth quilt, made in Mathry, Dyfed, Wales. Featuring stylized tulips in centre and very fine background quilting, and alternating narrow and wide borders. 249 cm x 259 cm (8 ft 2 in x 8 ft 6 in).

variety of patterns such as starflowers, daisies, bellflowers and lotus flowers. It was the earliest quilt showing a quilted strippy layout.

The other two quilts from the Lomas family were wholecloth with two very similar frame layouts. They had many flower patterns in common with the strippy.

A strippy quilting layout was seen on a wholecloth quilt from the Otterburn area of Northumberland. The quilt was probably made from local Cheviot wool, which was homespun and woven in a local mill, in the mid-nineteenth century. The strips were quilted with triangles and squares-on-point down the length of the quilt, with infilling of alternating flower sprays, leaves, hearts and lines.

Patterns

It is likely that utility quilting had always been practised as a matter of need with no thought to decorative effect. With the spread of interest in quilting as a fashion from the upper social classes to the middle and working classes, however, there would have been great impetus to reproduce the attractive quilts seen in the large houses.

Designs for quilting patterns would have been obtained from a variety of sources and it is interesting to speculate upon the possible influences at this time. Textiles from the eighteenth century were an inspiration for quilt patterns as well as layouts; it can be assumed that a quilter would also have drawn on the domestic items which surrounded her such as pottery (including English delftware) and carved furniture. A study of carved furniture from the seventeenth and eighteenth centuries reveals a wealth of decorative patterns such as cables, arches, church windows, strap work and waves. A number of motifs seem to have evolved from sources popular over the previous two centuries, but they would appear side by side with motifs such as hearts, clamshells and spirals, which were folk motifs seen in decorative art for hundreds of years.

Floral motifs continued to be used. In the case of earlier quilts, often they were freehand drawn, inspired by the fantastic floral motif seen in older textiles rather than reproduced in a rigid design from templates. A quilt seen at Halifax, dating from about 1810, is an excellent example; full of flowers, it demonstrates the quirky originality of the quilter who created them. Motifs from this quilt, together with a number of other flower and leaf quilt patterns from the early nineteenth century, are illustrated in figure 5.19.

It was noted that a small length of cable was used occasionally as part of a botanical motif either as a flower, as seen later in figure 5.25 on page 92, or as a leaf (see fig. 5.19). Alternatively, it was used as an infill, as demonstrated in the quilt layout in figure 5.13 on page 80. The cable infill was seen alongside the more usual infill patterns such as diamond, clamshell, wineglass, spirals and wave.

Opposite: Fig. 5.19. Leaf and flower quilting motifs from 1810-35.

Fig. 5.20. Border detail of eighteenth-century linen bed cover illustrated on page 78, featuring pot with flowers. Probably French.

Fig. 5.21. Centre detail of cotton wholecloth quilt made about 1820, in Dyfed, featuring vase with flowers and leaves.
210 cm x 224 cm (6 ft 11 in x 7 ft 4 in).

Fig. 5.22. Centre detail of reverse of pieced cotton quilt, illustrated in fig. 5.14, featuring vase with flowers and spirals.

Fig. 5.23. Centre detail of cotton wholecloth quilt made in 1934 in South Wales, featuring cornucopia with flowers and leaves. 180 cm x 198 cm (5 ft 11 in x 6 ft 6 in). *(Photo: Pauline Adams)*

The Halifax quilt has fine examples of an enduring eighteenth-century motif – the floral container. It has a central circle enclosing a basket of flowers and the corners of the first border feature cornucopia-style containers.

The floral container was a popular motif frequently seen in all kinds of eighteenth-century design, as was noted in the large corded quilt from Edinburgh which features a pot with flowers in the border (see fig. 5.20, p.86). It continued to occur frequently in the first half of the nineteenth century as a pot, basket or vase and was an ideal design to feature in the centre of a framed quilting layout, as demonstrated in figure 5.16 on page 82. A wholecloth quilt made by Elinor Thomas in Trevine, Dyfed, in about 1820 contains a vase with a variety of flowers and leaves at its centre, together with tiny vases with flowers in the corners of the central area (see fig.5.21, p.86). The quilted layout on the pieced quilt made by Mary between 1845 and 1850 again features a vase with five petalled flowers (see fig.5.22, p.87).

With the simplification of the quilting layouts and a change in style of quilting patterns in the second half of the nineteenth century the container motif seems to have faded in popularity. There does, however, appear to have been a revival of interest in the twentieth century and a number of Welsh quilts from the 1920s and the 1930s featured a pot or a vase of flowers.

A white cotton wholecloth quilt made for an Eisteddfod competition in 1934 demonstrates fine workmanship and an effective layout. A central square-on-point is edged by the wording 'Castell Nedd Eisteddfod Genedlaethol Frehinol Cymru 1934' – 'Royal National Eisteddfod of Wales Neath 1934'. Adjacent are four strongly worked cornucopia which are perhaps allusions to the Eisteddfod Horn of Plenty. It is interesting to speculate whether the maker of this fine quilt realized that she was reproducing a motif used by quilters two hundred years before and it would be fascinating to discover whether she won an award at the Eisteddfod (see fig.5.23, p.87).

One quilting motif was remarkable for its almost complete absence during the early 1800s. Assumptions had been made that the feather was often used, since it is a pattern commonly seen in more recent quilts; however, the feather was noted on only a few quilted items from the early nineteenth century and in some examples the certainty of its identification was in doubt. Motifs viewed initially as a feather proved more likely to be leaf patterns and this conclusion was strengthened when the motifs were considered in context.

This is illustrated by an example from the eighteenth century. The fully corded quilt in figure 5.10 on page 75 features motifs which, when seen in association with a pattern of stems, fruits and flowers, could only be interpreted as segmented leaves: taken out of context, though, they could be assumed to be feathers. The quilt made by Mary, shown as a quilt layout in figure 5.14 on page 80 and illustrated in figure 5.22 on page 87, has two motifs which are arranged along the inside edges of the border. The context of the design and their arrangement in close proximity suggest that they are both leaf patterns.

It has been shown that botanical images featured extensively in domestic textile designs over a long period, so it is more likely that leaf forms were a significant design source for quilt motifs during this period. Similarly, close examination of repeated patterns often occurring as circular wreaths in the centre of a quilt or as an undulating running design in a border showed features far more leaflike than featherlike. Images such as the circular leaf wreath have been popular since classical Greek and Roman times, while within the period discussed running patterns of vines, ferns and seaweed were popular in cotton fabric printing.

A quilt recorded at Halifax, dated 1810, features a pattern which examiners interpreted as one of these undulating fern patterns. It occurs both as a border and on the rim of the circle and is illustrated in figure 5.19 on page 85. In the same figure, another pattern can be seen which, at first glance, was considered to be a feather, but then comparisons were made with illustrations of leaves on a number of Indian printed textiles. It has a segmented leaf shape with three lines outlining the pattern and parallel lines running out from the central vein.

If quilt researchers of the twentieth century are sometimes uncertain of the identity of some early-nineteenth-century leaflike quilt motifs, it is possible that quilters of that period also were confused. When copying quilting patterns or incorporating a motif from another decorative discipline they may well have misdrawn or misinterpreted what they had seen. Thus a motif that originally had botanical origins may have evolved on occasions into a feather. This proposition requires further consideration and would benefit from more data and discussion.

Some regional variation in choice of patterns was noted for this period. While the majority of the quilts examined at many of the venues featured combinations of the motifs already mentioned, some quilts made in south-west Wales had a different style. In these examples floral motifs did not feature, while strong large leaf motifs, often arranged in groups of four set in a cross or in pairs set zigzag style, were frequently seen. Some leaves showed the curved bent-over shape of a pattern later called 'Paisley pear' and many were strongly infilled with lines.

A number of quilts from this area of Wales had an undulating border pattern set in very deep horseshoe-type curves, as seen in the quilt made by Ann Morse in Dyfed (fig.5.13 on p.80). This pattern sometimes showed a variation in width of the curved lines, which created prototype bell shapes.

Elizabeth Hake in *English Quilting* suggests that a regional variation could also be detected in quilts from the south-west of England. She ascribes a floral style to this area but the quilts of this period from the south-west did not appear to be different from those of the same period seen in other areas. She studied a large number of old quilts from the south-west for her book and it is suggested that she confused region and period when coming to her conclusions about the regionalization of floral motifs.

Alice Orange

It is rare to find a date on a wholecloth quilt and indeed it is usually very difficult to date a wholecloth quilt unless it contains some exceptional fabric on the top or back. It is even rarer for a wholecloth quilt to be signed and dated by the maker, so a surviving group of five quilts signed, dated and with the name of the recipient is an exceptional case.

The five quilts made by Alice Orange (see fig.5.24) for the rector of the parish of Dinnington in Northumberland date from 1851-6 and are still owned by his family. Little is known of the maker except what is shown in the 1851 census: born in Newton Underwood, Northumberland, she was unmarried and aged thirty-eight at the time of the census, and was the rector's housekeeper. By the next census, in 1861, the rector had moved away to take up family responsibilities and Alice no longer lived in Dinnington. The only contact with Alice Orange is through these quilts – it is not known where she learned quilting, whether any more of her quilts survive, or what happened to her.

The quilts are an interesting collection which demonstrate the design style of one mid-nineteenth-century quilter, before the time that quilt layouts in north-east England developed from the earlier contained frame style (with defined areas of quilting) into much freer and looser designs.

Four of Alice's quilts have a layout of a central motif and defined borders, and the fifth is a very early strippy made in 1855. While some of the background quilting is closely spaced, with patterns such as hanging diamond, wineglass and a double-lined clamshell, and the motif and border outlining is of double or triple lines, the patterns making up the central motifs, borders and strips generally stand on their own without background quilting around them. However, Alice Orange introduced some unusual, probably

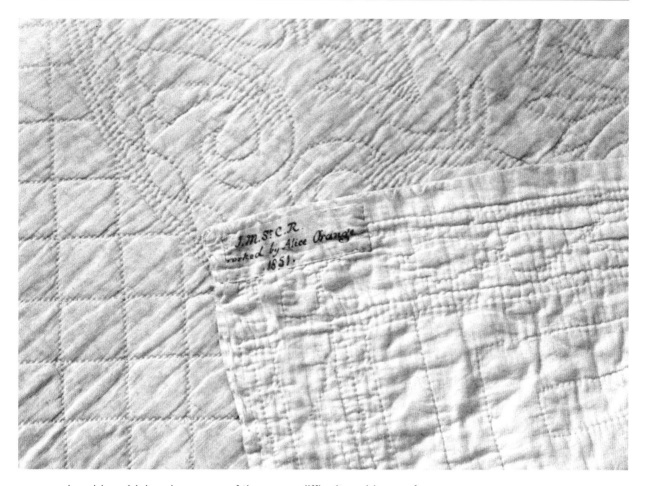

Fig. 5.24. Label from Alice Orange's 1851 quilt, tape and marking ink. *(Photo: Bridget Long)*

personal, quirks which solve some of the more difficult problems of turning corners and filling gaps. Figure 5.25 on page 92 shows the composite central motif of the 1851 quilt and a selection of Alice's patterns, traced from slides. Her patterns, usually employed as simple repeat of each motif, include the usual stars, fans, two Paisley shells (with three or four lobes and a very curved tail), a lined squares-on-point border, Northumberland half-plates and Northumberland simple chain, hearts, and tulips and unusual border patterns of tear drops, 'esses' and Greek keys, a four-line dog's trail with leaf corner treatment, lined trail segments with leaf infill, a running flower vine and gryphon heads.

The gryphon heads are in the central circular area of one of the two 1852 quilts, which also contains naive flowers and a central circle of four hearts. The gryphon, which was part of the rector's family crest, was used in plasterwork and stained glass in his family home; unusually, it was also reproduced in one of his bed quilts. Because of the complexity of the pattern, it was difficult enough to identify and impossible to reproduce legibly. Alice Orange's favourite patterns seem to have been the Paisley shells, which are in all five quilts, and the tear drop and running vine which are each in four of the quilts.

QUILTING 1850-1960

This period of over one hundred years witnessed many changes in quilting in Britain. The Alice Orange quilts mark the end of an era: the sewing machine was soon to become a useful tool to the seamstress and quilter; fashions in home decoration changed and this brought a new emphasis on decorative, rich types of patchwork – what could be termed conspicuous handiwork.

There was, however, still poverty and a continued need for warm, cheap and serviceable bed covers. Aside from the decorative patchwork in silk and velvet, there was, perhaps, an outlet for creativity in what was a necessary domestic chore: that of making utilitarian patchwork or wholecloth quilts. It is hard to imagine how else such work could have been approached. If the need was purely for utility and warmth, then quilting could quite adequately be done with simple straight lines, crosshatch or wave quilting: patchwork need have been no more than the stitching together of squares and rectangles of cloth scraps.

Many of the quilts seen were indeed the remaining band of those utilitarian items made in desperate need. These quilts from the South Wales coalfields and elsewhere, however, did not contain random and formless patchwork; nor, generally, was the quilting without thought and pattern. In the Isle of Man, it is true, there was a tradition of all over quilting in a 'square wave' pattern, which, since it was often worked over thick Log Cabin patchwork, was far from perfect. Indeed, it would be difficult to execute delicate quilting designs on such an intractable base and over such a dominant pattern.

As far as can be seen, there was a fairly common vocabulary of quilting layouts and patterns at the beginning of this period throughout Britain – flowers and leaves in both naturalistic and formalized forms; vases, pots and urns; and many geometric patterns based on the circle and square. One marked characteristic of this quilting tradition was the 'delineation' or defining of the areas of the layout: the pattern elements were arranged within outlined areas, as was the background quilting.

The documentation data show that there were unexplained changes in this situation, probably around the period 1870-80, and only in the north-east of England. One was the virtual abandonment of the very structured quilt layout featuring the 'delineated central motif and borders' just described (and illustrated in fig.5.47 on pp.122-3) and the other was the introduction of the feather in many varieties as a quilting pattern. Quilters in other areas seem to have continued with their traditional ways. In some places, such as the south-west and the East Midlands, the art and craft of quilting withered away completely. In

Opposite: Fig. 5.25. Tracings from slides of Alice Orange's quilts. Centre: 1851 central motif 50 cm (1 ft 8 in) diameter; clockwise from top left: 1856 fan and floral vine corner, 28 cm (11 in) wide: 'esses' from 1855 strippy: 1852 Paisley shell and teardrop borders, 15 cm (6 in) wide; 1856 lined-trail segments with leaves, 24 cm (9½ in) wide; 1852 clamshell central field, with dogtrail border, 12 cm (5 in) wide; 1851 tear drop and Greek key borders, 32 cm (12½ in) wide total. *(Photo: Pauline Adams)*

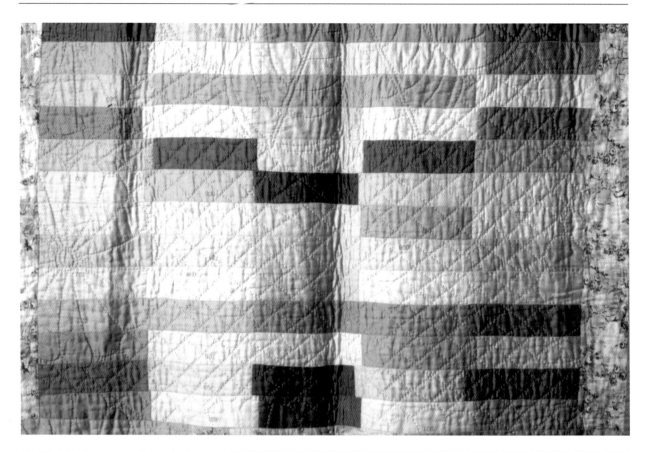

Fig. 5.26. Detail of reverse of pieced quilt, 1926, showing cotton sateen samples. 125 cm x 202 cm (4 ft 1 in x 6 ft 8 in).

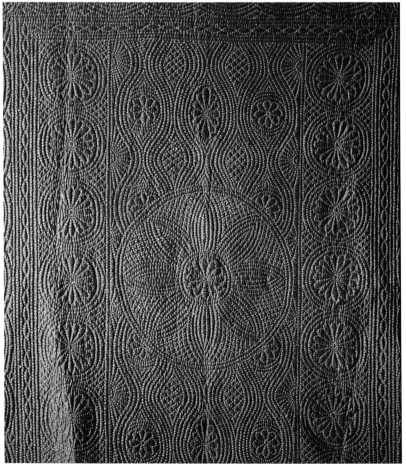

Fig. 5.27. Black wholecloth quilt, cotton sateen, 1920. Quilting layout: strippy with motif centre and borders. 194 cm x 233 cm (6 ft 4 in x 7 ft 8 in).

Fig. 5.28. Salmon pink and gold cotton sateen strippy, strippy quilted, twentieth century. 189 cm x 250 cm (6 ft 2 in x 8 ft 2 in).

Wales and the north-east it remained alive probably only because of the revivalist efforts of various agencies in the 1920s and 1930s and the efforts of a few dedicated teachers and enthusiasts.

Owing to the particular difficulties presented by photographing and otherwise recording wholecloth quilts, it is possible to illustrate here only a few of the many seen from this period. Very few of the examined quilts were signed and dated and family records and memories tend to go no further back than 1900. Of the 641 quilts made between 1850 and 1900, only nineteen were actually dated. Of those, five were Alice Orange's quilts, a further two celebrated Queen Victoria's Golden Jubilee (1887), one was started in 1877 and finished in 1989 and one was machine-quilted and dated 1868 – which leaves just ten quilts: not enough to be fully representative. The owners of the quilts were able to provide information about only a very few of the makers from the last century. There were proportionately even fewer signed and dated quilts in the period 1900-60 than in the previous fifty years, even though 1,541 quilted items from this period were seen.

In the absence of more helpful data, the wholecloth quilts have been grouped by type: strippies; Welsh; and north-eastern English. First, however, mention should be made of a true sampler of that favourite of all quilting fabrics – cotton sateen. This material was available from about 1880 to 1940 and its lustre beautifully highlights the relief surface of quilting. This single quilt, seen in Dorchester, has a patchwork top of cotton sateen, but of more interest is the back: each of the pieced rectangular sateen samples still carry stamped reference numbers. This is a superb collection of the many colours and shades that were available, including pastels and bright and dark colours. The quilt (see fig.5.26, p.94) was stated to have been made in 1926, in Durham.

Strippy Quilting

The black quilt in figure 5.27 is also of cotton sateen, but with a print backing. It was made in 1920, in the Sunderland area, as a wedding present. Worked in the 'strippy with central motif and borders' layout, it has two, three or even four parallel lines delineating the different quilting areas. The central area contains a wide strip of bellows pattern, with a central daisy motif, and two side strips of sixteen-petalled flowers. The main border of lined cable has flowers in each corner and is flanked by narrow borders of simple chain.

Unfortunately, nothing is known of the origins of a fine but startlingly coloured strippy seen at Halifax. It has nine equal strips of salmon pink and gold sateen, and is quilted in a strippy layout. The symmetrical layout of patterns includes a large lined trail, a bellows pattern with fillings of flowers or crosshatch, and squares-on-point filled with flowers or crosshatch. The most unusual pattern is a wavy strip of parallel lines (see fig.5.28, p.95).

Three more strippy quilts are shown with diagrams taken from the quilts themselves or from slides. The first, in figure 5.29, is a dark pink and white strippy of eleven unequal width strips. It dates from the early twentieth century and is interesting for the fine quilting and the unusual use of a large flower in each corner. The other patterns are goose wing end to end, nestling hammocks with trefoil tops, squares-on-point filled with flowers, and a centre strip of sixteen-petalled flowers. Spots of blue-pencil marking could still be detected at the flower centres.

Some innovative quilters did not confine their patterns within the strip widths: a red and blue check strippy of nine equal strips is illustrated in figure 5.30 on pages 98-9. The two outside strips are the same running feather; the remaining strips are all different and include Paisley shells, a pattern the documenters nicknamed 'Sweetie Papers' because of the splayed ends, and two unusual patterns for enclosing a square-on-point. More notable is the variety of patterns used to fill the gaps across strip seams: Paisley shells,

Fig. 5.29. Patterns from dark pink and white cotton strippy, early twentieth century. 223 cm x 244 cm (7 ft 4 in x 8 ft).

Fig. 5.30. Patterns from blue and red check cotton strippy, c. 1900.
211 cm x 222 cm (6 ft 11 in x 7 ft 3 in).

Fig. 5.31. Patterns from feathered strippy, twentieth century.
205 cm x 228 cm (6 ft 9 in x 7 ft 6 in).

flowers and leaf fronds among them. The owner said that the quilt came from Northumberland. The piecing is by machine, except for one seam. Because of the way the light plays across a quilted surface, it is sometimes difficult to decipher the pattern - hence the diagram has one or two gaps.

Another fine North Country blue and white feathered strippy of seven strips has outline quilting in the little triangular sawtooth patches. The owner called this pattern 'Tree Everlasting'. Three strips are illustrated in figure 5.31: a lined arches pattern, filled with straight and curved chequers; a running feather; and a strip with half-flowers facing each other. The quilt was ascribed to the period 1900-60.

Thus even the humble strippy gave scope for the choice and balance of patterns, innovation in pattern design and alteration, and unusual ways of filling the awkward spaces between the patterns. The earlier strippy by Alice Orange is clumsy by contrast, with one strip made up of two different-width patterns.

Welsh Quilts

The striking quilt in figure 5.32 on page 102 was made in Pembrokeshire (Dyfed), west Wales, in about 1870 and passed down in the family to the present owner. The patchwork is made from hand-spun and hand-woven wool, charcoal (mixed of black and white fleeces) and red, in a counterchange borders pattern, with a red appliqué heart in the centre. The filling is wool, and the backing red cotton. The quilting layout conforms to the boundaries of the central square-on-point only, totally ignoring both the heart and the rest of the patchwork. All the areas of quilting – square-on-point, centre field, borders and corners – are delineated with a double line of quilting. The central motif is quilted with a radial arrangement of spirals, flowers and leaves, with vases of flowers in each corner of the central field. The inner border is of filled squares-on-point, the next of filled circles and the outside border of a Welsh trail variation.

Said to have been made in about 1905 by a farmer's wife in Pembrokeshire, the exuberant gold quilt in figure 5.33 on page 102 would brighten the darkest morning. Was it possibly a wedding quilt, with the association of pennies and hearts? In any case, it contains remarkably little background quilting, being composed of a skilful assemblage of motifs. The central square-on-point contains a flower made of four heart-shaped petals, set on point, with a rose in its centre. These are all outlined with small circles. Triangular leaves fill the rest of the central square. The first border has veined leaves in a triangular arrangement with a large Tudor rose in each corner, and the outer border has hearts on their sides, again outlined in pennies. This quilt appears to be identical (although it has been confirmed that the backs are different colours) to one illustrated in a centre close-up on page 50 of *Quilts*[5], a book about the collection of quilts at the Welsh Folk Museum at St Fagans. That quilt is reliably stated to have been made in Maesteg, Mid-Glamorgan, in the 1920s – fifteen years and perhaps fifty miles apart! However, both bear striking similarities to a quilt brought to Carmarthen and made by Miss Fanny Lewis (not illustrated).

Miss Lewis's other quilt, shown in figure 5.34 on page 103, was also seen at the Carmarthen documentation day. Miss Lewis, who was a professional quilter, lived at Whitland, Dyfed. She made quilts for Liberty's, the London department store, as well as for local customers. Liberty's paid fifteen shillings (75p) per quilt, with the materials provided – but for locals she charged only two shillings and sixpence (12½p), one-sixth of the London rate! The quilt, of cream cotton on one side and cream and pink floral stripe on the other, was made in 1925. The circular central motif, outlined with a narrow chain border, contains a cross of four diagonally lined leaves, with the spaces filled with a formal arrangement of linked large and small spirals that resemble scissors. The central field has fan corners. The inner border is a zigzag of lined leaves, and the outer a church-window variation.

The second of her quilts is white, and made in the 1920s to 1930s for a wedding. The centre square-on-point is identical to the yellow Pembrokeshire quilt (pennies-and-hearts flower), except that the corners of the central square are filled with back-to-back Paisley pears rather than triangular leaves. The two borders are like the

Pembrokeshire quilt seen at Pontypridd. These strong similarities do suggest that Miss Lewis was the maker not only of the quilt illustrated in figure 5.33 but also of the three pennies-and-hearts quilts – her own white one, described above (fig.5.34), and the one at St Fagans – or that, at the very least, she drew the quilting patterns for them. The quilt in figure 5.34 seems much less of a folk-art piece than the three pennies-and-hearts quilts and was presumably made after she was recruited to supply the sophisticated and discerning London market.

Margaret Williams (see p.140), who was described as a 'quiltwife', made a quilt which was brought to the Knowle documentation day by her granddaughter. Mrs Williams lived in Gwaun-cae-Gurwen, on the borders of Dyfed and West Glamorgan, and her quilt of gold cotton with an apricot cotton back was made in 1930 for an exhibition. The central circular motif is illustrated in figure 5.35 on page 103. It consists of a circular band of spirals, within which are four large plain leaves filled with the Welsh equivalent of freehand floral (flowers, leaves and spirals) surrounding a complex flower shape made up of overlapping tear-drop shapes. The spectacular outside corner of a naturalistic horse-chestnut leaf is also illustrated, with its ivy-leaf border, in figure 5.36 on page 103.

The preceding succession of Welsh quilts shows that, while a gradual formalization of traditional patterns did occur, they still adhered to the strict 'delineated motif and borders' format. There is no doubt that the Rural Industries Bureau and other agencies influenced this. In the process, perhaps, some of the natural *joie-de-vivre* of the design was sacrificed for a perceived upgrade in quality and the fortunate continuation of the craft.

North Country Quilts and Feathers

Three North Country quilts dating from the first quarter of the twentieth century that were brought to the Bowes Museum documentation day had been made by two sisters who lived in Allendale. They are now owned by the sisters' great-niece. Two are described and illustrated below. The sisters, the Misses Barron, made quilts during the winter and ran a guesthouse in the summer. The quilting patterns were drawn for them by 'someone in Allendale' and it is believed that a number of their quilts went to America. The examining expert commented: 'Style of quilt characteristic of Allendale/Weardale school – certainly a designed quilt – confirmed by historical information from owner.'

The first Barron quilt is made of pink cotton sateen and has an old gold backing. Its quilting layout is that of a central motif and borders, undelineated except for a double line between the two borders. The large, complex, circular motif in the centre is

Fig. 5.32. Carmarthenshire (Dyfed) woollen
quilt of patchwork, appliqué and quilting,
cotton back, wool wadding, 1870.
198 cm x 216 cm (6 ft 6 in x 7 ft 1 in).

Fig. 5.33. Gold cotton wholecloth quilt,
Pembrokeshire (Dyfed), c. 1905. Motifs
used: hearts, leaves, spirals, pennies.
205 cm x 224 cm (6 ft 8 in x 7 ft 4 in).

Fig. 5.34. Cream cotton wholecloth quilt, wool wadding, made by Miss Fanny Lewis in Whitland, Dyfed, 1925.
182 cm x 217 cm (6 ft x 7 ft 1 in).

Below left: Fig. 5.35. Detail of centre of cotton wholecloth quilt, made by Margaret Williams, Gwaun-cae-Gurwen, South Wales, 1930.
190 cm x 228 cm (6 ft 3 in x 7 ft 6 in).

Below: Fig. 5.36. Detail of corner of quilt shown in fig.5.35.

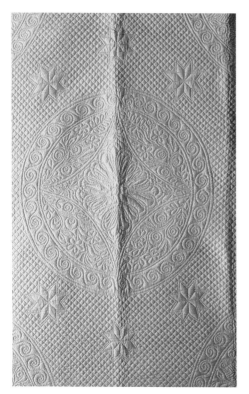

composed of a central double rose surrounded by circuits of small clamshells. Eight infilled 'flatirons' radiate from the centre. Between these are concentric circles or 'targets', with chevron quilting radiating outwards, topped by a fleur-de-lis variation. The inner border has lined hammocks, topped with fleurs-de-lis, and outside of these is a rose in each corner and an infill of freehand leaves. The narrow outer border is of small scrolls (see fig.5.38, p.106).

The second Barron Allendale quilt is again of pink cotton sateen with an old gold backing, and the layout a central motif with one border. The large, complex motif in the centre consists of a central rose in a double circle, then eight large curved feathers with freehand leaf and scrolls between; two roses on stems protruding from leaves are at top, bottom and each side, with a five-lobed leaf on the diagonals. Figure 5.39 on page 107 shows a detail of the corner, which has a pattern of ribbon-like cabbage leaves spreading from a knot shape to the centre of each side. The edge infill is freehand scrolling and feather and there is a large lined clamshell filled with a small rose, scrolls and feather in each corner.

The Barron sisters' third quilt, sashed block patchwork in pink and white, is quilted in a design similar to the other two. In this case, though, the quilting bears no relation to the patchwork.

Six hundred and forty-one quilted items dating between 1850 and 1900 were seen during the Project. Of these, feather patterns were recorded for fifty-nine quilts, or 9.2 per cent. Unfortunately, not one of them was signed or dated, but one, with good documentary back-up, was stated to have been made in 1870 – in Salisbury, Wiltshire – and to have been taken to the gold mines in South Africa with the grandparents of the present owner. It was rediscovered on the death of the owner's mother, still in the steamer trunk along with a hoard of diaries and maps detailing their stay in South Africa. On their return in 1909 they survived (how is not explained) a shipwreck.

The quilt is a yellow and white Streak of Lightning patchwork, in which the quilting completely ignores the patchwork. The illustration in figure 5.37 is a reproduction of a sketch made of the quilt at the Chelmsford documentation day. Note the similarity of the patterns in the centre to those of Alice Orange's on page 92: the delineated layout, and the feather hammocks. When it was realized that the makers' names were Sarah Scott and Alice Lawrence, hopes were raised that Alice Orange's trail had been found. Unfortunately, Alice Lawrence was the daughter of Sarah Scott and her maiden name was not, therefore, Orange! While there may be some residual uncertainty about who actually made this quilt, and when, and where, there is no doubt that the motifs used and their arrangement are quite consistent with the date attributed by the owner.

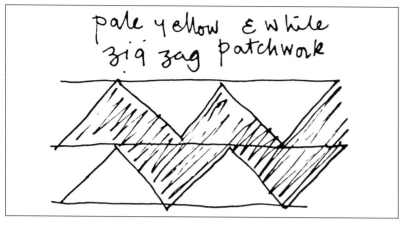

pale yellow & white zig zag patchwork

Fig. 5.37. Streak of Lightning quilt. Salisbury, Wiltshire, 1870. Rough sketch of patchwork pattern and quilting layout made at Chelmsford documentation day.

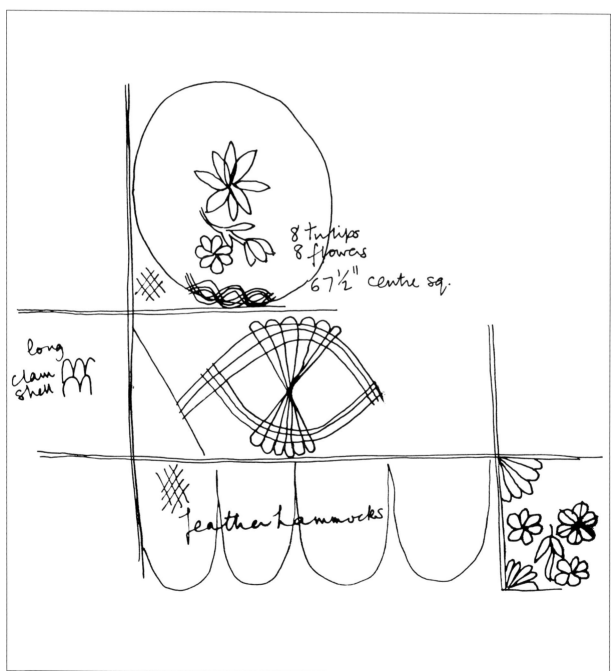

8 tulips
8 flowers
67½" centre sq.

long clam shell

feather hammocks

Fig. 5.38. Cotton wholecloth quilt, made by the Misses Barron, 1900-25, in Allendale, Northumberland, where it was also marked. 213 cm x 240 cm (7 ft x 7 ft 10 in).

Opposite: Fig. 5.39. Detail of corner of a cotton wholecloth quilt, made by the Misses Barron in Allendale, Northumberland, 1900-25. 208 cm x 232 cm (6 ft 10 in x 7 ft 7 in).

It is well known that by this same period of 1870 feather quilting patterns were commonplace in North America, and one American quilt was seen which contained very fine feather wreath quilting, and had a good provenance of 1870. For the period 1900 to 1960, 246 quilted items out of a total of 1,541 contained feather patterns, giving a proportion of just over 17 per cent compared with the 9.2 per cent of the second half of the 19th century.

The complex centre of a cream feathered quilt is shown in figure 5.41 on page 110. It is not known where the quilt was made, but, stylistically, it was dated to the first quarter of the twentieth century. The quilting layout is that of an undelineated central motif and border on a background of hanging diamonds. The patterns include straight and curved feathers, a double rose, plain lined leaves, ferns, clamshell and hammocks, with infill freehand floral around the edge, which is frilled. Note that the area around the individual quilting motifs is more prominent than the motifs themselves, because of a lack of background quilting. Note also the

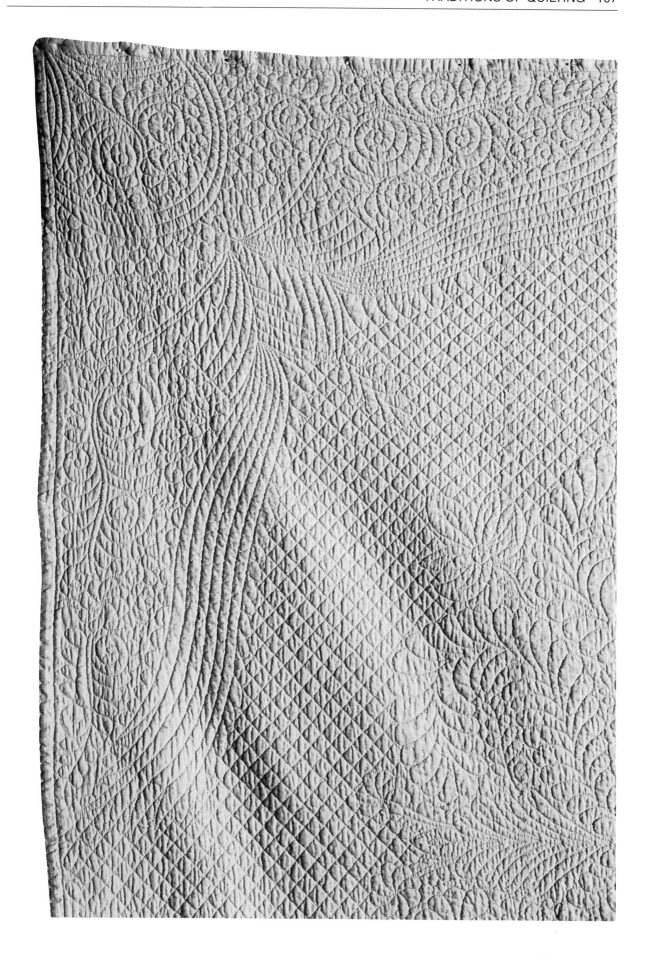

pierced type of feather design, typical of the Allendale/Weardale quilt stampers – their original blue-pencil marking is still visible.

Another feathery quilt (see fig.5.42, p.110), this time made of pale green and pale pink cotton, was examined at Edinburgh. It was made in north Northumberland in about 1919, by a professional quilter for a wedding, and came down through the family to its present owner. The centre star is composed of two outlined squares, set square and diagonally, and enclosing a large curved-petalled flower, surrounded first by a ring of small concentric circles (targets) and then by a circular feather wreath. Pairs of long curved feathers enclosing a leaf are at corners and centre sides, and the whole is surrounded by a running feather border – one of the few borders seen which did not break at the corners.

Twenty-five Sanderson Star quilts (named after the well-known stamper Elizabeth Sanderson) were brought to documentation days. While the patchwork is probably the best-known British pattern after the hexagon, it is generally believed that no two of these wholecloth quilts were quilted the same. Quilters will say that small differences were always made. Sanderson Stars involved complex piecing with no less than sixteen set-in corners, and they were made in Sanderson's workshop and probably marked for quilting as well. The quilting patterns do exhibit some small variations, mainly in the pattern used for the outside border, but also for that within the large star points.

The green and white quilt shown in figure 5.43 on page 110 was machine-made in about 1920 and, of course, hand-quilted. The quilting patterns are typical: the white star at the centre has a central flower within a circle, and all the star points are freehand floral, which make the running pattern for two of the borders. The other borders are lined cable or flower-filled Weardale chain. All the border corners are quilted in contrast to the borders themselves. The quilting layout can be assigned to type 8 (see fig. 5.47 on pp.122-3) – 'enclosed by patchwork motif and borders'.

Patterns traced directly from a pink-and-pink (overdyed) Sanderson Star quilt quilted by Regina Hetherington of Chopwell, Newcastle, in 1920 and seen at Carmarthen are reproduced in figure 5.40. They include the filling for the star centre and points and the two outside borders, which are freehand floral and Weardale chain.

Another striking example of both patchwork and quilting was seen at Chester-le-Street – a feathered star, where the quilting layout is, again, 'enclosed by patchwork motif and borders' (see fig 5.44, p.111). This quilt was made in the Hexham, Northumberland, area in 1910 by family members of the present owner. The striking, almost optical illusional, block patchwork of strong pink and white left

Fig. 5.40. Typical Sanderson Star quilting patterns, star section and two outer borders from a quilt made by Regina Hetherington in Chopwell, Newcastle, in 1920.

squares, diamonds and stars to be filled with quilting. The stars themselves are outline-quilted a half-centimetre (¼ in) from seam lines. The shapes of the stars and the background spaces are filled with subtle and symmetrical variations on the theme of a central curved-petalled flower with various outlinings and infilling patterns, including hearts, shells, semicircular bowls and much freehand scrolling. The blue-pencil marking lines are still visible. Thus, with subtle variations on a simple repertoire of patterns a stunning quilt was made, owing as much to the impact of the quilting as to the patchwork itself. Not only that, the backing includes flour sacking where the lettering, though turned inwards, is still visible in mirror image: 'Diploma of Honour, London 1884; gold medal, Capetown 1887; First Award, Adelaide 1887'; and the edges are machined!

Above: Fig. 5.41. Centre of wholecloth quilt made in north-east England, early twentieth century.
202 cm x 233 cm (6 ft 8 in x 7 ft 8 in).

Above right: Fig. 5.42. Cotton wholecloth quilt from Northumberland, c. 1919, featuring feather quilting patterns.
187 cm x 216 cm (6 ft 2 in x 7 ft 1 in).

Fig. 5.43. Sanderson Star patchwork quilt, Allendale, Northumberland, c. 1920.
199 cm x 208 cm (6 ft 6 in x 6 ft 10 in).

Fig. 5.44. Feathered Star patchwork quilt, pink and white cotton, made in 1910 in the Hexham area of Northumberland. Simple quilting patterns are adapted to suit the varying large patchwork shapes.
215 cm x 247 cm (7 ft 3 in x 8 ft 1 in).

Fig. 5.45. Patterns (quarter centre and
borders) from bordered wholecloth quilt.
Probably Co. Durham, about 1910.
214 cm x 244 cm (7 ft x 8 ft).

Coincidences

Textile examiners were very gratified when coincidences were noticed. Already detailed is the similarity of central-motif designs between Alice Orange's quilts and the early feathered quilt made in Salisbury, and between the Welsh pennies-and-hearts quilt and the ones made by Miss Fanny Lewis.

Two other 'coincidental' quilts were seen at the widely separated venues of Chester and Carmarthen. They are North Country wholecloth quilts but have borders of rose-printed sateen. These quilts are the pink versions of a quilt with blue print owned by Beamish Museum which dates back to 1910 and was made in Bowburn, Co. Durham. The patterns from the Carmarthen quilt were traced and the centre and border are shown reduced in figure 5.45.

Fig. 5.46. Pattern (quarter of quilt) from Welsh-style wholecloth quilt, 1930s, one of four nearly identical quilts.
244 cm x 236 cm (8 ft x 7 ft 8 in).

Note the skilful way in which an awkward meeting of motif and crosshatch background has been avoided by the insertion of a small length of simple chain at difficult points. The coincidences made it possible to date these two quilts whose known history previously amounted only to: 'they came from the North Country'.

Even more surprising, perhaps, were no fewer than four quilts that were almost exactly the same except for small variations that had been made to cope with slightly different sizings. These were seen in the three far-apart venues of Swavesey, Exeter and Kelso. There is some uncertainty about the maker: the Swavesey quilt was purchased in London, with no provenance; the two Exeter quilts have no maker's name and the Kelso quilt was said to have been made in 1920 'in a village on the North Yorkshire moors behind Whitby' and 'inherited from late father-in-law who bought it from the maker'. Three of the quilts were made of rayon, while the Kelso one was of cotton and also had cut-out corners to accommodate bedposts. The illustration on page 113 (fig.5.46) shows a quarter of the Swavesey quilt. The distinctive double-hearts are shown in figure 5.50 in the section on patterns. The documenter at Kelso commented: 'This is a quilt with very strong Welsh influences despite being made in Yorkshire.' It is easy to speculate that a Welsh family moved to Yorkshire and continued their traditional style of quiltmaking.

The similarity between a Devonshire quilt illustrated by Mrs Hake and one documented in Inverness (see figs. 5.15 and 5.17, pp.82-3) has already been noted.[6] Probably there are many more identical quilts – only the most distinctive quilts (and those recorded in print) are likely to be recognized as such. It was fortunate that such a large sample of Britain's treasury of quilts came forward for recording.

MACHINE-MADE QUILTS

The sewing machine is now a commonplace tool for making patchwork and it is often used for quilting. Most people imagine that it was invented by Singer, but this is not the case: Isaac Merritt Singer did indeed patent a lock-stitch sewing machine in America in 1851, but earlier inventors had first developed the chain-stitch machine and later the lock-stitch machine. After a court case, it was found that Singer's machine infringed one of these patents and he had to pay royalties to the inventor, Elias Howe. Nevertheless, Singer's name has become virtually synonymous with the sewing machine, thanks in part, no doubt, to his excellent salesmanship: his company was the first to offer hire-purchase terms to its customers. But it was the firm of Wheeler and Wilson that sold the most sewing machines in America in the 1850s and 1860s. In 1856 the two firms combined with Howe and another manufacturer to form a Combination, which by 1860 had sold 500,000 machines in America. Many more were exported to countries around the world. Attachments for the machines were also produced, which as early as 1865 included a 'quilter' – a spacer bar for ensuring lines of quilting were parallel.

At documentation days, members of the public often expressed the belief that all quilts should be completely handmade: that only these were 'proper' quilts. This, however, is more a case of wishful thinking. It is clear that sewing machines were used as soon as they became available for the tedious job of joining long seams in the quilt backings, sewing blocks together, adding sashings and borders and, finally, binding. If it was considered worthwhile to produce a 'quilter' attachment, then machine quilting must have been started at least before 1856 – almost as soon as Singer's first machine came on the market.

When dating quilts, the presence of machine stitching will indicate a date later (probably) than 1860, but of course many quilts were still being wholly handmade much later than this as machines were expensive and there was no sudden conversion. One quilt came to the Penrith documentation day that was fortunately signed and dated 'M. Myers 1868'. It was strippy patchwork with machine quilting of parallel lines running vertically and diagonally to form slanting diamonds. If the backing of the quilt had not given the date, it might have been assumed that a strippy top had been quilted at a later time. A quilt brought to Chester had been made in Gateshead in 1890: it was machine-quilted in hanging diamonds. Another, at Chelmsford, was machine-quilted on a Cornely machine, and another quilt, seen at Pontypridd, was dated 1893 and of machine appliqué and machine quilting.

Wholecloth quilts from north-east England commonly have butted (both edges turned in) and machined edges, while their Welsh counterparts tend to have butted and quilted edges.

One quilt, brought to the Edinburgh documentation day, was machine-quilted in chain stitch; it dated from about 1900. Many of the Canadian Red Cross quilts from 1939-45 were machine-quilted: machining was also used for the patchwork and construction. In all, the Project recorded 243 quilts as being machine-quilted.

That notable quilter Elizabeth Sanderson, renowned for the quilt-designing-and-making workshop she ran in the village of Allenheads, in Allendale, Northumberland, produced the instantly recognizable pieced and bordered Sanderson Star quilt on the sewing machine, although the quilting was by hand (see fig.5.43, p.110).

More than one firm manufactured machine-made quilts during the interwar period. The best known is the 'Comfy': fifty-six were recorded during the Project, and one 'Cushonia' quilt. The Comfy quilt is thickly wadded with cotton, and instantly recognizable. The quilts were made with a printed cotton fabric on one side and a matching plain cotton fabric on the other. The fabric-and-wadding sandwich was quilted in an all-over 'square wave' pattern of zigzag parallel lines. Once quilted, it was cut, leaving, for instance, a diamond in the centre and a border at the outside. The cut sections were reversed, leaving a centre diamond and border in one fabric and the remaining part in the other. The cut edges were covered on both sides by binding strips – the cuts can be felt through the binding. The quilts were all labelled. Unfortunately, it is not known exactly where the factory was, nor for how long it operated.

In Inverness, Scotland, the Project discovered a type of machine-made quilt that was previously unrecorded by quilt historians. These quilts were made to commission by a number of women in the east-coast fishing town of Fraserburgh after about 1940. The customer provided the fabric (often a rayon) and a filling (often a blanket). The three layers were simultaneously quilted and embellished by the stitching-on of ruched strips of contrast fabric. Sometimes they had some additional widely spaced machine quilting.

Seven of these distinctive cottage-industry quilts were seen, which the documenters nicknamed 'Fraserburgh Frillies'. The makers' names were given as Margit Craig, Maggie McWilliam, Jeannie Carne and Maggie Sutherland. Later information from a local quilter produced more names: Grace Jack, Maggie Noble and Barbara Noble. Grace Jack (who was a widow) and her contemporaries were also fish workers, following the herring fleets from Shetland to Great Yarmouth in order to gut and pack the catch. Barbara Noble, who made this type of quilt from 1941 to 1981, called the technique 'rucken'. The quilts were often made for a girl's 'providings' or trousseau, or were taken to sea on the fishing boats. It is not known whether the technique originated in Britain – it seems that the word 'rucken' has Scandinavian origins.

METHODS OF WORKING

While most of the information about methods of quilting came from interviews with older quilters or their relatives, some clues were derived from the quilts themselves. The advantage of studying closely such a large number of quilted items during the Project was that many comparisons of work standards were possible.

Standards of stitching examined were variable, this an inevitable result of the varying social status of the quilters involved. The balance of necessity with fashion is highlighted by the stitching. Quilts made at speed using thicker waddings for warmth are bound to have a cobbled look when compared with fashion quilts made by ladies of leisure. It has been suggested that there has been a general lowering of sewing standards over time, but since no specific note was made of levels of stitching skills when the quilts were examined no theory can be proved. It could, rather, be explained by the fact that older, poorly stitched utility quilts are less likely to survive than older masterpiece quilts which merited preserving. Some later nineteenth- and twentieth-century quilts are, admittedly, weakly sewn, but many examples of items made by well-trained or even professional quilters of the period would stand comparison with any earlier quilts.

A good example of a well-made quilt that is in The Quilters' Guild collection demonstrates fine stitching of a well-designed and drafted quilting layout. The quilt is made of soft white cotton and the spacing of the rows of stitching is less than half a centimetre (¼ in) apart. Although thought to be a twentieth-century quilt it has a style of layout and combination of patterns reminiscent of an earlier time and illustrates well the skill required in order to produce an effective quilt.

Markings

Transferring patterns on to the fabric before quilting has always been a difficult exercise. When outline quilting is used, the lines of sewing can be defined solely by eye, as illustrated by the variability of the stitching line seen in some quilts; more complex patterns need to be marked on to the fabric used as the quilt top.

Mention has already been made of the problems encountered in defining which of the two sides of a quilt is the top when one of them is pieced and the other displays complicated quilting at its best. In such examples it is more likely that for practical reasons the quilt design was marked and worked on the plain cloth side. This was confirmed on a quilt seen in Hereford, which was thought to have been stitched between about 1820 and 1830. Made in patchwork, it still had strong pencil markings defining leaves, flowers, diamonds and wineglass infill on the plain side.

Assumptions have been made in the past about the regional variation in the use of different marking media. It has been suggested that chalk was less popular in the North of England, but Mrs Moody from Goole, Humberside, when describing the activities of her aunt who ran a quilt club there, having moved from South Shields, said that after the fabric and wadding was rolled on the quilting frame the patterns for that piece were laid on and marked round with chalk. When quilting was complete the surface was lightly brushed to remove the marks. A collection of quilt templates made from paper, card and metal, acquired in the Barnard Castle area and now in the Quilters' Guild collection, shows evidence of chalk marking around the edges of the templates.

A quilter who favoured using dark fabric for her quilt top was very likely to select chalk to mark fabrics, since it would produce an easily seen line. Similarly, a coarsely woven fabric such as wool flannel could only be marked with a very soft medium – and, again, chalk meets the bill. Since quilts made of wool or of darker fabrics were more often seen in South Wales, there could be a bias towards chalk there.

Another correspondent describes Mrs Cockayne, a Northumbrian quilter, who taught members of her Women's Institute to quilt just before World War II. She and her mother 'cut quilt patterns out of brown paper which they laid on the quilt in the quilt frame and scratched around them with their needles as a guide to stitching'.

Elizabeth Hamilton, who made the Land Army quilt (see Chap.1, fig.1.11, on p.14), used the prick-and-pounce method with carbon to mark her complex design on to the quilt. The family of Elizabeth Morgan, who quilted in South Wales, gave an account of the method she adopted for marking spirals on to her fabric. She used her forefinger to anchor one end of a piece of string at the planned centre of the spiral and tied a marker at the other end, the string length thus dictating the radius of the spiral. The marker was drawn in a circle around her forefinger and, as the string wrapped around the finger and shortened, the marker spiralled inwards.

Quilt Markers

It is well known that professional quilt markers operated in the north-east of England in the last half of the nineteenth and into the twentieth century. Tops for marking were delivered to them and a quilt design was drawn in blue pencil – sufficiently durable to last the return journey – using templates and a lot of freehand designs. A number of quilts were examined that still retained the blue marking. It seems that quilts needed a number of washings before all the blue disappeared and the marks tended to survive in areas of dense quilting.

One of the markers was Mrs Peart of Allendale, Northumberland, who was apprenticed to Elizabeth Sanderson, the doyenne of markers. Mrs Peart started her apprenticeship when she was fourteen years old and worked without pay for a year, during which time she had to provide her own food.[7] She marked the top of the quilt (seen at Basingstoke) made by Allendale Methodist Church members for church funds and also marked the pattern for a quilt made by the Sunderland Women's Institute which was presented to the Queen Mother.

A quilter from Musselburgh, near Edinburgh, learned to quilt when in service in Newcastle in the early twentieth century. She made quilts for all her grandchildren and sent away her fabrics 'to have the patterns put on'. The daughter of Jane Hunter, a quilter from Consett, Durham, remembers that the tradition was for the stamper man (quilt marker) to visit the area to mark out quilt patterns. No record survives of his identity or of his method of working.

Fillings

The warmth-giving properties of a variety of materials were an important consideration when quilt fillings were selected. Utility quilts, where the need for warmth was paramount, revealed fillings of old blankets or clothing, while recycled old worn quilts were frequently seen, particularly in areas of the country that had experienced periods of depression and hardship. Seventy-three re-covered old quilts were recorded, several of which had been re-covered more than once.

Cotton and wool were the two most common fillings, with the wool ones in the form either of loose fleece or woven blanket. While wool was usually used for filling quilted items of the eighteenth century, by the first half of the nineteenth century cotton wadding had become more popular and was easily available from that period onwards. The attraction of cotton wadding was great even for quilters in sheep-rearing parts of the country: of all the quilted items examined, 68 per cent had a cotton filling, 12 per cent had a wool filling and 16 per cent had a blanket filling.

The proportions of fillings in quilts examined at the two venues in Wales during the Project were different. Two-thirds of the fillings seen were wool or wool blanket, and at Carmarthen only 20 per cent had a cotton filling. A large number of small woollen mills were operating in the western part of South Wales until comparatively recently and information received at Carmarthen showed that quilters in this area frequently obtained their materials from local mills.

The Isle of Man was another area known for sheep rearing, but only one quilt that had a woollen filling was examined there. The majority of Manx quilts were flat-quilted with no wadding at all.

Two examples of seasonal differentiation of fillings were discovered. Jane Hunter made summerweight quilts with lightcoloured fabrics and thin cotton fillings, while blankets, or dark-coloured quilts that in many cases were filled with old blankets, were used in the winter.

Two quilts from the south-west of England that were made in the period 1825-40 had pieced tops and many of their fabrics in common. One had a thinnish wool filling for summer, while the other, the winter quilt, contained a thick firm blanket. Clearly the summer season was considered to be shorter at that time, since the winter quilt shows far more wear.

Fabrics

The wide variety of fabrics used in the quilts is discussed in detail in Chapter 9. However, mention should be made now of some fabrics favoured by twentieth-century quilters.

The majority of wholecloth quilts of this period appear to be made from cotton with a sateen weave. Cotton sateen, often described as Roman Sateen, was very popular, as demonstrated by the wide range of colours available (see fig.5.26, p.94) and easily obtainable in local shops. A club quilter in Chester-le-Street, Durham, records that she bought sateen under the brand name Silver Sheen at her local Co-operative Society branch. She also bought no. 9 Brookes thread for quilting. In South Wales two fabrics – Sparva and Opaline – were mentioned specifically during the Project.

Finishings

Study of the data regarding quilt-edge finishing techniques reveals a difference between the technique favoured in Britain and that in the United States. In Britain, by far the most popular method was butting. The technique requires the raw edges of the top and back fabrics to be turned in and stitched together, either by machine or by hand with a running stitch. Machining the edge provides a stronger finish, but it does lend an incongruous touch where quilts demonstrating hours of hand stitching are completed by machine stitching. Machine stitching of the butted edge was seen in 57 per cent of quilts examined. It was noted that there was a regional variation in the method of stitching the butted edge. Fewer quilts with machine finishing were seen at the two Welsh venues: in Carmarthen, 67 per cent were hand-finished.

The most popular finishing method on the quilts from the USA was binding. Lapping, where the edges of the top or back fabric are brought round to the other side and sewn down like a binding, was seen fairly frequently, while the butting technique was rare.

Tying

The quickest way to hold the layers of the quilt together is to run a thread back and forth through the layers and tie the ends together. This method of tying or knotting serves the purpose of creating a functional quilt, but does not contribute anything to the quilt design by enhancing the fabric or the piecing. Tying was likely, therefore, to be used most often in the sewing of utilitarian quilts, where speed of production was more important than any aesthetic consideration. It also was an ideal method to employ on quilts with very ornate patterning, such as crazy patchwork, or on quilts with many thick seams, such as Log Cabin, where no further enhancement was necessary.

No-nonsense functional quilts made solely for warmth are very likely to be used until they wear out. Crazy and Log Cabin patterns were very popular patchwork styles from the second half or the nineteenth century onwards. It was not a surprise, therefore, that no pre-1850 quilts with tying were noted: the majority of tied quilts were found to be from the twentieth century.

The tying occurred either as discreet knots on the quilt back or as flamboyant additions to the quilt top with the use of brightly coloured threads and long loose thread ends. This was seen on the twentieth-century quilt illustrated in full in Chapter 9 (see fig.9.39 on p.215), which has very obvious knots with added tufts in a style reminiscent of mattress buttoning.

QUILTING LAYOUTS, PATTERNS AND TEMPLATES

Layouts

A quilt is designed by arranging one or more quilting patterns into a pleasing layout. After viewing nearly 1,359 wholecloth quilts during the documentation programme, it was evident that these layouts could usefully be classified into a number of distinct types, whether the quilting was by hand or machine. Figure 5.47, which is illustrated overleaf, on pages 122-23, shows the different types, with further explanation. It should be noted that the quilting layout can be, and surprisingly often is, completely unrelated to any underlying patchwork.

As in any handiwork, especially rural or folk handiwork, there will be exceptions that do not fit these observed categories, and instances where the worker 'does her own thing'. The use of different layouts may also vary over time or with location: prior to about 1870, it is thought, the 'delineated motif and borders' layout (no.6) appears to have been used throughout Britain in conjunction with the 'all-over' (no.1) and the 'strippy' (no.2) and its variations. These remained in use throughout all areas of Britain except north-east England, where the 'delineated motif and borders' layout was supplanted by the 'undefined motif and borders' layout (no.7). In the Isle of Man and north-west England it is more usual to have all 'all-over' layout (no.1) than any other.

Patterns

Just as the quilting layouts have changed over time, so have the patterns used. Earlier quilting (up to 1860 or so) made much more use of flowers, leaves and pots and vases of flowers, than is common today. Some are shown in figure 5.19 on page 85. It is difficult to say exactly where and when the exuberant and elegant feather patterns of north-east England appeared – possibly around 1870. While

Fig. 5.47. Diagram of standard quilting layouts.

1. All-over. Only one quilting pattern is used over the whole surface – for example, a background pattern such as hanging diamonds, clamshells or square wave, or a single strip pattern such as bellows. (This is not to be confused with quilting over the whole surface with a number of different patterns.)

2. Strippy. The strippy layout consists of at least two alternating strip or border quilting patterns generally running up and down the quilt, but occasionally they are set crosswise. While strippy patchwork usually has an uneven number of strips in order to create a pleasing visual effect, the strippy quilting layout may instead consist of an even number of strips.

3. Bordered Strippy. Here the quilting is laid out as a conventional strippy, but the side patterns are continued around top and bottom to form a border.

4. Motif and Strippy. These quilts have a motif or arrangement of motifs set in the centre of a strippy layout.

5. Motif and Border(s) Strippy. This is a bordered strippy with the addition of a central motif.

6. Delineated Motif and Border(s). With this type, the outside edge of the central motif is defined by a single, double or triple line or quilting, as are all the borders. Generally the border corners are separated by quilting lines and filled with a different pattern from those in the borders themselves.

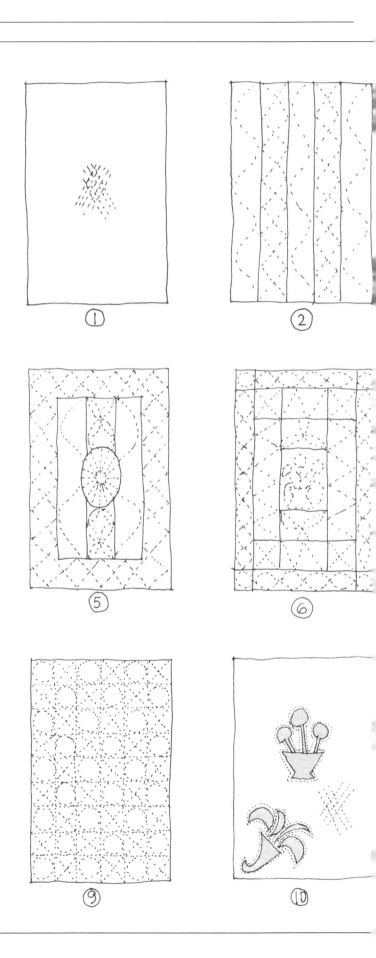

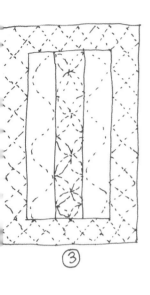

(3)

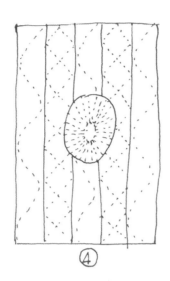

(4)

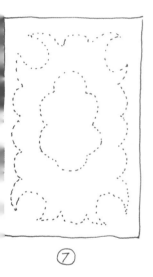

(7)

(8)

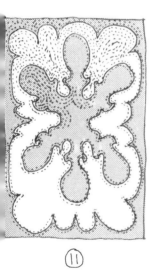

(11)

7. Undefined Motif and Border(s). The central motif, which may be an arrangement of repeats of several different quilting patterns, is set in a field of background quilting, which runs right to the edge of the motif and the border. There may be additional small motifs scattered over the background. In a variation of this layout the border is inset, with further background quilting extending to the edge of the quilt. The main distinguishing feature of this layout is the lack of delineated areas.

8. Enclosed by Patchwork Motif and/or Borders. This category includes the Sanderson Star, the Feathered Star, and some Welsh quilts. In this layout, the large patchwork areas and borders have appropriate quilting motifs within the different shapes. This layout also includes those quilts where there is no central patchwork motif, just a different fabric border or borders.

9. Chequerboard Layout. This is alternating arrangement of squares of quilting patterns, generally but not always enclosed by block patchwork – some wholecloth quilts were seen with this layout. It is a common layout for American quilts but is also seen in British quilts – using baskets, for example.

10. Following Piecing/Appliqué. A serviceable and practical way of quilting either patchwork or appliqué is to stitch a seam's-width – traditionally a half-centimetre (¼ in) – away from, and parallel to, all patchwork seams. In this category, normal background or patterns of quilting are outside the appliqué or patchwork elements.

11. Contour Quilting. Parallel lines of stitching are worked echoing the shape of the appliqué pieces on the quilt top, both inside and outside, to fill the whole quilt.

superficially similar to American feather patterns, which have been confirmed from very much earlier dates, they are recognisably different in profile and detail: Averil Colby discusses and illustrates this point in *Quilting*.[8]

There must be literally hundreds of quilting patterns, many with small individual variations, and often with marked regional uses. It is not possible within the scope of this book to do more than highlight a few of them. As usual, they can conveniently be divided into categories, according to the way they are used: backgrounds, borders and strips, and motifs (see figs.5.48-5.52 on pp.125-29). Often a motif can be repeated to make a border or strip (such as the Alice Orange Paisley shell repeated back-to-back for borders), and a background pattern can be enlarged, elaborated and infilled to form a border or motif pattern – such as the wineglass pattern, which can become large diagonally crossed leaves (used as both border and motif), or clamshell, seen as a motif in the corner of figure 5.39 on page 107.

It is difficult to classify some patterns: the spiral, so popular in Wales, may be used as an infill in pattern areas but would classify as a motif, and the freehand floral or scrolling of north-east England is used as filler in combination with various motifs, such as the flower/rose in the star points of the Elizabeth Sanderson Star quilts.

Another difficulty lies in naming patterns: nothing creates more argument among traditional quilters than calling patterns by the wrong names. When it is considered that there are at least five or more names for the Welsh spiral (snail creep, snail shell, spiral, whirl, twirl), it is easy to see how problems of communication can arise. One of the flower-pattern templates in the Guild's ownership was labelled 'Star' and another one was called 'Blow Bellows'! In the absence of known names for quilting patterns, it has been necessary to make some up. It would be interesting to know the traditional names.

It is often asserted that heart motifs in the quilting indicate that the quilt was made for a marriage. There may be some truth in this, but the proportion of Welsh quilts with hearts far outweighed those in north-east England, so possibly this is a romantic but incorrect idea. Horseshoes were also said to be good luck on wedding quilts, and a number did appear, as did the Lover's Knot in varying degrees of accuracy (it is very easy to get this pattern wrong if it is not taken from a correct source). Two quilts from Wales had hearts outlined with small circles, like coins – perhaps love and good fortune were signified! Also shown (see fig.5.51, p.128) are a heart and thistle head from the Scottish borders (probably Hawick), an unusual double heart from a Welsh quilt and a selection of leaves, flowers and feathers.

Pages 125-129:
Fig. 5.48. Diagram of background quilting patterns.

Fig. 5.49. Diagram of typical border or strippy patterns.

Fig. 5.50. Diagram of typical Welsh quilting motifs.

Fig. 5.51. Diagram of typical North Country quilting motifs.

Fig. 5.52. Diagram of typical country-wide quilting motifs.

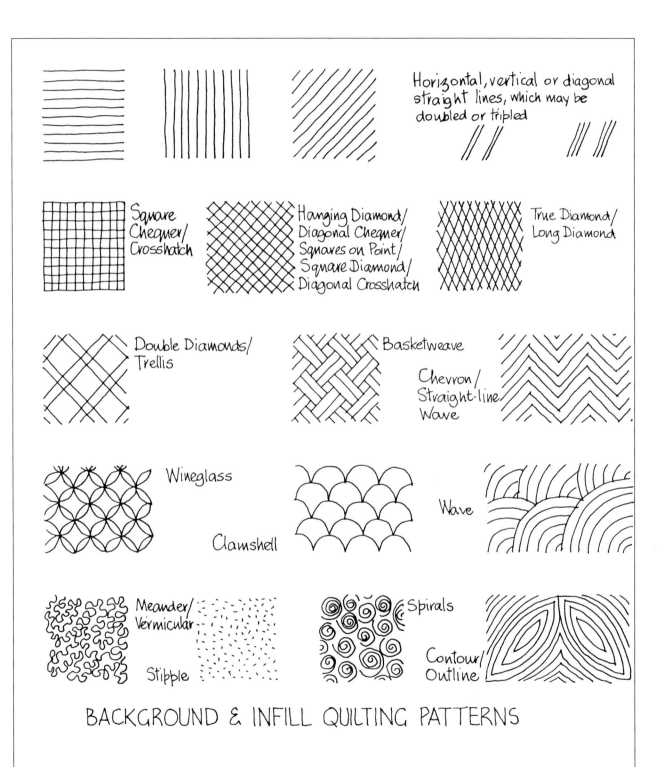

Horizontal, vertical or diagonal straight lines, which may be doubled or tripled

Square Chequer/ Crosshatch

Hanging Diamond/ Diagonal Chequer/ Squares on Point/ Square Diamond/ Diagonal Crosshatch

True Diamond/ Long Diamond

Double Diamonds/ Trellis

Basketweave

Chevron/ Straight-line Wave

Wineglass

Clamshell

Wave

Meander/ Vermicular

Stipple

Spirals

Contour/ Outline

BACKGROUND & INFILL QUILTING PATTERNS

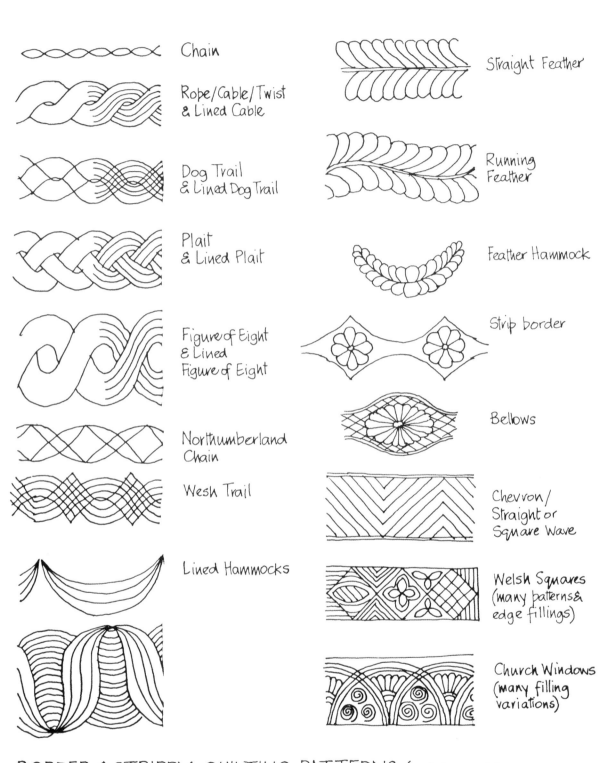

Chain

Rope/Cable/Twist
& Lined Cable

Dog Trail
& Lined Dog Trail

Plait
& Lined Plait

Figure of Eight
& Lined
Figure of Eight

Northumberland
Chain

Wesh Trail

Lined Hammocks

Straight Feather

Running
Feather

Feather Hammock

Strip border

Bellows

Chevron/
Straight or
Square Wave

Welsh Squares
(many patterns &
edge fillings)

Church Windows
(many filling
variations)

BORDER & STRIPPY QUILTING PATTERNS (not to scale)

WELSH QUILTING MOTIFS (not to scale)
1, 2, 3 &   various leaves, infilled.   4 - heart   5 - border of tulips, leaves & hearts
6 - triangle infilled spirals & trefoils.   8 - flatiron (various fillings)
9 - double-heart corner from fig. 43

Feathers

Fern in Stand

Flower Pot

Sheaf of Corn

Wheatsheaf

Weardale Wheel

Fleurs de Lys

Flower

Pine

Oakleaf

Paisley Flower

TYPICAL NORTH COUNTRY & SCOTS
QUILTING MOTIFS (not to scale)

Scottish Borders
Heart, Thistle & Fleurs
de-lys Cross

Roses

Double Knot

Single Knot

Fans

True Lovers' Knot

Paisley Pear

Paisley Shell

Stars

Shells

Flowers

Leaves

Tulip

Fern

TYPICAL QUILTING MOTIFS, not to scale
Flowers, leaves etc.

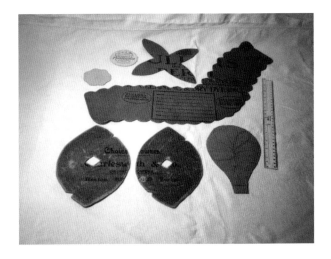

Fig. 5.53. Quilting templates made from metal, paper and card.
(Photo: Pauline Adams)

Fig. 5.54. Quilting templates made from card and cardboard-box lids.
(Photo: Pauline Adams)

Templates

The techniques for marking the quilting patterns are described on page 117. When it was necessary to use templates for repeating patterns, they were traditionally made from available materials. The Quilters' Guild has several sets of templates. Part of one set is illustrated in figures 5.53 and 5.54. These templates date from about 1917. Although originally purchased in Barnard Castle, the set contains templates made of local newspapers of the Penrith area and the *Northern Echo*, printed in Darlington, and parcel wrapping paper addressed to Loftus near the North Yorkshire coast. Four of the templates are made from sheet metal and have handles; others are cut from thick cardboard-box lids, old brown wrapping paper (complete with address label), grocer's sugar paper and the newspapers. The sturdier templates could be drawn around with pencil or needle, but the flimsy paper templates confirm that an alternative method was also used: their edges have traces of white and coloured blackboard chalks, showing that the chalk was drawn over the edge of the template rather than round it. The set includes some tiny templates that look as though they have been traced from tea-caddy spoons.

It must be emphasized that a template merely provides the outline of a quilting motif and that all but the smallest require additional infilling to be added. Figure 5.54 clearly illustrates a paddle-shaped template with an infill pattern drawn on.

It constantly surprises people to see the very great range in size of quilting patterns – note the cable 'eye' shapes ranging from tiny to very large.

THE SOCIAL VIEW

Nearly one-third of the quilts studied in the Project were wholecloth. Quilts relying on decoration achieved from quilting on plain fabric, or on a pieced strippy or large star, survive in large numbers and bear witness to countless hours of repetitive hand stitching. It is intriguing to speculate about the lifestyles of all the quilters who worked hard to produce these wholecloth quilts over the past three hundred and fifty years.

Many writers have already recorded the social benefits that women over the ages have derived from sewing in groups. Quilting, as a sewing technique, lends itself very easily to such a communal activity. Quilting, after all, met the requirements of an ideal female occupation, where idle hands could be kept busy in a safe social environment while conversation ranged widely. Quilt frames such as the 'twilting frame' recorded in the Thornton sisters' family inventory – see Chapter 2 – not only helped the quilting process but also enabled other quilters to join in the activity.

A strippy quilt recorded at Penrith, made by Mary Brown in 1860, was finished by a local group at a quilting party in Nenthead, Alston, in the north Pennines. Apparently the maker eloped to Gretna Green when eighteen years old and married an upstanding member of the community who was a local leadworks manager as well as a farmer and Methodist minister.

Mrs Cockayne regaled her Women's Institute with descriptions of 'twilting' (quilting) parties held in Northumbria in the 1880, when relatives, friends and neighbours were invited into a home to help the hostess finish a quilt in exchange for refreshments and a chance for a good gossip. Such social events were eagerly anticipated as a break in the usual domestic routine. Mrs Cockayne's mother could not afford to buy refreshments for these occasions, so, sadly, they never held a quilting party.

Since the time of the Guild of Linen Armourers in the Middle Ages, quilting has been a skill often employed as a source of income: it is interesting that nine of the named makers of quilts in the Project were described as 'professional' quilters when their occupation was defined.

Some of the eighteenth-century quilted garments viewed on documentation days gave rise to speculation about their professional makers. It is very likely that later generations of local dressmakers continued to offer a quilting service along with other skills.

Miss Puddicombe, the maker of the Wellington panel quilt (see Chap.9, p.207), was described as a dressmaker in north Devon who had the capability to produce a striking pieced and quilted quilt. Miss Maggie Davies of Cilycwm, Llandovery, Dyfed, was the village quiltmaker in the early 1900s and she had a quilt 'rig' (squarish) in the front room, where she did her work, clearly visible from the road outside. At the same time, in Pontygwaith, Rhondda, South Wales, Sarah Rees and Co., Building Contractors and Undertakers Ltd, had a haberdashery shop on the premises, where homemade quilts, household linen, dress materials and tailored suits could be purchased. The shop provided employment for the three Rees daughters as well as sixteen young women who made quilts and other items in the upstairs workroom.

A pieced frame quilt quilted in a Welsh-style defined layout, and made in the second half of the nineteenth century, was seen at Hereford. It was stitched by two sisters who were described as itinerant weavers. They used to travel from farm to farm in South Wales and stay for six to eight weeks making all the clothes and household textiles, including quilts, before moving on.

Church Groups

Fund-raising sewing activities, particularly quilting, were organized by many churches in the nineteenth and twentieth centuries. In Hawick, in the Scottish borders, all the church guilds in the town quilted and once a year there was a two-day sale of quilts. Production of the 'Hawick-style' quilts in the 1920s and 1930s must have been quite considerable, since the distinctive designs on these quilts were recognised at East Grinstead, Edinburgh and Swavesey, as well as locally, in Kelso. (See also Chap.6.)

Some motifs that were incorporated in a motif and border layout and were commonly seen in these quilts included an ornate heart with a spiky leaf infill, a circle divided by a curve yin-yang style and a thistle flower sometimes with thistle leaves (see fig.104 on p.128). The background infill frequently used was clamshell and the quilts were often finished with a single row of clamshell that looked like scallops. One of the few examples of a black quilt seen during the Project was a Hawick quilt that contained large hearts and thistles stitched in bright pink thread.

Quilt Clubs

At the same time, for women in straitened circumstances quilting was a way of earning a living. Mrs Elizabeth Morgan, one of the nine named professional quilters, supported herself and her widowed mother by quilting in the early 1900s. Quilt clubs were very popular in north-east England. Fourteen quilters who run clubs were named during the Project in an area stretching from North Shields, Tyne and Wear, to Redcar, Teesside. Details of clubs run by groups of miners' wives in Ynysybwl in Glamorgan, Newcastle and Durham were also received. Each club usually had about twenty members and the quilter supplied each member with a quilt over a number of weeks. The quilts were paid for by weekly instalments of, usually, one shilling (5p), although one club in Southwick, Sunderland, was said to charge four shillings (20p) a week in 1926.

Quilts were still used extensively as everyday household linen at this time and the club system provided non-quilters with bed covers as well as allowing philanthropic local people to provide an income for poorer families where the mother was the breadwinner. A quilt owner records that his family farmed in Fulwell, Sunderland, in the 1920s and that they bought quilts for their live-in servants to help needy local families; the quilts were not considered of value at the time. Another quilt was recorded as having been bought in Leeds in 1926 as an 'act of charity'.

Edith Hutchinson (née Kendrew) ran a quilt club with her widowed mother for twenty years, from 1919 to 1939, at home in Plawsworthgate, Chester-le-Street. She made one quilt a week, working every day except Sunday and starting at 6 a.m. She charged club members a total of 27/6d. (£1.37½), from which she reckoned on a profit of about 7/6d.

Mrs Moody describes leaving school at fourteen in 1928 to help her aunt run a quilt club. She can remember collecting one shilling a week from club members whose names were drawn out of a hat to decide the order in which the members received their quilts. Two weeks before their turn, she gave them the sateen fabric samples so they could choose the colour of their quilt and posted off the order to Grattons in the Market Place, South Shields, who supplied the fabric by mail order. Her aunt made mobcaps, selling for sixpence (2½p), and aprons with the leftover fabric.

The income from a quilt club was obviously hard earned. Mrs Moody and her aunt made a quilt in four-and-a-half days and, like Edith Hutchinson, worked long hours. Her niece reported: 'Everyone who called on my aunt when she was sewing was kept busy threading needles while chatting.'

Revival

A revival of interest in quilting in South Wales and north-east England in the 1920s and 1930s was encouraged by the Rural Industries Bureau, the Women's Institute and the Northern Industries Workrooms' Clubs, as described in *Traditional British Quilts* by Dorothy Osler. By promoting an expansion of the market for quilts and small quilted items in places such as London and by encouraging the training of new quilters in order to maintain a high quality of workmanship, the interested bodies were able to help increase the income of a number of families in the areas. The Quakers also played a part in the revival of quilting in Wales – their work is described in Chapter 6.

Some of the quilters who were noted during the Project supplied quilts to shops in London and made items such as dressing gowns and bed jackets for members of the Royal family, who supported the

Rural Industries Bureau scheme. Jane Annie Pattinson (neé Stobbs) of Upper Weardale, Durham, made quilts when a young girl with her sister Amy. After her husband's early death, she was too busy earning a living as a dressmaker to quilt, but she returned to quilting after her daughters were married. She was one of a number of women who made a quilt which was presented to Queen Elizabeth (the late Queen Mother) 'in recognition of her encouragement and support in promoting the craft of quilting instigated by the Women's Institute and the Rural Industries Bureau'.

Evelyn Jones recalls attending the Northern Industries Workrooms' Clubs centre at Barnard Castle, Durham, in 1938 to learn to quilt and she still has the bag which she made as a learning piece. To qualify as a quilter she had to work for three weeks without pay and then earned two shillings and sixpence (12½p) a week.

The Barnard Castle centre was run under the guiding force of Lady Headlam, who also had contacts with a group in West Auckland, Durham, which was run by Elizabeth Black. A quilt made for a family wedding by Elizabeth Black in 1941 was seen at Chelmsford. She and other members of the group made quilted items for Princess Marina, the Duchess of Argyll and the Marchioness of Zetland. The family record that Mrs Black was very proud of the fact that she made the original quilts for the Durham room at the Women's Institute Denman College.

Two of the Rural Industries Bureau centres in South Wales were at Abertridwr, Glamorgan, and Porth, Rhondda, Glamorgan. They are described in the book by Dorothy Osler. Three quilts made by Katy Lewis, a member of the Abertridwr class, were seen at Pontypridd. The quilts, one of which won second prize at the 1951 Quilting Exhibition at the Welsh Folk Museum, demonstrate design skills and workmanship which are a tribute to Miss Owen, who was the original tutor of the group.

A cushion, now in a very fragile state, made by Mrs Pugsley also won a second prize at the same exhibition. Mrs Pugsley was taught to quilt by Miss Jessie Edwards, who was the inspirational tutor of the Porth group and also a teacher at Merthyr Tydfil College, Glamorgan. Miss Edwards encouraged her to enter the competition at the Folk Museum and drew out a design for her on parachute silk – the only silk easily available after World War II.

Mrs Rossiter was another pupil of Miss Edwards in the 1950s. She had a lesson about every three months in her home in Merthyr Tydfil. Mrs Rossiter describes working on an old frame which was only 91 centimetres (36 in) wide because she could not use a full-sized frame in a small house. She worked the centre section of a quilt first and then stitched the sides in one piece with a space left down the centre of the fabric to allow for cutting the two sides apart when finished. The side pieces were joined to the centre after quilting. Mrs Rossiter said that it was very important to mark the pattern accurately in order that the pieces matched after quilting!

Wemyss School of Needlework

Very fine quilting on silk with wool domette wadding was one of the techniques taught at the Wemyss School of Needlework in Coaltown of Wemyss, Fife, Scotland, until the 1940s. The school was set up in the late nineteenth century by Lady Henry Grosvenor, who had been inspired by the establishment of the Royal School of Needlework in London. The school was opened to provide needlework training for the daughters of miners from the area. They entered at the age of fourteen and took an apprenticeship for six months, after which time they easily found a situation elsewhere as a ladies' maid or stayed on in a waged position making or restoring embroideries and other household textiles as well as creating items for trousseaux and layettes. The school's teacher believed it was better for young women to spend their time over the needlework than to waste it over 'trashy' stories.

Decline

By the late 1930s the fashion for wholecloth quilts was waning. Many of the quilts that were examined from this period do not appear to have been used and were apparently put away in drawers or airing cupboards. One quilt owner explained that her quilt, made for a family wedding, was regarded as old-fashioned by the relative for whom it was made. This was very likely the reason why many other quilts languished unseen. The coming of World War II was the reason for the fading in popularity of quilts when fabrics were in short supply and quilting was not a priority. Thirty-one quilts were examined which were made in 1940, while only nineteen were seen which were made in the rest of the decade. After the war, despite the publicity created by such events as the 1951 Welsh Folk Museum exhibition and the efforts of teachers such as Miss Edwards and quilters such as Mrs Lewis, there was no revival in quilting, since fashions had moved on: only thirty-three quilts dating from the 1950s were recorded by the Project.

Above top: Figs 6.1 and 6.2. Two rare examples of quilts bearing names.

Above centre: Fig. 6.3. Over 100 years in the making. See the Cobb family story on p. 138-140.

Fig. 6.4. Blue cross stitch was used to record the name of Margaret Pickering on this quilt. See p. 33 and p. 188.

CHAPTER 6

THE
QUILTMAKERS
Margaret Tucker

CERTAIN SOCIAL, historical and industrial milestones appear in the history of patchwork and quilting which affected not only the quiltmakers but also what they produced.

The development of Turkey Red dye in the eighteenth century, the printing of floral and commemorative panels in the early part of the nineteenth century and the introduction of roller-printing techniques for cotton had an obvious bearing on the types of fabrics that were available. The invention of the domestic sewing machine in the middle of the nineteenth century made another kind of impact, as did the Great Exhibition at Crystal Palace, London, in 1851, which glorified classical design sources. Britain's role as a colonial power during the Victorian era – both in war and peace – was directly responsible for the military-style quilts, many of which were made in India. The middle-class obsession with 'fancy' needlework on silk, satin and velvet in the later 1800s was another kind of landmark because it threw up an abundance of decorative embroidery and embellishment techniques that were used in crazy patchwork quilts and table covers as well as on such fripperies as watch cases, pen wipes and matchbox covers.

Two World Wars and the Depression era in between were other turning points in patchwork and quilting – milestones which affected not only the availability of materials but also a woman's place in society. During wartime, when women had to go out to work, there was less time to spend on sewing and other household pursuits. In contrast, during the Depression, there were some women who had to take up sewing to support their families, mainly in the mining districts of north-east England and South Wales.

Travel and the development of communication made another kind of impact on British patchwork and quilting. Patterns and quilts alike crossed the ocean from North America, while intrepid travellers or missionaries abroad acquired fabrics and new ideas to add to their own basic skills. Along with all these general influences were the circumstantial ones reflected in the stories of the individual quiltmakers from every walk of life and every part of the country.

Anne Laughton, who made the multi-coloured silk, satin and ribbon Log Cabin cover in figure 6.5 on page 138, was a quilter who kept a record of important events. A notebook of hers contained an entry dated 7 October 1857. It read: 'The day set apart for humiliation and prayer for the rescue of our poor suffering country and people in British India, their day 7th, Anne' (a reference to the Indian Mutiny).

Another entry, dated 5 October 1858, said: 'Between 7 and 8 o'clock, in the sky, saw the comet pass and apparently very near to a magnificently bright star, so that the star was shining through the comet's tail …'

Anne's notebook, found in a trunk with her quilt, also recorded recipes and tips on household management. The recipes included one intriguing set of directions for cleaning fabric: 'To clean silk – ¼lb honey, do [the same] soft soap, 2 wine glasses of gin, 3 gills boiling water. Mix and let stand till blood warm. Lay the breadths on a table and brush with a nail brush, then rinse in cold soft water and iron before quite dry.'

The Log Cabin cover made by Anne is believed to have been constructed between 1860 and 1870. When she died, she left it to her nephew, who in turn deposited it with a friend for safekeeping. He had put the quilt in a tin trunk, along with Anne's notebook and the silver buttons from his Seaforth Highlanders dress uniform, when he emigrated to California in 1886. The trunk was never reclaimed and lay unopened for years. In 1975, the present owner, a great-great-granddaughter of the woman who had taken the trunk

Fig. 6.5. The Log Cabin quilt made by Anne Laughton lay in a trunk for many years. Silk, satin and ribbon, c.1860
123 cm x 149 cm (4 ft 1 in x 4 ft 11 in).

Opposite: Fig. 6.6. The quilt started by Alice Rebecca Cobb in 1877 was finished 100 years later by her granddaughter, Dorothy Alice Cobb. Appliquéd diamonds on squares. Cotton, including fabric from railway signal flags.
212 cm x 222 cm (7 ft x 7 ft 4 in).

in care, added a 10 centimetre (4 in) black velvet border to the quilt and had the work framed and put under glass.

Another quilt begun in the same period as the one made by Anne took more than one hundred years to finish! Alice Rebecca Cobb started her appliqué diamond quilt in 1877 at the age of seventeen and just after her wedding, She was a dressmaker and when her son was born in 1878 she put aside her patchwork. It was not picked up again until 1927, when her eleven-year-old granddaughter went to stay with her after her husband died. Alice taught Dorothy Alice Cobb to sew the quilt and Dorothy eventually finished it in 1978 (see fig.6.6).

Alice's husband was a railwayman and pieces of fabric from his red signal flags are included in the quilt. The resourcefulness of the maker is also recorded by her inclusion of white nappy fabric and pieces of material left over from sewing her husband's shirts. Dorothy Alice added scraps from dressmaking: the grey and white stripe cotton is the material which was used to make her

Fig. 6.7. Barbara Whitehead, née Metcalfe, who married in 1859.

Fig. 6.8. A celebrated Welsh quilter of the 1920s and 1930s, Margaret Williams died in 1937 at the age of sixty.

A SOUTH WALES QUILT WIFE

South Wales "quilt wives" are much in the public eye at the moment, and their work is being eagerly sought in London.

Our photograph is of one of the most famous and skilful of these ladies, Mrs. James Williams, of Gwaun-cae-Gurwen,

MRS. JAMES WILLIAMS.

who was the winner in the "quilt for double-bed, hand-sewn," class at the Treorchy National Eisteddfod this year.

The winning quilt, a beautiful specimen of work, was purchased by Mrs. David Davies, of Llandinam. Other ladies who have possessed themselves of examples of Mrs. Williams's work include the Countess of Dunraven and Grace Countess of Wemyss.

Mrs. Williams was also the winner in the quilt making competition at the Ammanford National Eisteddfod. She is very well known in the Gwaun-cae-Gurwen district.

probationer's uniform for Guy's Hospital, while the plain mauve is from the material used to make her midwifery uniform when she worked at Royal Buckingham Hospital in Aylesbury. Dorothy finished with tie quilting.

A pair or quilts made by a farmer's wife in Yorkshire in 1890 demonstrate a similar resourcefulness in the use of fabric. Cottons, wools and printed shawl fabric were used by Barbara Whitehead (see fig.6.7) to make a quilt or squares turned on point as diamonds. Barbara, née Metcalfe, married her husband, Robert, at Gretna Green in July 1859 and the quilts she later made (see fig.6.10, p.142) have been handed down in the family to her great-granddaughter.

Earning a Living

Those women who earned their living from patchwork and quilting often had to be quite ingenious in their use of available materials. The quilt in figure 6.11 on page 143, which looks anything but English, is made of a loosely woven mixture of cotton or linen warp with a wool weft, which was teased for a fluffy, effect. It was manufactured in Cumbria from the 1880s onwards and intended solely for export to Central America, North Africa and the Middle East, where the fabric was used for shawls, sometimes worn poncho style. A Mrs Foster of Canonbie, near Carlisle, used the available offcuts in a more imaginative way. After being widowed at a youthful age, she supported her family by making and selling quilts from the blanket-like material. They were in great demand during the Cumbrian winters, their warmth and bright colours being much appreciated.

Margaret Williams (1877-1937) of Gwaun-cae-Gurwen, South Wales, worked in a more traditional way with quiltmaking (see fig. 6.8). She made and sold quilts to order, which went to America and to such notables as Dame Margaret Lloyd George, Lady Davies of Llandinam, the Countess of Dunraven, and the Countess of Wemyss. A letter from the Countess of Wemyss in 1929 thanks her for the quilt and encloses a cheque for £5 1s 3d in payment.

As well as being an adjudicator in several Royal shows in Wales, she was an Eisteddfod winner at least four times. She frequently gave quilting demonstrations at Women's Institute meetings and exhibition centres and taught sewing in schools. On top of all this, she had qualifications as a home nurse and for ambulance work and was noted for making and icing wedding cakes! Among her remaining quilts is one made in 1929 to celebrate the birth of a grandson. Executed in simple Irish chain, it is backed with a flour bag with the label 'Daren Mills Dartford. Made from the life of the wheat, discarding all its indigestible parts.'

Fig. 6.9. A quilting group working around a traditional frame in the Maes-yr-Haf Educational Settlement in the Rhondda in the early 1950s. (From *Quakers in the Rhondda* by Barrie Naylor.)

The Quakers

The 1930s saw a craft revival in the Rhondda Valley, fostered by the Quakers. The long strike in the Welsh coal pits in 1926, followed by the General Strike, had led to the closure of pits and great deprivation.

One woman who was greatly moved by the plight of the miners and their families was Emma Noble, a Quaker from Swindon. She went to the Rhondda and talked to local officials and teachers. On returning home, she wrote a letter to the Quaker Crisis Committee in London outlining the situation in Wales and detailing the need for material help and 'loving sympathy'. She was particularly interested in the plight of the women and children:

> In several secondary schools I visited, the teachers are giving part of their salaries to provide one meal a day for necessitous children. They, knowing the homes of children and the circumstances, fear there are more needing help. In some of the schools it is obvious there is distress and there is a marked need for boots. Many of the children travel long distances on foot ... Where ever I visited I found that boys of fourteen upwards who had started work are not allowed any relief. They have one meal at the soup kitchen in the Rhondda; but at Aberdare I found no soup kitchens for men and in some homes there are three or four of these lads ... The needy children in the secondary schools in Aberdare are given one meal a day for five days a week. These children need help over the week-ends.[1]

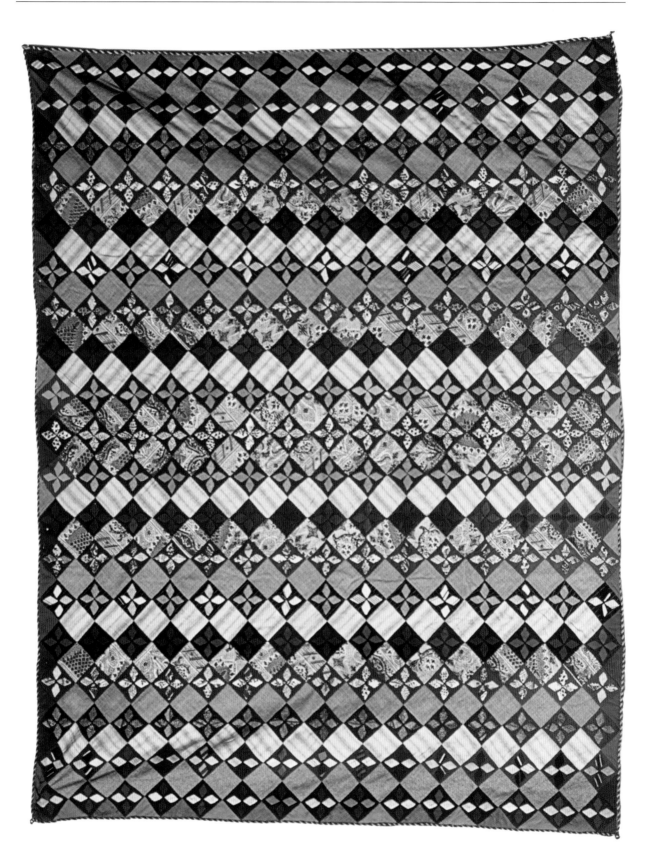

Fig. 6.10. Cotton and wool squares-on-point
made effective use of colour in this Yorkshire
quilt. 1890.
144 cm x 185 cm (4 ft 7 in x 6 ft).

There was a quick response to Emma Noble's letter and an effective appeal for clothing, boots, food and money. This relief work in turn led to the establishment in 1927 of Maes-yr-Haf, the Quakers' Educational Centre in the township of Trealaw, initially run by Emma Noble and her husband. Here programmes were launched in adult education, youth work, and cultural and leisure activities. The Quakers set out to teach new skills to the unemployed and to promote various self-help schemes. Classes were held in shoe repair, dressmaking, weaving, pottery, furniture making, music and drama and clubs were established for women and the unemployed (see fig.6.9, p.141).

Fig. 6.11. The blanket material in this quilt made many a Cumbrian winter more comfortable. Late nineteenth century. 177 cm x 185 cm (5 ft 10 in x 6 ft).

Quilting became an important craft activity at Maes-yr-Haf. It developed through the sewing activities of the Women's Clubs members who were initially charged with remaking donated clothing. Dressmaking grew as a prime activity and Emma Noble bought at cost price thousands of yards of calico, shirting, winceyette and cotton prints, which she in turn supplied to the clubs. She also purchased Sparva to make quilts at a cost of sixpence (2½p) a yard. Quilters paid for the fabric by instalments, at the rate of one penny a week.[2] The quilts they made were all wholecloth (they did not do patchwork) and although some occasionally were sent to London for sale (London was also a very profitable outlet for the settlement's woven rugs and furniture just after World War II) the quilts were generally made for personal use.

The Women's Clubs, with their focus on sewing, spread to other parts of the Rhondda and, for a time, yearly exhibitions and rallies were held at Maes-yr-Haf. By 1939, there were thirty-nine clubs in total, with 2,650 members over three valleys. The clubs were so popular that some had as many as 150 members.

In 1986, Maes-yr-Haf was purchased by Rhondda Borough Council for use as a community centre. Various classes are still held there and it also provides accommodation for a play group and different charitable and social activities. The quilting activity also continues sporadically in the Rhondda: a few of the women who either learned or improved their quilting skills through the Quakers' programme in the 1930s still quilt today even though in their seventies and eighties.

One such group, who came together at a Quaker Centre in Evanstown, Gilfach Goch, Porth, in 1939 still meets once a week in the winter to quilt and socialize. At the height of the group's popularity (in the 1940s and 1950s) they would be working five frames simultaneously, with between six and eight people on a frame. They have made numerous quilts for family and friends in years past, and they make one quilt yearly to raffle in aid of the local Old Age Pensioners' Centre. Some of these women learned quilting at an early age.

'We used to buy lengths of printed cotton from the drapers and stitch the lengths together. The filling was an old Welsh blanket and we didn't have a frame but worked on the kitchen table and the designs weren't so adventurous. I used to help my granny with the quilting after school ... I was the only grandchild and we lived with her. She had me making tarts as well.' [3]

'I made my first quilt on a table without a frame. The fabric was very cheap – about 1s. a yard – and the colours were muted pinks and blues. I used it at home for many years' [4].

The women acquired sewing skills at an early age at both home and school and were generally accustomed to making clothes and soft furnishings – basic plain sewing. Once brought together in groups, however, the use of more decorative quilt patterns began. Over the years, they drew and cut paper and cardboard patterns from whatever source happened to be at hand. Paper and cardboard templates made by individual quilters never had names other than something purely to identify them, such as 'star' or 'flower' or 'leaf', but each quilter always put her name on her own templates so that they would be returned if she loaned them.

To this day the group still retains their own 'marker' and work on traditional wooden frames where pegs are used to keep the quilt taut (traditionally the holes in the end of the wooden slats were made by a hot poker because no one had a drill). The frames are placed on trestles and the quilting is done from one side to the other, rather than from the centre outwards.

Mrs Lorraine Bryant, the marker, uses chalk to trace around her templates, preferring the 'knob' chalk once used by miners on drums of coal. 'It is softer than the hard chalk you buy nowadays.' As far as design is concerned the group seem to have abandoned some of the Welsh wholecloth-making traditions in that they never consciously incorporate such familiar Welsh patterns as the snail or seed pod. The background infill which they call 'trellis' is made by chalking the string and then snapping it on to the fabric to create lines. They prefer working with washable satin but will also tackle cotton and polycotton nowadays, although they find the latter fabric 'hard' to work with. They always used coloured thread and if one happens to prick a finger and get blood on a quilt they follow a time-honoured prescription for removing it.

'What you do is spit on the spot and rub it in. Then you get a bit of white cotton thread and rub the spot. When this has soaked up the blood you get a clean piece and rub some more,' explained one. The 'magic', it seems, is in the spit – and it has to be spit from the person who pricked her finger in the first place.

This particular group working in Wales will eventually disappear since they have trouble recruiting new members. 'People don't want quilts any more – it's all duvets now,' said one.

Heal's Mansard Gallery

Yet another kind of professional endeavour involving handicrafts, including quilts and textiles, was that launched in 1917 by the London-based furnishing store Heal's, in Tottenham Court Road. The store's Mansard Gallery, on the fourth floor, had been opened for the purpose of enticing customers to the top floor, but its regular exhibitions of textiles, pottery and furniture made

Fig. 6.12. An example of a Mansard Gallery quilt made of military cloth. It is backed with striped brown and beige wool and bound with a mauve and white machine-made braid. 152 cm x 187 cm (5 ft 1 in x 6 ft 3 in).

it a popular venue for new ideas in art and design. The Gallery was run by Prudence Maufe from 1917 until the 1960s, closing during World War II when the store was completely taken over by hundreds of machinists who made parachutes and blackout material.

Mrs Maufe, described by Sir Hugh Casson as 'formidable, centreparting, full skirts and buckled shoes',[5] set up the textile department in the store and in 1939 became a director (her husband, Sir Edward Maufe, designed Guildford Cathedral). She proved very enterprising, especially after World War II when materials were scarce. She went around country houses and fabric manufacturers looking for old and interesting fabrics which could be recycled into quilts and wall hangings for the Gallery's selling exhibitions. Held once a year, these exhibitions were immensely successful and gave a great deal of work to talented needlewomen. The standard of work was very high. The quilt in figure 6.12, purchased at the Gallery in 1953, is made of military uniform material, men's suitings and tweeds, barathea and livery cloth, all accurately machine-pieced in geometric shapes.

Fig. 6.13. Made from offcuts of livery uniforms by a small tailoring firm in Berwickshire in 1898.
194 cm x 198 cm (6 ft 5 in x 6 ft 7 in).

Fig. 6.14. Fabric from several family wedding dresses went into this Isle of Man quilt made as a present in 1934. It contains 2,600 patchwork pieces.
204 cm x 222 cm (6 ft 10 in x 7 ft 5 in).

Fig. 6.15. Jane Purves before her marriage in 1898.

Family Life

When Jane Melrose Purves (see fig.6.15) wed Robert Harrower on 16 August 1898, the employees in her father's firm in Allanton, near Chirnside in Berwickshire, made the bride a quilt. It was an unusual wedding quilt in that it was made of offcuts of livery material used to make uniforms for the staff of the Blackadder Estate, belonging to the Houstoun Boswall family. Jane Purves's father was a tailor and the PURVES label was on the back of the quilt. The quilt, in red, black, green, gold and beige, is finished with a wool fringe and backed with beige cotton (see fig.6.13, p.147). It was worked in much the same manner as the military quilts described in Chapter 8. In 1924, Jane's husband, Robert, bought one of the ten farms that had been part of the Blackadder Estate and the quilt has now passed down in the family to their grandson.

A completely different kind of wedding quilt, also made as a present, was that stitched by Edith Young and Isabel Aspinall on the Isle of Man. Made in 1934, over a period of seven months, it was given to David Young and Dorothy Maud Kerr when they married. What made it unusual was that it contained fabric from different family dresses dating back to 1860. The elaborately pieced quilt (see fig.6.14, p.147) has a centre panel with blue and pink brocade from a fancy dress worn by Mrs John Budge Aspinall, great-grandmother of David Young, in 1860. The cream brocade pieces were from the court train worn by Mrs John Aspinall (David's maternal grandmother) in about 1880, while six white moire pieces came from Edith Aspinall's wedding dress of 1902. David's mother, Mrs Smelter J. Young, initialled pieces of white satin, sent from New Zealand, from a wedding dress belonging to Helen Maria Teilby, another relative married in 1907. Fabric from Dorothy Maud Kerr's bridal gown was also initialled and included in the quilt. The initials are embroidered in blue silk cross-stitch. The rest of the quilt, made in both cotton and brocade, includes several patterns such as elongated hexagons and Baby Blocks – there are 2,600 pieces in total and the diamond template used by the makers is still in use.

Another example of a quilt made as a family project is the red and white appliqué quilt made by Matilda Adelaide Hughes in 1880 (see fig.6.18, p.150). Matilda and her husband, Herbert, lived in Wednesbury in the West Midlands, where he was a coal-mine owner and also a member of the Masons. Husband and wife made the quilt as a pastime: Herbert cut out paper shapes - birds, fish, domestic animals, ships, keys, bellows, gardening tools and Masonic insignia – which Matilda in turn used for her patterns, applying each red cut out with buttonhole stitch. Herbert was Welsh and Matilda was English and both the Welsh Dragon and British Lion emblems on the quilt emphasize this.

Needlework skills were taught at an early age in the nineteenth century and often to boys and girls alike. In some cases, sewing patches was the accepted method of teaching either a running stitch or oversewing (as with papers). Entertainment was probably the motivating force, however, for the quilt started by seven-year-old Henry Fisher in 1855 (see fig.6.16). Perhaps he was convalescing from an illness when he started – sewing patches would after all have been an ideal way to pass the time – or perhaps the quilt was simply started as a hobby. Whatever the reason, with three sisters and a mother to egg him on and also to pick up where he left off, the quilt was eventually finished, though probably not by Henry. Made in a frame layout (of the type described in Chap.2) and with simple large squares and oblongs of furnishing linens and cottons, the quilt eventually ended up large enough for a king-size bed, measuring 240 cm x 252 cm (8 ft x 8 ft 5 in). It is obvious from the fabrics used that the quilt took some years to finish and it was not wadded. It was quilted in a diamond grid with linen thread. Henry died in 1916 at the age of sixty-eight. In his adult life he became an artist and his watercolours and other paintings are still in the family.

Fig. 6.16. Henry Fisher was only seven years old when he began to sew a quilt.

Hannah Selina Sealy, who grew up on a smallholding at Atworth, in Wiltshire, would also have learned needle skills at an early age – and because she was the only daughter. The hexagon quilt with single rosettes and central medallion that she made in 1890 (see fig.6.19, p.150) is filled with dress and shirt scraps. She made ample use of her skills too when she married a plasterer and tiler. Her competency as a needlewoman was certainly challenged with her family. The four children that she is pictured with in figure 6.17 (William Henry, Frederick Charles, Eva Dorothy and Phyllis Irene May) were completely outfitted by Hannah. Her skills ran to gents' suits and shirts and she also regularly outfitted her husband. Little wonder that her hexagon quilt is believed to have been a one-off, made prior to her marriage. When she died in 1914 her husband, Lewin, remarried and the quilt eventually passed to one of Hannah's daughters, who lived in Epsom. She used it as a blackout curtain during World War II.

Fig. 6.17. Lewin and Hannah Sealy with their children, William Henry, Frederick Charles, Eva Dorothy and Phyllis Irene May. Hannah made all the family's clothes.

The role of the church in family life in the nineteenth century also encompassed patchwork and quilting and, as indicated in Chapter 8, the needle skills of the women in the church's congregations were often used to raise funds. Then, as now, the women who quilted did so in whatever time was available.

Mary Jane Wood (1860-1940), the village midwife in Metal Bridge, Co. Durham, used to do her quilting if up in the middle of the night to deliver a baby. She used to rock the cradle of her own baby with one foot while quilting, her first child being something of a poor

Fig. 6.18. Herbert Hughes drew the pattern
for his wife, Matilda, when she made this
appliqué quilt in 1880. Turkey Red on white
cotton embroidered with initials and name of
maker.

Fig. 6.19. Hexagon rosette quilt made by
Hannah Sealy in about 1890.
215 cm x 260 cm (7 ft x 8 ft 6 in).

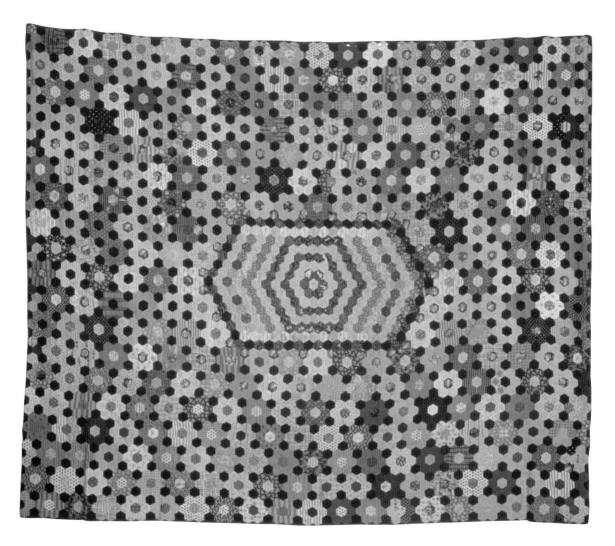

Fig. 6.20. A detail of Janet Reid's quilt made during her journey to Australia in 1890. One of the ship's sailors helped her with the nautical embroidery designs.

Fig. 6.21. Detail of a pillow from the quilted bed set made by Jeannie McClay during her voyages. She used back-stitch quilting, achieving an average of eighteen stitches to the inch.

Fig. 6.22. Mary Jane Wood (seated), the village midwife in Metal Bridge, with her daughter, Edith Mary, and granddaughter, Mary Jane.

sleeper, and she sewed to help raise funds to build a Methodist chapel in her village, An important and active member of the community, Mrs Wood was easily recognizable (see fig,6.22): if going somewhere special she wore a long black quilted petticoat and black quilted cape. When her own children were born, Mrs Wood covered their cradles with quilted covers and frills and she quilted her son's christening cape in blue and beige. When her daughter married, Mrs Wood gave her two quilts and these were subsequently passed down to her granddaughter. Mrs Wood's great-granddaughter still has the cardboard and tin templates that Mrs Wood used.

Quilters and Their Journeys

When sisters Agnes, Janet and Harriet Sloan Reid sailed aboard the Loch Sly for Australia in about 1890, they took with them their piano, sewing machine, cat and remnants of dress fabrics. The sisters, experienced dressmakers, were originally from Creetown, Wigtownshire, where their father worked as a blacksmith and also was the owner of a tanner's yard. After the death of their mother, the father remarried and the three girls left home for Glasgow to continue their dressmaking business.

The sisters had two brothers in Australia and when the unmarried brother needed a housekeeper they decided to set sail. During the three-month voyage, each sister made a crazy quilt in silk and velvets helped by one of the ship's sailors: he drew anchors, flags and a tiller on fabric for Janet to embroider (see fig.6.20, p.151). After many years of successful dressmaking in Melbourne, the three ladies returned to Glasgow aboard the same ship. The piano and sewing machine were still part of their luggage, but not the cat – it had been replaced by a talking parrot!

Agnes eventually died in Glasgow and the two remaining sisters returned to Creetown. Janet died in 1943 at the age of eighty-one but no family records about Harriet have survived.

Another seafaring quilter was Jeannie McClay, who married the master of a cargo steamer about 1900. The steamer, owned by the Burrell Line in Glasgow, travelled around the world, and Jeannie and her husband and eventually their small daughter, Nessie, visited many ports (see fig.6.23). To occupy herself on board, Jeannie quilted a bed set using a printed furnishing fabric of trailing flowers and branches with crested birds. She outlined the patterns in the fabric with back-stitch quilting in cream silk, achieving an average of eighteen stitches to the inch (2.5 cm). (See fig.6.21, p.151.)

Yet another eventful life was that of Jean McGregor Young, SRN, born in Lanarkshire in 1884. In 1923, Jean sailed to China, where she nursed for eighteen years in a mission hospital in the Provinces

Fig. 6.23. Jeannie McClay with her daughter, Nessie, and husband, Captain Archibald McClay.

of Acheng and Hailong. She and her nurses led an often precarious existence, having to travel long distances and sometimes through bandit-infested areas. She returned to England in 1941 to become matron of a Red Cross convalescent home and retired seven years later. The Dresden Plate quilt that she made dates from this period and shows the influence from another continent – North America. She spent the last ten years of her life in Stonehouse Hospital, where she died (see fig.6.24).

Fig. 6.24. After an active life as a missionary in China, Jean McGregor Young spent the last ten years of her life in a nursing home. She is shown here being visited by a newlywed couple. The present owner of the quilt is the youngest bridesmaid.

Fig. 7.1. Detail of Fig. 7.3 *opposite*.

Fig. 7.2. Detail of a table cover made in Russia by the wife of an English ribbon maker. *C.* 1880.
140 cm x 169 cm (4 ft 5 in x 5 ft 5 in).
(Photo: Tina Fenwick Smith)

CHAPTER 7

THE
OUTSIDERS
Pauline Adams & Margaret Tucker

QUILTS BOUGHT ON HOLIDAY, given as presents, or passed down through families, often travel far and wide with their owners. This fact was frequently in evidence during the course of the documentation programme. There were occasional examples from such places as Bermuda, Egypt and China and a few quilts from Europe – from France, Holland, Germany and Sweden. The Swedish quilt was of particular interest, although the purpose it was intended for was unclear: the present owner thought it had either religious or wedding connections. A silk wholecloth quilt, made in the last half of the nineteenth century, it had been embellished with embroidery of sprays of flowers, and quilted with biblical references (e.g. 'Psalms 30:6; Cor 5.19; John 13.34')

An elaborate table cover made in Germany also proved noteworthy, since it had been pieced by a young British woman who had gone there as a bride in the 1840s, possibly the wife of a diplomat. Created in the crazy style, a style made popular in both

Fig. 7.3. Austro-Prussian velvets from the second part of the nineteenth century together with unusual decorative embellishment were used in this German crazy quilt.
139 x 243 cm (4 ft 7 in x 8 ft).

America and Britain in the nineteenth century, it was made of velvets, ribbons and satin (scraps from clothing worn at a German court). The table cover contained one border of tumbling blocks and had been bound with ribbon. It was particularly interesting because of its surface decoration of ornamental braids and other embellishments (see figs.7.1 and 7.3). Of equal interest was a table cover made in Russia by the wife of an English ribbon maker who worked in that country between 1870 and 1880. He was either a dyer or manager in a mill staffed entirely by English workers, and his wife, maker of the cover, travelled between the two countries – returning home each time she was about to give birth (she had six children in all). The cover (see detail in fig.7.2) is made entirely of ribbons and some are very unusual. The ribbon with a raised chevron design is a case in point.

The largest number of recorded quilts made outside Britain came from North America – 126 from the United States and 89 from Canada (including the Canadian Red Cross quilts). Owners of American or Canadian quilts who brought them for documentation generally knew their origins. Many British quilters in recent years have purchased old American quilts for their own use or because they are collectors. American quilts from the 1930s were perhaps the most numerous – and, because of their patterns and colours, the most easily recognized. Not all of these, however, were recent purchases: some had been in British ownership since they were made.

A much earlier example of American appliqué was the Rose of Sharon quilt made by Sarah Ann Sobey, who emigrated to Memphis, Tennessee, in the middle of the last century. She became caught up in the American Civil War (1861-1865) and lost everything except the quilt (see fig. 7.4, p.158), which she brought with her when she returned to Liverpool. She subsequently married a farmer and lived the rest of her life in Lancashire.

Several quilts with Australian connections were also recorded, including a silk hexagon quilt made in the early 1950s by Amelia Lambert, widow of the Australian artist George Washington Lambert and mother of Constant Lambert, a well-known composer and conductor in Britain. George Lambert married Amelia Beatrice (Amy) Absell in 1900 in North Sydney and the couple sailed two days later for England. George Lambert had a distinguished career, being elected an associate of the Royal Academy in 1922; he was an official war artist during World War I and, in 1921, a retrospective of his work was held in Melbourne.

After her husband died in 1930, Amy Lambert went to live with their eldest son, Maurice, a sculptor and associate of the Royal Academy. They lived in Kensington in London and Amy subsequently developed friendly ties with her next-door neighbours. The hexagon quilt she made for the twelve-year-old daughter of the neighbours in 1950 is composed of scraps of silk, velvet, brocade and grosgrain; and the back, a linen tablecloth, carried a tape label hand-written with the name Lambert (see fig.7.5, p.159). Amy was particularly gifted at handiwork and sewed not only quilts and patchwork cushions but other items as well.

CANADIAN RED CROSS QUILTS

'Has it got a Canadian Red Cross label?' was a frequent query at documentation days when an obviously 1930s to 1940s quilt was being examined. The team was already aware that there were in Britain large numbers of these relief quilts dating from World War II, but did not know how many to expect. In fact, fifty-four quilts bore the Canadian Red Cross Society's label and other owners spoke of removing labels. Thus the provenance of other likely quilts lacking labels could not be established. These quilts and their interesting and sometimes harrowing background stories deserve a special section to themselves.

The Canadian Red Cross Society archives show that during the 1939-45 War, the Society sent large amounts of aid, including quilts, to the war zones, including Britain. Their National Women's War Work Committee chairman, Mrs C. McEachren, OBE, visited England in October and November 1944 and, in reporting on her visit in January 1945, said:

… while I was in England 25,000 quilts were assigned to Women's Voluntary Services and plans were made for large shipments to Greece and Jugoslavia.

And later:

Nothing has been more popular than the quilts we make and send Overseas. Here again there has been a considerable increase of use during the past three months, and large numbers have been distributed both in England and on the Continent.

This visit is recorded as coming after the Blitz of February 1944 and the Doodle-bug (V1) and V2 rocket raids which peaked in June and July of that year.

All the goods made and distributed by the CRCS were made to strict patterns – except the quilts. In a later report on the work of the Women's Committee for the years 1939-46, Mrs McEachren said: 'One outstanding exception where no samples were required should be noted, namely the patchwork quilts which were made by hundreds of Canadian women in their own homes. They went overseas by the thousand and proved a boon to the British people, especially when the air raids began. Many found their way to the liberated countries in Europe at the end of the war. Perhaps no single output of Canadian women is remembered with more gratitude than these quilts. Lady Reading, chairman of the Women's Voluntary Service in Great Britain, a post which she still holds [this was written prior to 1958] said in a message to the Canadian Red Cross Society that: "… no quilts anywhere in the world equal or rival yours." '[1]

The distribution of the quilts was put in the hands of the British Red Cross Society, the WVS (now WRVS), the Salvation Army, other such charities, and the ARP (later, Civil Defence). It is known that many were sent to hospitals and the armed forces.

Bundles for Britain

Another category of aid quilts similar to the CRCS quilts were those donated by the 'Bundles for Britain' organization. Four quilts came to documentation days that were stated to be from this source, one from 'Quilts for Comfort', plus a further three which were made for the Canadian Officers' Club in London. None of these seems to have been labelled. It was surprising to hear from quilt owners that it was possible for quilt groups or makers to designate recipients of both Canadian Red Cross Society and Bundles for Britain quilts. The labels on Canadian Red Cross quilts are machine-stitched to a back corner, and are almost always the same. They are woven in red on white, carry the words 'GIFT OF CANADIAN RED CROSS

Overleaf, p158: Fig. 7.4. After being caught up in the American Civil War, Sarah Ann Sobey returned to Liverpool with her Rose of Sharon quilt. *c.* 1850-60.
221 cm x 282 cm (7 ft 3 in x 9 ft 3 in).

Overleaf, p159: Fig. 7.5. A mosaic-floor style of hexagon quilt created by Amy Lambert in 1950. Amy, widow of Australian artist George Lambert, was a prolific sewer and recycler of old fabrics.
120 cm x 188 cm (3 ft 11 in x 6 ft 2 in).

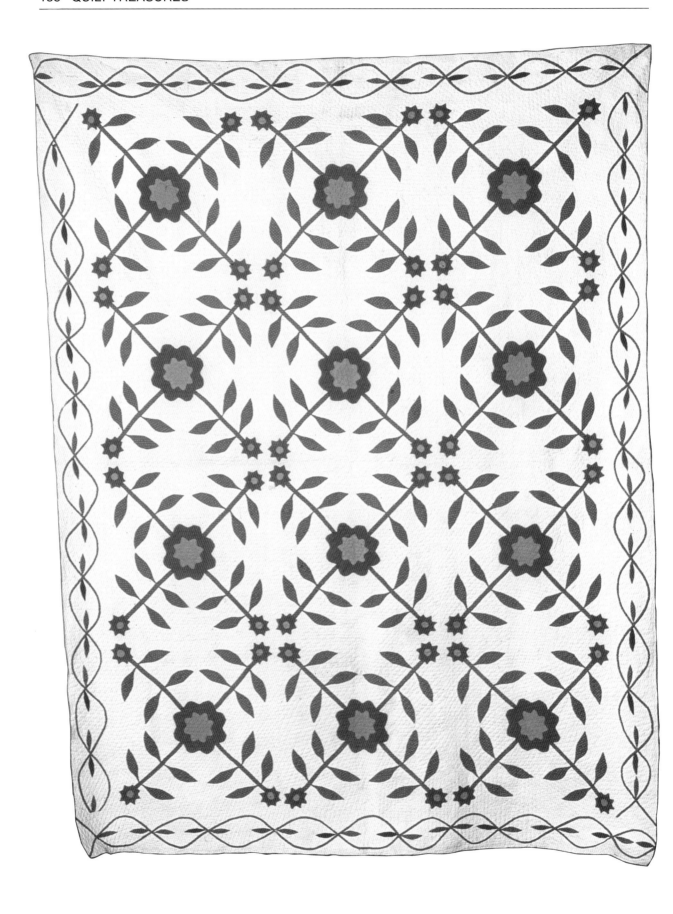

Fig. 7.6. Standard Canadian Red Cross Society label from the World War II relief quilts. Red, white and blue fabrics printed with V-for-Victory sign. See p. 162.

SOCIETY' and have a red cross in the centre of the label (see fig.7.6). Unusually, two quilts documented at Exeter, and belonging to the same person, had labels which included the town and province: one was made in New Glasgow, Nova Scotia, and the other in Edmonton District, Alberta.

Unfortunately, not much is known about the makers, although it is understood from a Guild member who was born in Canada that church sewing groups produced quilts.[2] This is borne out by the only makers' label found, which was stitched to the front of a quilt documented at Chester: CIRCLE 6, GREENWOOD CHURCH, WINNIPEG, MANITOBA, CANADA' (see fig.7.7). This was on one of two quilts given to the owner's mother-in-law, who was expecting to house two Dutch refugee children. They were never finally billeted with her, as her home was considered to be in an area vulnerable to air raids.

Fig. 7.7. Makers' label from Canadian Red Cross Society quilt.

The Quilts

One can envisage that attics were searched and linen cupboards raided to fill the first urgent wartime appeal by the Canadian Red Cross Society. This first flush would be of 1930s or even earlier quilts and tops. After that, donated unquilted tops would be quilted and then the many thousand quilts needed made as quickly and simply as possible.

Most of the quilts documented were in simple block patchwork, often of crazy patchwork, with or without sashing. Much use was made of the sewing machine, for piecing, joining blocks and quilting. Many quilts were tied, not quilted. One typical white-sashed crazy quilt (see fig.7.8, p.162) was given to a family who were bombed-out five times. This quilt was unusual in containing red, white and blue fabrics printed with the Victory V-sign and the morse code dot-dot-dot-dash for the letter V.

Another quilt had red centres in its machine-stitched crazy blocks and minimal quilting. A third (a Bundles for Britain quilt) seems to have been the product of two distinct scrap bags and may have been one of a series of quilts made 'by the yard', as part blocks showed at top and bottom. It was tied, with a striped winceyette backing. Much use seems to have been made throughout of striped pyjama fabrics, shirtings and printed dress cottons. Some quilts had flour sacking as a backing and/or flour-sack prints used in the patchwork. One quilt documented at Harlesden had been issued to the ARP for distribution, but was never needed, and after the War was given to a newlywed. It is typical block patchwork of the period (see fig.7.9, p.163), in the pattern Lady in the White House.

Where They Went

It was very clear, in talking to people who brought these quilts to be documented, that those who had received them as Blitz victims were greatly attached to their quilts (sometimes the bringers were the children of the original recipients) and still expressing immense gratitude to the Canadian Red Cross. One of the documentation team joined the First Aid Nursing Yeomanry (FANYS) in 1938 and in 1943 was issued with a dark blue, red and white Double Irish Chain quilt – probably a Bundles for Britain quilt rather than a CRCS donation. She had to relinquish it in 1944, when she entered officers' training, and has been hoping to find it ever since. Some double quilts were cut in half and issued to the Auxilary Territorial Service (ATS).[3]

At the Exeter documentation day, three quilts that were brought had been issued to families evacuated from the coastal areas in the pre-D-Day troop-training period – one was from Slapton Sands, Devon, and two were from the Kingsbridge area of Devon.

Fig. 7.8. Sashed blocks of machined crazy patchwork which include fabrics with V-for-Victory prints. The backing of this Canadian Red Cross quilt is red, white and blue fabric with cotton wadding. It is hand-quilted in parallel lines and the edges are finished with back turned to front. The label of this quilt is shown in fig.7.6.
164 cm x 200 cm (5 ft 4 in x 6 ft 6 in).

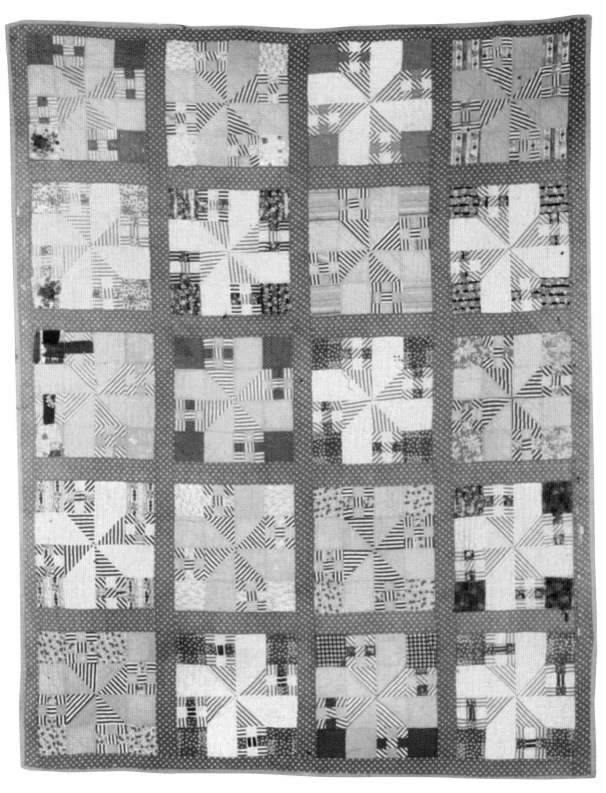

Fig. 7.9. Lady in the White House pattern in machine-sewn sashed block patchwork quilt made for Canadian Red Cross Society. Backed with cotton flannelette, filled with cotton wadding and quilted in parallel diagonal lines with edges lapped. Bears standard CRCS label with words 'Wheatley Branch' added. 176 cm x 195 cm (5 ft 9 in x 6 ft 5 in).

One owner reported that her husband's adoptive grandmother and grandfather were in a house demolished by a V2 rocket in 1944: 'Grandfather died, grandmother was entombed for four days but survived for another 30 years. The Canadian Red Cross supplied quilts as bedding for such unfortunate people. This quilt survived too.'

The stories are important, but the quilts themselves provide a superb historical record of utility North American quilts of the period up to 1945, both as patchwork pattern and as fabric archive. The labels should not be removed, as they are vital in verifying the source and date of the quilts.

Where are all the others?

If 25,000 quilts were distributed in Britain and Europe in a six-week period in the autumn of 1944, how many more were sent before and after that date? The documentation programme recorded only fifty-four quilts – what happened to all the others?

QUILTS OF NOTE

One of the more unusual block quilts recorded during the Project featured swastikas. Machine-made in Toronto, Ontario, in the first quarter of this century, its colours are faded red, ecru and green, and each pieced block is surrounded with sashing (see fig.7.10).

The swastika will, no doubt, for ever be associated with Nazi Germany. In fact, the word is Sanskrit in origin and the swastika is one of the oldest symbols in both India and China.[4] In the Indus culture of Mohenjo-Darso (2500-1500 BC) it was used mainly as a symbol of good luck.

The swastika can be angled either clockwise or anti-clockwise. The version that is angled clockwise (the one used by the Nazis, who turned it on point) was considered an emblem of immortality in ancient China. The same clockwise version represents the seal of the heart of Buddha and is often to be seen on the breast of statues of Buddha. In China the symbol was also a very old form of the character Fang, meaning the four regions of the world. From about AD 700, it has been used to mean the number ten thousand, symbolizing infinity. This meaning is implicit in the emblem's use as a decorative motif, but over the centuries artistic licence has often been taken with the original shapes, particularly in printed fabrics.

The maker of the Canadian quilt, who used what later became the accepted Nazi version of the swastika, quite possibly took the design from a book because of its visual impact or from a logo which had been adapted from native Indian culture and used by a girls' ice-hockey team in Alberta in 1916: she could not have foreseen its worldwide notoriety one or two decades later.

Fig. 7.10. Made in the early twentieth century when the design had different connotations. 190 cm x 178 cm (6 ft x 5 ft 10 in).

The American Kits

During the 1930s, when appliqué was particularly popular among American quiltmakers, it was possible to buy kits containing pre-cut fabric, tissue paper shapes to make templates, threads for embroidery and instructions. These kits also contained a stamped background fabric to show the quiltmaker where to place her appliqué pieces, leaving no opportunity for individual creativity. These, as well as appliqué patterns, could be purchased in craft shops or through newspapers and magazines throughout the United States, where they were advertised.[5]

Although experienced quiltmakers decried this trend as being unoriginal, the kits and patterns were very popular with beginners who did not want to design their own quilts or who simply were not capable of drawing the desired shapes (patterns for a pieced quilt were more easily originated because of their regular geometric shapes).

Many of these 1930s American appliqué quilts were brought to documentation days. Two identical ones, in the more unusual Dogwood pattern on a soft green ground, appeared at Chester documentation day within an hour of each other. Most of these 1930s quilts were easily recognizable from their colour and design – bright pastels on white, cream or yellow backgrounds and many cottons with small pastoral prints. So many Sunbonnet Sues and Sunbonnet Sams, Crinoline Ladies, Baskets of Flowers and Dresden Plates. Although the designs were the same, the quilting and finishing were often quite different. One at least had very poignant associations: it was a Sunbonnet Sue pattern made by a young Cheshire woman, Dorothy Clarke, who moved to Pasadena, California, where she had a career training horses in dressage for the film industry. She made the quilt from her old clothes and to remind her of life in England. Unfortunately she was killed in a riding accident while still in her twenties – her ashes, the quilt, and a trophy she had won in a competition, were the only items brought back to England by her father.

Another American pattern of the 1930s – one with political associations – was also recorded. Although the quilt had been purchased in London in about 1980 and made in Ontario in the late 1930s or early 1940s, it nevertheless carried the logo of the American Republican Party – the elephant. Both the elephant and the donkey (representing the Democratic Party) were used in wall hangings and bed covers. Their origins were the two political cartoons created by Thomas Nash (1840-1902), a well-known political cartoonist.[6] He first drew the figures for *Harper's Weekly* in 1877, after the disputed election of 1876 between Rutherford Hayes and Samuel Tilden in which the outcome was determined by an Electoral Commission appointed by Congress. The figures of the

Above: Fig.7.13. Detail of a wholecloth quilt with several different examples of resist-printed indigo on a white ground. Made in the nineteenth century and found in an abandoned house in France.
179 cm x 181 cm (5 ft 10 in x 5 ft 11 in).

Left: Fig. 7.12. The discovery of King Tutankhamun's tomb was a boon to the tourist trade and commemorative items made included these appliqué panels.
97 cm x 190 cm (3 ft 2 in x 6 ft 3 in).

Opposite: Fig.7.11. Believed to have been made before World War I, this cover of printed flags was painstakingly pieced by hand and the seams decorated with feather stitching.
178 cm x 261 cm (5 ft 10 in x 8 ft 6 in).

Fig.7.14. The elephant and donkey, symhols of the Republican and Democratic parties, were used as quilt designs. Although the pattern, was American in origin, this example was pieced in Ontario and quilted with overlapping rainbow shapes.
178 cm x 217 cm (5 ft 10 in x 7 ft 2 in).

elephant and donkey became so recognizable that they were adopted as logos for the two parties.

The quilt in fig.7.14 was pieced in melon, grey and white, and backed by white cotton. It was hand-quilted, all over, with overlapping rainbow shapes, the lines spaced 2.5 cm (1 in) apart. This was a favourite Ontario quilting pattern.

A cover purchased in an antique shop in Maine and taken to London a few years ago also roused considerable interest (see fig. 7.11, p.166). It is made of printed cotton flags –150 in total. The national flags include those of Austria, Hungary, Persia and Russia and Japan – the latter's, with the rising sun, was instantly recognizable. American state flags, mercantile flags and Britain's red ensign are also included.

The flags have been pieced very carefully, the quiltmaker having to juggle with the different sizes. The largest flag measures 19.5 cm x 28.5 cm (8 in x 11½ in), the smallest 14 cm x 20.5 cm (5½ in x 8in). The printed flags have been stitched together by hand and each seam is covered by feather stitching in a variety of different cotton threads. There is no wadding or quilting but the cover has been lined with beige cotton hemmed around the edges.

Nothing was known about the origins of this cover, but one would assume it was made by an ardent flag collector. The flags, called cigar flannels, were printed in America between 1890 and 1925 and were included in cigar packaging in much the same manner as the cigarette cards and silks. The names of some of the countries represented have changed now – for example, Persia is now Iran. The style of the designs and colouring suggests it could have been made just before World War I.

Indigo Blue

An interesting wholecloth quilt, found in an abandoned house in France a few years ago and subsequently taken to London, contains several pieces of fabric resist-printed indigo blue on a white ground. What makes it unusual is that, although the design of the fabric is the same, the printing has been undertaken by two different textile printers, the details being finer in some pieces than others.

There was, and still is, some controversy about the original 1750 indigo design and whether it was printed in France or England and exported to America, or whether it was printed in the three different countries.[7] The design used in the fabric of the quilt in fig.7.13, p.167 was used as an illustration in a book on America's indigo blues. The presence of this material in the quilt does show that the design was still being printed in the late nineteenth century.

The quilt is backed with a dark brown and white floral striped cotton. The wadding, a very thick cotton wool, is of a thickness that allows little quilting; however, some hand quilting has been executed in a diagonal pattern, the lines ten centimetres (4 in) apart. It has been well used and washed and is not in pristine condition.

Tutankhamun

Two appliqué panels from Egypt, relating to Tutankhamun, were documented in London. Made to commemorate the discovery and excavation of Tutankhamun's tomb in the Nile valley in 1922, the panels were specially created to sell to the many tourists who visited the country.

The background of these panels is a coarse cotton: the appliqué figures are a finer cotton but the cloth is not of good quality and the original bright pastel colours have faded. Each piece of appliqué is applied in the traditional way, with edges turned under and blind-stitched by hand with matching cotton. There is decorative embroidery on the stems and laid work of embroidery silk couched with cotton thread. The hangings have been finished with a crepe binding in deep mauve attached by machine but finished by hand.

The top of the panel, shown in fig.7.12 on page 167, is a frieze of lotus flowers from the lintel of a doorway. The next section depicts figures from temples and tombs, each holding an ankh, the symbol of life. The winged sun disc with the snakes is a symbol of protection. Beneath, the king is holding the flail (a sign of royalty) and making an offering to the god Amon-Re. Behind the king is the goddess Isis, mother of all things. She is wearing a headdress of cow horns, with the sun disc between, and holding a staff.

The presence of the god and goddess is based on the king's jubilee festival. Above them is the sacred eye of Horus and the cartouche, a carved or cast ornamental tablet in the form of a scroll enclosing hieroglyphics expressing royal and divine names. Either side are two columns with decorations of the papyrus plant, the sacred scarab, the serpent and some male figures. The last section has the Pyramids and the Sphinx, which were probably added to appeal to the tourists.

In Egyptian antiquity, the Sphinx, Pyramids and Obelisks were never shown with perspective and indeed some of the symbols and characters in the hanging are not quite authentic. The maker has taken considerable artistic licence and used personal interpretation of Egyptian mythology in order to make the panel more effective or possibly to make it easier to work.

Fig. 8.1. A detail from a soldier's quilt which shows the Prince of Wales feathers applied using punched shapes from small circles cut for the buttonholes on uniforms.
191 cm square (6 ft 3 in square).

Below: Figs. 8.2 and 8.3. Details of Crimean quilt on p. 175 and Bible quilt on p. 183.

CHAPTER 8

QUILTS
WITH
SPECIAL
ASSOCIATIONS
Janet Rae & Margaret Tucker

MILITARY QUILTS

MILITARY QUILTS and covers submitted for documentation were all made between 1850 (the Crimean War began in 1854) and 1910. This was a period in British history when patchwork and quilting was most prolific and when there was a fashion for the elaborate and colourful. Military quilts represent a unique chapter in the history of the craft: such was their popularity that The Great Exhibition of 1851, at Crystal Palace in London, included more than thirty examples submitted by military personnel.

Military quilts (often called Soldiers' quilts or Crimean quilts) cannot be verified by fabric alone. Authorities at the Royal Army Museum in London are cautious when attributing quilts to soldiers or regiments, holding that such attribution is not bona fide unless the quilts are made from genuine military fabrics as described by 'dress regulations' and sewn by military personnel. In addition to these two requirements, they insist on further evidence in the form of regimental letters, War Office records, photographs or the maker's name and rank before they will allow that a quilt is 'military'. Understandably, few of the present owners of these quilts could provide this level of provenance at the documentation days. 'It was handed down in the family', 'it was rescued from a bonfire' and 'it was known to be a Crimean quilt': often only these small pieces of information were offered as the means of identification.

A Yorkshire firm, Abimelech Hainsworth, has produced cloth for civilian and military needs since 1783, when the company was started. The firm has specialized in the highest-quality uniform cloth for home and overseas requirements, from Trafalgar (1805) to the present day. 'However, uniform fabrics are not only for battle and bloodshed but for pomp and pageantry too,' they say. 'We supply cloth for Livery uniform, for the Woolsack and benches in the Palace of Westminster, as well as for hunting and other outdoor wear. Qualities and colours are often interchangeable.[1] Given this wide use of the fabric, it is easy to understand why it is perilous to assume that quilts made of military-type fabric were invariably sewn by soldiers.

Made in India

Among those quilts documented that did possess a provenance, 50 per cent had been made in India between 1850 and 1900 by various military personnel.

Samuel Attwood, an Army tailor who served in India in the 1850s, was one such quiltmaker. The whereabouts of the quilt with which he appears in figure 8.5 on page 172 is, unfortunately, at present unknown. However, a second cover that he made, measuring 150 cm x 155 cm (5 ft x 5 ft 1 in), has been beautifully preserved and is owned by a member of his family. Unused and unfaded, it is a fine example of this soldier's skills.

Research has shown that not all India-based military personnel did their own sewing: a lot of tailoring work, in the British regiments, was handed out to Indian civilians who were attached to the Army. It seems quite possible that these civilians might have been delegated to do some of the sewing in the quilts. India had a profound effect on British soldiers of all ranks. The photograph in figure 8.4 on page 171 of Lt.-Col. Hall-Dempster of the 1st Battalion of the South Lancashire Regiment with his household staff serves to remind us of a particular lifestyle.

Brightness of colour is the key feature of those quilts or covers made in India. An example which typifies this is the table cover

Fig. 8.4. Lt.-Col. Hall-Dempster with his household staff. India. 1890s.

Fig. 8.5. Samuel Attwood wearing off-duty mufti with his quilt made in India in the 1850s to 1860s.

given to Lt.-Col. Hall-Dempster as a present from his orderly (see fig.8.6, p.174). He made it from dress uniforms worn by various regiments stationed there during his own service in India between 1895 and 1905.

The Crimean quilts, with their controlled colouring, are in contrast to those military quilts made in India. The small cover with the repeated variable eight-point star in figure 8.7 on page 174, reputed to have been made during the time of the Crimean War, is an example. The previous owner of the cover, who died in 1984 at the age of eighty-one, had used it as a horse blanket. Her son-in-law, turning out her possessions, was about to burn it, when the present owner remonstrated and saved the quilt.

Sewn While Convalescing

Other military quilts or covers were made by soldiers convalescing in hospital or serving a sentence in a military prison, as we are reminded by the famous painting of a soldier sewing a quilt in a hospital bed. The painting is owned by the Royal College of Surgeons of England and it shows Pte. Walker recovering from a fractured skull he suffered at the Battle of Inkerman, again in the Crimea.

Another quilt made while convalescing is that in figure 8.8 on page 175. It is a Mariner's Compass variation with geometric pattern borders. Every seam and shape is outlined with narrow braid. Made by a soldier in India, the quilt was presented for documentation with an envelope carrying relevant information: the quilt contained 7,000 pieces of fabric, 48,000 inches of braid and 168,000 stitches. Not only a soldier and quiltmaker but also a mathematician!

Cloths Most Used

Cloth used in military quilts was difficult and unusual for women quilters to work with because of its thickness, so it is unlikely that any of these quilts were made by women. Certainly, none was documented. The cloth was woollen but of different qualities and weaves, the pieces used being left over from uniform tailoring or uniform alterations. In some cases the cloth used came from the uniforms of soldiers who had died in battle.

The types of cloth most frequently used were: wool serge or woven worsted twill weave with a smooth face, which tended to shine with wear owing to the hard twist in the yarn and the compact weave structure; Melton, a plain base weave with a nap finish, closely sheared to give a smooth surface (this was first made in Melton Mowbray in Leicestershire); doeskin, originally made from real doeskin (but later from Botany wool), closely set in the warp to give a smooth finish so that the twill weave became almost invisible; and worsted plain woollen cloth, long staple wool dyed to the required colours, as were all the other cloths.[2] This last-named cloth, when dyed in bright colours, was used as facings on the jackets, usually on the sleeves and collar, or sometimes on the trousers as a stripe to identify a particular regiment. Colour in itself, however, did not help a great deal with identification, since several different regiments might use the same facing colour, relying for identification on many other regimental exclusivities – for instance, different braid, different buttonhole positions, badges and collar embellishments.

In his book, *Uniforms of the British Army, The Infantry Regiments*, W. Y. Carman tells us that facing colours were standardized in 1850, and again in 1881 when many of the regiments were amalgamated. The following colours were used: blue was reserved for Royal regiments; black for the rifle brigades; and, for other regiments, dark green, bright Lincoln green and grass green, sky blue, dark blue, purple, scarlet, pale yellow, yellow, white and buff. Various shades of grey to blue-grey, navy and black were used for jackets, trousers and overcoats. As a rough guide for facing colours, white was used for the English and Welsh regiments, yellow for the Scottish and green for the Irish regiments. Some of the brighter shades of turquoise, vermilion, salmon and orange were largely Indian colours. This entire range of colours was found in the military quilts examined during the documentation sessions. The qualities of fabric in these quilts differed also. Officers had to pay tailors for their own uniforms, so the quality of cloth rather depended on how much the individual officer could afford – obviously a colonel could pay more than a junior officer. Uniforms worn by other ranks were standardized.[3]

Fig. 8.6. Table cover made by Lt.-Col. Hall-Dempster's orderly 1890-1905. 188 cm square (6 ft 3 in square).

Fig. 8.7. Military fabrics from Yorkshire regiments. The quilt is embroidered with the White Rose of York. 1850s-1860s. 112 cm square (3 ft 8 in square).

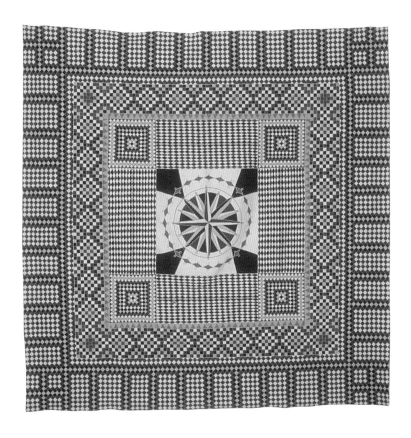

Fig. 8.8. Mariner's Compass variation. India, late nineteenth century. 235 cm x 240 cm (7 ft 8 in x 8 ft).

Fig. 8.9. Meticulous piecing in a subtle hexagon centre (*C.* 1850-1900). 188 cm x 205 cm (6 ft 3 in x 6 ft 8 in).

Pieced With Precision

The recognizable feature in all the quilts examined was the design arrangement and the accuracy of the piecing – one might almost say, the 'military precision' of it. The shapes were confined to squares, triangles, elongated triangles, oblongs, diamonds and rhomboids and sometimes arc-shaped leaves. There was little embroidery, apart from that used to enhance the crowns on Prince of Wales feathers and various symbols such as stars, thistles and the leaf shapes worked in silk and cotton thread in chain, herringbone or straight stitches.

The embellishment used most often consisted of small cloth circles appliquéd singly in clusters to form a stylized flower head, or solidly to form shapes, as in the Prince of Wales feathers in figure 8.1 on page 170. They were attached by a single stitch in linen or cotton thread through the centre of each circle. Where used they were identical, either 2 or 4 millimetres in diameter. They came from buttonhole punching. Originally the fabric would be placed on a slab of slate. A hollow sharp-edged metal tube would be placed in the required position. This would be knocked by a hammer to cut out the circle of cloth. 'When the metal tube was full of the circles, they would be hooked out and discarded. Later, a more efficient cloth and leather puncher, similar to the ones used today, was developed. It had five or six different-sized hollow spindles on a wheel that could be rotated for the size required. It punched out the circles of cloth with a pincer-like movement.[4] Thoughtful tailors made use of these discarded circles as embellishments for their personal sewing.

Another immaculately pieced quilt was documented at Chester. Again, it is from the Crimean period and made in military-type fabric. There is no provenance except that it has been in the family for three generations and has always been known as the 'Crimean quilt'. A large six-pointed star of green and red diamonds forms the centre medallion. The spaces between the points are filled by six small stars and black triangles to complete a hexagon shape. The sides of the hexagon are filled in to form a square by the use of rhomboids, diamonds and Tumbling Blocks and triangles. A further five borders consist of triangles, diamonds and oblongs, in different arrangements and colours. The final border is pieced in rhomboids in red and black (see fig. 8.9, p.175).

Piecing of these quilts was all by hand and generally done by a simple running stitch: however, one quilt documented was pieced by flat oversewing. Every seam in this particular quilt was then decorated on the upper side with a herringbone stitch in white silk. None of the quilts had any wadding or quilting and the edges were plain, bound with braid or fringe added at a later date.

A superbly made cover illustrating the herringbone decoration was made by Joseph Rawdon for a Mr Bootland of Bradford (see fig.8.11, p.178). A letter dated 2 April 1872 states that it took Joseph 'all of six years on and off to make the quilt from different uniforms, more than a few pieces from poor fellows that fought hard for their country and fell in the struggle'. It was also made in India. The census figures of 1871 confirm that the families of both men lived in York and Bradford, as per the addresses in the letter. Joseph talks of buying English silk thread (superior quality) in India to sew the quilt. All that is certain is that he finished the quilt and was back in England in 1872.

Other quilts merit description. Sgt. Instructor Porter of the Staffordshire Regiment showed his ability for meticulous piecing when he made a quilt between 1890 and 1896. Sgt. Porter left the Army in 1896 and was presented with a watch and a china teapot, with his name inscribed in gold leaf. His quilt, 225 cm x 230 cm (7 ft 5 in x 7 ft 7 in), is made entirely of squares and triangles in red, white and navy. He has made a most interesting quilt with the use of only three colours and two shapes: the layout is a large diamond, forming the central medallion, and six borders.

The last quilt, made of military-style fabric with no provenance, was something of a red herring. However, it was so unusual and dramatic that it called for documenting. Undoubtedly from the Edwardian period, it had the names 'A.E.' 'Edward' and 'Alexandra' embroidered around each of the Prince of Wales feathers. The stars, borders around the feathers and Maltese crosses consisted of hundreds of punched circles solidly sewn together, with a coloured or crystal bead in the centre of each. The rest of the heavily beaded cover had a multitude of cut-out shapes appliquéd to the foundation fabric, with tiny glass beads on top. In addition, each triangle in the border was outlined with stringed crystal beads, while the four outside crowns consisted of the stringed beads sewn solidly together on to the foundation fabric. Bead work was an extremely popular craft in the Edwardian era and this cover appears to have been made by someone with expert beading skills.

QUILTS BEARING NAMES AND OTHER WRITING

Friendship/signature, autograph and bazaar quilts – all quilts bearing names or initials of people – were a familiar sight on documentation days. The difficulty lay in trying to label such items if the provenance was unknown, especially if other motives for making the quilt (e.g. wedding gift or commemoration) were also introduced.

The Turkey Red and white quilt made for a Shropshire school-teacher in 1900, for example, was both a symbol of friendship

Left: Fig. 8.10. A wedding gift for Lady Rosalind Howard, Countess of Carlisle, in 1890.

Opposite: Fig. 8.11. Six years in the making. India. 1866-1872.
160 cm x 222 cm (5 ft 3 in x 7 ft 5 in).

Fig. 8.12. Detail of West Kent Women's Institute commemorative hanging.
229 cm x 262 cm (7 ft 6 in x 8 ft 7 in).

and a gift. The alternate red and white squares were each embroidered with the names of the pupils who had made the quilt – itself a parting wedding gift.

The quilt made for Lady Rosalind Howard, Countess of Carlisle, by a church group also served the dual purpose. Again made in Turkey Red and white, this quilt's square-on-point centre carries the inscription: 'To the Countess of Carlisle from the Primitive Methodists of Brampton and District 1890'. The quilt's white centre square is surrounded by white triangles with blue embroidered flowers and red triangles with the embroidered names of W. Saul, E. Dalton, J. Foster and J. S. Nightingale. It has a scalloped edge embroidered with blue floral detail and is bound with blue silk ribbon. Unusually for this type of quilt, it is quilted – with random zigzag to fit in with the embroidered centre and with other patterns, including clamshell, diamonds, parallel lines and a Welsh leaf (see fig.8.10, p.179).

This particular quilt, inherited by Lady Cecilia Roberts (née Howard), was given back to the Brampton Church in 1989, in time for its centenary, and is now displayed there.

A different type of friendship or commemoration hanging was that presented to Frances J. Heron Maxwell, chairman of the West Kent Federation of Women's Institutes 1918-22. Each panel, representing one Institute within the Federation, is cross-stitched on neutral coloured linen with various insignia, mottoes etc. (see detail in fig.8.12, p.179). The panels were then stitched together with herringbone embroidery. The completed item bears a tribute:

Queen Bee of West Kent Women's busy hive!
Who bore the heat and burden of the day
For four long years, and underneath whose sway
These eighty Institutes were born and thrive
Accept this token at our hand who strive –
Inadequate and humble though the way.
In this a tribute on your feet to lay
You, who, unsparing self, did ever give
Us of your best, would now a measure take,
Of well-earned ease, we would be with you still
As you with us, so does the needle move
With three fold zeal this coverlet to make,
To tell, if so its purpose it fulfil
Our grateful Homage, Loyalty and Love.

Turkey Red Feature

The Women's Institute quilt is not typical of the British commemorative, friendship or, indeed, other quilts with names and writing. The distinguishing factors were usually the use of Turkey

Red and white cotton and the absence of quilting. Several American quilts embroidered with names also surfaced during the Project but they were quite different in character: two were the Dresden Plate pattern, using different-patterned cotton scraps, and another was made of crazy patchwork blocks incorporating cotton, silk, velvet and ribbons. The two Dresden Plate quilts were made in the early 1930s but only one had a definite provenance: it was stitched by the women of the Methodist Church in Genoa, Nebraska, as a present for Sara Battles, a Sunday-school teacher who was about to marry.

Quiltmaking and fund-raising have been companionable activities for well over a hundred years. But the nature of the quilts being made for this purpose has changed: nowadays, individual makers or groups will piece or make a wholecloth quilt in either traditional or original patterns for raffle. The idea that you work with only two colours and collect money from sponsors in return for embroidering their name on a patch seems to have died out. Quilts made in this fashion are generally labelled Bazaar quilts although, as expected, the purposes of the fund-raising varied.

Some of the funds raised to build Easton Wesleyan Church, for example, came from a bazaar held in 1897. The square-on-point centre, with the embroidered picture of a church, carries the legend 'Easton Wesleyan Day School Bazaar April 21st 1897' (see detail in fig.8.13, p.182). There are numerous names, initials and some embroidered motifs on the quilt, which again is executed in Turkey Red and white. No one knows who benefited from the quilt made in 1905 at the Ebenezer Baptist Bazaar in Haslingden, Lancashire, but it is known that people were charged two pence to have their names put on the red and white squares.

Autograph quilts – where signatures were exactly replicated – were less in evidence during the Project. Such quilts, of course, could have been used as gifts and gestures of friendship, as some kind of commemoration or in order to raise funds. A red and white quilt of squares made in 1896 in Llanddulas has 500 autographs but little is known about its purpose. However, a red and white quilt made in Ireland (where these types of quilts were particularly popular) is believed to have both fund-raising origins and political relevance. Its centre panel carries the legend 'Taylorstown North National School Autograph Quilt 1901' and the names included are those of Winston Churchill; the Rt. Hon. William Ellison Macartney, who was an MP for South Antrim and later a Governor of Tasmania; and the Revd John Gray Porter, Macartney's son-in-law. This particular quilt also has stylized flower embroidery – and one of the blocks has four hands on it, probably a graphic reference to the 'red hand of Ulster', a symbol of the history of Protestant Ulster, originating in Irish folklore.

Fig. 8.13. A fund-raising quilt associated with Easton Wesleyan Church. 1897.
199 cm x 260 cm (6 ft 6 in x 8 ft 6 in).

Opposite: Fig. 8.14. Colourful example of rare Bible quilt made from printed fabric texts.
127 cm x 202 cm (4 ft 3 in x 6 ft 8 in).

Insert opposite: Fig. 8.15. Detail of printed texts from fig.8.14.

Fig. 8.15. Made by members of Rehoboth Welsh Methodist Chapel as a World War I fund-raiser.
153 cm x 216 cm (5 ft x 7 ft).

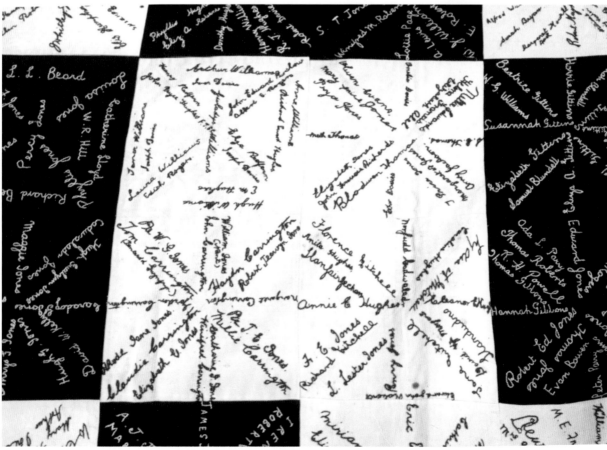

Two of the more interesting quilts with signatures that surfaced during the documentation sessions were made as fund-raisers for the 1914-18 war effort. One at least departs from the tradition of red and white in that the makers chose the more pacific colour of blue. Alternate blue and white squares are, however, embroidered in red, the signatures radiating outwards from the centre of each block. Made by chapel members of the Rehoboth Welsh Methodist Chapel in 1914, this quilt has grouped family names, indicating that blocks or sections of the quilt were sold in units. It is backed with a red Paisley cotton print (see detail in fig.8.15, p.182).

Another World War I fund-raiser, brought to Paisley documentation day, carries names of national import: including those of King George, Queen Mary, Asquith, Kitchener, Connaught, Joffre and Jellicoe. There are 49 blocks, each with between 14 and 16 signatures – a total of 685 signatures in all. The blocks themselves are an unusual pattern in that they all have a semicircle at each corner, but nothing is known about the makers (see Chap.4 fig.4.15 on p.60).

Bible Quilts

The use of Turkey Red and white with contrasting embroidery is a British tradition that also extended to Bible quilts – quilts with Scripture, hymns or familiar biblical phrases instead of names. The reason for making such quilts and how they were used remains something of a mystery. Were they, for example, intended for chapel wall hangings (reminding the faithful of their Christian duty)? Were they used on hospital beds as a means of comforting the sick? It must be remembered that these were pious people, living in a less secular age, for whom the use of such Christian texts was an integral part of their lives and an entirely natural form of decoration.

There is some evidence that, at least among one religious group in the Scottish Highlands, they were used to cover the coffin during a funeral service, such quilts having been made by the ladies of the parish especially for this purpose. Called 'mort' cloths, these coverlets were sometimes embroidered with passages suitable to the occasion, i.e. 'My presence shall go with thee and I will give thee rest.'

Most of the red and white Bible quilts date from the second half of the nineteenth century and this was certainly true of those brought to documentation days. One had Wesleyan connections, having come from a family who lived at Morecambe, the father working as a lighthouse keeper in the mid-1880s. The white centre of this quilt, an irregular-shaped piece almost like a puzzle piece, had the words 'Faith', 'Hope' and 'Charity' in three outside corners while the centre of the panel was inscribed:

Jesu lover of my soul
Let me to thy bosom fly
While the nearer waters roll
While the tempest still is nigh
Hide me O my Saviour hide
Till the storm of life is past
Safe into the haven glide
O receive my soul at last.

The quilt had been made in red and white squares, the total measuring 202 x 221 cm (6 ft 7 in x 7 ft 4 in), and it had been left unquilted.

One Bible quilt that did include quite elaborate quilting, however, was brought to the documentation day at Bowes Museum in Barnard Castle. It, too, had been designed with a central white panel, for inscription, and alternate red and white squares. The hand quilting, however, was in strips and featured four bellows infilled with small squares. The patched squares included some of the Ten Commandments, lines from the Lord's Prayer and exhortations such as 'The just shall live by faith'; 'The Lord is mighty to save'; 'Flee from the wrath to come'; and 'Continue in prayer'.

Another very distinctive style of Bible quilt, also from the same period, is the type sewn of cotton blocks printed with biblical texts, proverbs and pictures, some of which are numbered and carry the artist's name or initial (see figs.8.14 and 8.15 on p.183). They are rare, but two were documented in the course of the Project. One of them gives a clue to the origin of these fabric texts –which are printed on a variety of colours, including gold, pink, white and grey. This quilt carries a printed label with the words 'Francis Whitehead, Crayford, KENT' and the additional information: 'Executor & Sole Manager for 'the Invalid Widow'. Designed by R. Mimpriss. Set of patterns from 3d upwards.' Such texts were obviously sold by Mr Whitehead for various uses.

The Bible quilt with this label has been finished with a machine made tassel fringe and is unquilted. Its provenance is unknown. The other quilt made of texts, however, had come from a farmer's family with chapel connections who lived in Cheshire.

Fig. 9.1. (1815-35) Roller-printed dress fabrics, except at the top block-printed chinoiserie border for furnishing. Light-blue grounds typical of I820s, produced by printed resist under indigo. Twisting floral stripes often printed on the diagonal. Complex geometric design in lapis technique on right.
Below: see p. 206.

Fig. 9.2. (1815-35) Furnishing chinoiserie design on blotched tea ground. A good example of stippled roller printing giving three-dirnensional form in red monochrome. Other colours printed by block or possibly surface roller.
(Photo: Tina Fenwick Smith)

CHAPTER 9

READING
A QUILT

Deryn O'Connor & Tina Fenwick Smith

'I DO HOPE that you will be able to give me a date for it.' This was invariably the opening gambit as a quilt was spread out for examination during the documentation sessions.

Of the 4,183 items documented, 1,880 were pieced quilts or bed covers. It is these pieced items that are discussed in this chapter. Of the pieced quilts, less than 2 per cent were of wool, less than 2 per cent of silk, 3 per cent of linen and 5 per cent of velvet; 85 per cent were made of cotton. Man-made fibres accounted for about 3 per cent, and many of the quilts included quite a mixture of the latter. The great majority of fabrics were for dress and a minority for furnishings.

Owing to the volume presented at any venue, it was possible to spend, on average, only 15 minutes on each item. For absolute accuracy in identifying the fibres and the dyes that were used, chemical tests would have had to be made. This was not feasible without removing small samples, so visual analysis was relied on.

However, one member of the team had made extensive research into the techniques of printing and the dyes used pre-1850 and, together with historical context, judgements were made through experience gained over the years of studying cloth made since 1750.

The pieced cotton quilts were made almost entirely of printed cotton and thus they reflect the place of printed textiles in British society.

Quilts made up to about 1835 were sewn when printed cotton was a prestige material. In the late eighteenth century cotton even took precedence over silk for dress and furnishing fabrics. But the documentation days revealed very few of the most expensive prints: there were only eight examples of the painted cloths from India and only eight of the plate-printed furnishings.

Quilts made up to 1835 contained a large number of cloths of different designs – as if there were a practice of swapping to increase the variety. One quilt (see fig.9.22, p.207) dated 1834 contains 252 different fabric designs, of which three have three or four colourways each. In the late 1820s and 1830s there began to be more colourways of the same designs. Earlier, the same colours and printing styles tended to be carried out in different designs, showing probably that particular printworks specialized in certain techniques.

Quilts made after 1835 reflected the changing place of printed cotton. Cotton dress fabrics moved down the social scale as they became more abundant and cheaper. By then roller printing was well established, enabling very long runs of one design to be printed. Designs of dress fabrics became increasingly repetitive and were often versions of earlier designs printed in different scales and colours. Nevertheless, dress fabrics remained the main source of fabrics for pieced quilts. The numbers of colours in any one print became fewer, but included some striking combinations in the 1840s and 1850s based on Prussian blue. In the second half of the century, Turkey Red discharges were important, together with the classic purples in one or two tones. Cotton fabrics produced from 1850 and well into the twentieth century are difficult to date because so many roller-printed designs were produced again and again, year after year. There are some landmarks such as Art Nouveau designs in the late nineteenth century, but the main change in fabrics in quilts studied by the Project was found to be in the 1920s to 1950s, when styles, colours, designs and structures of cloth had different flavours. It is interesting that the Project failed to discover any quilts containing William Morris fabrics.

From the late nineteenth century to the mid-twentieth century, quilts included fabrics with less variety of design but more colourways and there were many pieced tops made partly or wholly

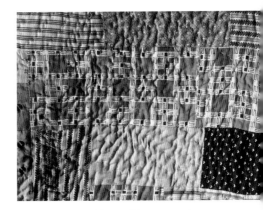

Fig. 9.3. (1920-60) 'Leaves' from a sample book of cotton dress fabrics showing colourways. Traditional styles, e.g. black (bottom right) and red (top centre) contrasted with a fresh geometric design echoing the graphic designs of the Thirties.

Fig. 9.4. (1920-60) Roller-printed, indigo discharge cotton for the African market, from a sample book.

from manufacturers' samples. They can be recognized by their similar size and shape and the many colourways of the same design. However, it is interesting that only a few quilts surveyed included fabrics made for export, or at least not those which were designed for specific markets abroad such as Africa or India. But two good examples are shown in figures 9.4 on page 187 and 9.34 on page 211. This is surprising as, until recently, end of rolls (fents) of such fabrics could be found in the markets of northern English towns.

As the status of printed cotton fabrics declined, wool and silk became more important in quiltmaking. Some wools and silks were printed for dressmaking from the 1830s, and especially in the 1840s and 1850s, but few appeared in quilts studied. The great change was the predominance of silk of many different weaves, sometimes accompanied by velvet, in the last quarter of the nineteenth century. The colour range reflected the dress of the period, with its emphasis on black and the extended range of colours now available from synthetic dyes. The silks were hardly ever printed, except for those in which the warps were printed before weaving (chiné), giving an easily recognizable effect created by the design shifting in one direction (see fig.7.2, p.154). Many quilts were made from ribbons. When a quilt was backed this was difficult to ascertain, but during the documentation sessions the team learned to recognize many more ribbons than were expected at first (see fig.9.6 on p.191, and figs. 9.36 and 9.37 on p.214).

Increasingly in the late nineteenth and twentieth century, quilts were pieced from everyday fabrics such as shirtings, tweeds and suitings (see figs.9.39 and 9.40 on p.215). These humbler fabrics, together with the cheap roller-printed cottons, probably survive only in quilts, since costume collections usually contain the 'best' garments of their day. Thus quilts are a wonderful repository of textiles that give us a unique glimpse into the society of their time.

Red Herrings and Pitfalls

What must be borne in mind throughout an examination is that 'a quilt, as a complete finished article, can only be as old as the youngest fabric it contains'.

Very, very few of the quilts were dated or signed. Even when dates and names were present they could not always be taken as evidence of the age of the piece: further questions had to be answered. It is not unknown for a piece of embroidery, signed and dated, to be the centre of a quilt. One example was signed in blue cross-stitch by 'Margaret Pickering, aged 14 years 1818'. However, the surrounding fabrics were about eighteen years younger than this date and it was not unknown for the difference to be considerably more. With this age gap, perhaps Margaret Pickering was not the eventual maker of the quilt: it might have been her daughter or, in the instance of a greater age gap, a granddaughter putting to good use an example of her ancestor's needlework skills. In this instance it could be said that the embroidery was the starting date for the quilt, not the finishing date, as tends to be the interpretation.

Other evidence which can be misleading is that handed down as family folklore. For example, it was not uncommon to be told by an elderly lady, 'The quilt was made by my grandmother who was ninety when she died thirty years ago, so the quilt must be about 120 years old, mustn't it?' Such a situation needed handling with diplomacy. On the table was a quilt clearly displaying fabrics of the 1920s, and somehow those fifty years had to be accounted for. By asking if the present owner might have been the first grandchild, a line of inquiry was opened up. If the answer was in the affirmative it could be pointed out that the grandmother might have made the quilt when she was about fifty years old because what better reason could there be than to celebrate the arrival of her first grandchild? Getting the owner to think about her family usually overcame the initial disappointment of owning a quilt of less antiquity than at first thought.

A further example of an older quilt centre surrounded by younger fabrics is the printed commemorative medallion. These were produced for a short time early in the nineteenth century, and an example from George III's Golden Jubilee of 1810 came to light in Penrith. In this case the fabrics were consistent with the medallion. Two medallions were printed to commemorate the victories of the Duke of Wellington. They were identical except for the name of the battle concerned. One was for his victory in 1813 over the French at Vittoria in Spain and the second was for his famous victory of 1815 at Waterloo (see fig.9.22, p.207). An example of this one was examined at Halifax, but in this instance the surrounding fabrics were younger and the date 1834 appears in the quilting.

Another known medallion had round it an inscription: 'PRINCESS CHARLOTTE OF WALES MARRIED LEOPOLD PRINCE OF SAXE COBURG MAY 2 1816'.

Incorporated in these commemorative medallions are invariably the rose of England, the thistle of Scotland and the shamrock of Ireland, but never any representations for Wales. This has been noted in other decorative schemes and the explanation given is that Wales as a principality is not represented in the Union Flag. There are other images which were printed as medallions, the most popular being a vase or basket of flowers, usually contained in a printed border of either a stylized 'beading', a wreath of leaves or flowers, or acorns and oak leaves. Borderless images such as 'Palm Trees and Pheasants' and 'Rustic Ruins set in a Leafy Arbor' were

Fig. 9.5. (1780-1815) Block-printed furnishings, full chintz.

also discovered. There was one particularly beautiful example that was documented at Penrith: a pair of black swans swimming before a waterfall with a bridge spanning the river, all beset with lush flowers and trees. Black swans are native to Australia, but perhaps Captain Cook brought back news of them from one of his three voyages made between 1768 and 1780. Surrounding this scene is a chinoiserie border, itself contained in two very narrow borders. The remarkable feature of this medallion is that the central picture and the border are all printed on the same fabric, necessitating the border to be printed with mitred corners (see fig.9.5). All these medallions would have been printed on fabric by the yard and, although appropriate for the centres of quilts, they would have been used for chair seats, fire screens or cushions, etc.

There are other pitfalls that make dating difficult. Some patchwork may have been started, many patches having been prepared and a quantity of them assembled as the beginning of a quilt. Then perhaps they all get put away for years. Someone finds them and decides to finish the work, supplementing what there is with current fabrics. A young girl starting a quilt might plunder her mother's or grandmother's scrap bag to augment her own, so once again we are looking at a wide spectrum of fabrics. We know for a fact that Averil Colby's scrap bag (see Chap.1) spanned 150 years.

Another example is a patchwork cushion or table cover which has been enlarged into a full-size quilt at a later date. On these occasions it was often found that there was a marked change of scale in the patches used. In keeping with the size of the original piece the patches would be quite small, but once it had been decided to enlarge the piece the patches used were much larger (see fig.9.32, p.211). A further example which provides many generations of fabric is a quilt that has been skilfully repaired, replacing damaged or rotted patches. This is the only exception to the rule that a quilt is as old as the youngest fabric contained therein, although there are purists who argue that this form of conservation is wrong, that repairs should be obvious and easily removable.

FIBRES, WEAVES AND FINISHES

Examination of a quilt should begin by looking at the constitution and structure of the fabrics presented. It is crucial that the basic fibres are identified, as dyes will vary in colour on different fibres. Fibres fall into two families: one is cellulosic or vegetable (cotton and linen) and the other protein (silk and wool). There is a third group, the man-mades, e.g. nylon and polyester. This last group was not of great significance in the Project's documentation. Nylon was not encouraged for use in patchwork up to our cut-off date (1960) because of its disparity in weight and 'handle' with other fabrics. At that time polyester appeared in combination with cotton and, as sheeting, was used as backing cloths for the most modern pieces of work. However, a poly-cotton sheet used as a backing on an older pieced top does reveal if it has been repaired/restored or rescued in the ten years prior to 1960.

The characteristics of each of the fibres as yarn and cloth may be helpful for analysis.

Cotton is of a short staple and gives a smooth, and unless mercerized, non-lustrous yarn that is strong but not elastic. As a cloth it has a soft handle. Linen has a very long staple producing a smooth lustrous yarn that is very strong but, again, non-elastic. The handle of linen is smooth, cool, at times almost crunchy, and creases very easily. Silk is a very fine continuous filament resulting in a very smooth and lustrous yarn that is strong and elastic. It has a soft but smooth handle.

Wool has the merit of giving us two yarns. One is woollen, which is spun from short staple fleece and results in a rough thread without lustre but is hard wearing, elastic and springy. Woollen cloth can be raised or napped when all signs of the weave are obliterated and then it can be felted too, as for baize. The other is worsted. This is spun from long staple fleece and produces a firm and smooth yarn with a certain amount of lustre. It is very hard wearing with an elasticity and springiness. This smooth but enduring cloth is most commonly used for men's suiting. Quilts were recorded made entirely from tailors' sample books of worsted suiting.

It should be pointed out that cotton yarn was used in conjunction with other yarns in the same cloth. In the nineteenth century these were known as 'unions' and therefore linen union, silk union or wool union may be encountered.

Several structures of material were recorded, but by far the most commonly seen was plain weave for both dress and furnishing use. Others serving the dual roles of dress and furnishing were brocades, damasks, ribbons, velvets and dimities. A fine white cotton with a textured weave, dimity had been used to give a ground to units of patchwork, e.g. Grandmother's Flower Garden, or, as in figure 9.21 on page 206, to isolate diamonds. This was a technique employed by Averil Colby, who liked to arrange her patchworks rather like a flower garden. By using these textured whites for her ground hexagons, she gave her quilts a richness and liveliness that would otherwise have been lacking.

Produced as furnishing fabrics exclusively were the cretonnes and sateens. Flannel and winceyette, loosely regarded as dress fabrics, were found in small quantities, as were piqué, taffeta and twill. Satin, too, thought of as a dress fabric, was encountered: one of two quilts was made entirely of corset satin in varying shades of

Fig. 9.6. (1880-1920) The great period of quilts made from silk ribbons, here used to advantage, together with black velvet. (Compare the grey checked ribbon with the purple roller-print in fig.164).

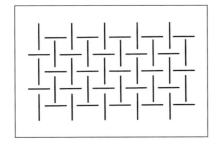

Plain weave.

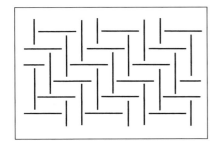

2/2 twill weave.

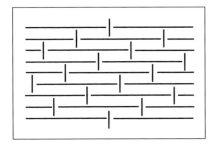

Satoon weave a weft faced broken twill.

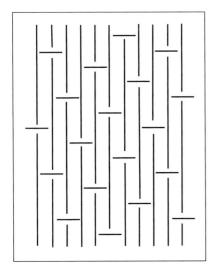

Satin weave a warp faced broken twill.

pink (see fig.1.7 on p11 in Chap.1). Muslin was a very popular fabric in the early nineteenth century and deserves a mention, but, as in the case of nylon in the twentieth century, was most unsuitable for inclusion in quilts because of its fineness and, in the case of muslin, its open weave.

In the eighteenth century both dress and furnishing fabrics were glazed by the calendering process. The purpose of this was to repel dirt and obviate the need for overlaundering a very prestigious and expensive fabric. By the end of the first quarter of the nineteenth century the habit of glazing dress fabrics had been dropped and confined to furnishings, which became very shiny. Calendering is a process whereby the cloth is passed between two very heavy revolving cylinders that touch one another and exert a pressure which smoothes and glazes the cloth. Linens also were calendered, but less often. Lustre can also be achieved if pressure is applied, especially with heat as in ironing. Silk, like cotton, was calendered, but this made the silk brittle. However, it is pressure, together with a small amount of water, on a ribbed silk that produces the watered or moiré effect. Another practice that affects silk is that of 'weighting'. During the preparation of the filament, the natural, gum-like sericin, which holds the cocoon together, is removed and, as the throwsters (persons who twisted silk filament or other long fibres into yarn) were paid by weight, they replaced the gum with metallic salts. It is thought that this practice has always gone on and, whereas the addition of a small amount of salts will not do any appreciable harm, the addition of excessive quantities causes the silk to become very brittle. This results in silk shattering completely. From about 1870 right through to the first quarter of the twentieth century, this reprehensible practice was employed, with coloured silks being weighted as much as between 50 and 100 per cent and black being weighted as much as 400-500 per cent. This treatment does produce the most wonderful 'rustle', but it renders the silk virtually incapable of being washed or laundered.

COLOURS AND DYES
It is important to understand that colours on fabrics in the quilts studied in the period covered by the Project's documentation were made with dyes that had technical limitations, as they depended on physical and chemical reactions with the fibres of the cloth. These limitations, however, were often exploited cleverly to give recognizable 'dye styles', or combinations of colours. It must also be remembered that only certain dyes are suitable for certain fibres, the main difference being between the cellulosic fibres (cotton and linen) and the protein fibres (wool and silk). Man-made fibres need special dyes, except for viscose rayon, which is dyed with cotton dyes.

Dyes for Printing Cotton and Linen

The Madder Style This refers to the plant dye, madder *(rubia tinctoria)* which gives different colours when dyed on cotton or linen that has previously been treated or 'mordanted' with metallic salts in solution –alum giving reds, iron giving purples, and mixtures giving chocolates and browns. Thus the red flower sprig in figure 9.12 on page 198 has been printed first with an alum solution thickened with a gum, and then the whole cloth has been dyed in a dye bath of stewed madder roots, the dye only attaching itself where the mordant has been. In 1868, the main colouring matter in madder, alizarin, was synthetized but it still had to be used in association with mordants, which by then included chrome. Synthetic alizarin with alum was used particularly to give roller-printed patterns in red and pink in the late nineteenth and early twentieth centuries and claret colours were produced with a chrome mordant.

Chintz This term has several connotations but in the British textile industry up to about the mid-nineteenth century it was used for the combination of colours seen in figure 9.20 on page 206. The term relates to the Indian painted cloths which were the forerunner of European printed textiles. The first print gave a black outline, then alum and iron mordants were printed and the cloth dyed in madder. Then yellow and blue were added, sometimes by printing, sometimes by painting on a dye or mordant, and this was known as pencilling. Compared with the clarity of the imagery produced by the first colours, these last yellows and blues often give a smudged effect when pencilled. Full chintz – that is, the full range of colours – was used for the most expensive dress fabrics until about the mid 1830s, but the style continued in furnishings (see fig.9.16, p.202). The earliest quilts of pieced fabrics found in the Project's documentation included chintz floral sprigs on either a white or on a dark background (usually referred to just as a 'ground'). Dark grounds – that is, a black background – were fashionable for dress fabrics from about 1780-95, but were revived, often printed on twill weave cloth, in the 1820s and 1830s (see figs. 9.11, p.198 and 9.22, p.207).

Blues The main dye throughout the nineteenth and into the twentieth century was indigo, a dye derived from plants grown in hot climates, chiefly of the family *Indigofera*. It was imported into Britain until artificial indigo was synthetized in 1880. Indigo gives the colour familiar to us in blue jeans, for which the weft yarn is dyed with indigo. The dye can be used to give tones from a light blue to a very dark blue. Both natural and synthetic indigo are very difficult to print, as the dye must be applied to cloth before it

Fig. 9.7. (1780-1815) Block-printed dress and furnishing fabrics. Medallion dated 1810. Note survival of good yellows and greens.

Fig. 9.8. (1880-1920) Cheaper roller printed fabrics in limited colours including novelty designs based on recreational motifs. Note new synthetic blue.

oxidizes in the air. The indigo pencilled on for chintz was made soluble by the use of arsenic, a practice naturally to be avoided if possible. In the pieced quilts dating from about 1790 to 1815 studied, a surprising number of printed blues were seen –mostly small patterns, often geometric, often in two tones of blue (see fig.9.21, p.206). These then petered out and were not encountered again, probably because the process of direct printing was a complicated one.

Instead, the main way of achieving indigo blues on printed cotton was by means of resists. These were made from mixtures of flour, powdered clay, gum, and often copper sulphate and were printed on the cloth. The cloth was then dyed in an indigo vat, with the resists protecting the printed area from being dyed blue. Figure 9.1 on page 186 shows several cloths in which the white and coloured areas have been protected by printing a resist after the mordant colours have been printed and dyed. Confirmation of this style can be found if the back of the cloth can be seen, showing that the colour is equally strong on both surfaces. It was only later in the nineteenth century that the knowledge of chemistry made it possible to take out the blue dyed by indigo, a technical process known as discharge and used particularly by William Morris from the 1880s. Examples of indigo-discharged patterns are shown in figure 9.7. Prussian blue, which is derived from iron, was discovered in 1710 but does not seem to appear as a colour in quilts until about 1815. It gave a greenish blue, as opposed to the reddish blue of indigo, and was a strong colour (see fig.9.26, p.210). It was an important colour in printed cottons (and wools) of the 1830s to 1860s, despite the fact that it was not fast to washing with soap. A bright blue appeared at the end of the nineteenth century often associated with black. This was one of the synthetic dyes discovered in the 1880s and 1890s that could be used on cotton (see fig. 9.8).

Yellows Yellow is the colour least seen in pieced cotton quilts, as it has often faded away, but figure 9.7 was chosen to show a furnishing fabric with very fresh yellows. On cottons up to the 1890s most yellows were achieved with dyes from plants and barks such as weld, persian berries, quercitron and fustic, which are all mordant dyes like madder and were used with alum, iron or chrome, the mordant giving different colours. The only clear yellows were found on an alum mordant – the iron gave an olive colour and the chrome more orange yellows. An exception to the yellows from vegetable dyes were the bright but rather crude yellows derived from chromate of lead, colours particularly seen in the 1820s and 1830s but which have also often disappeared from printed fabrics. Good fresh yellows from chromate of lead, often used in association with manganese brown, are seen in figure 9.23 on page 207.

Greens Until the very late nineteenth century, greens were made by a mixture of yellow and blue, with one exception. Because of the difficulty of printing indigo they were often achieved by taking a cloth dyed in indigo and then printing a mordant followed by dyeing in a yellow dye. These yellows have often faded, leaving just the indigo (see fig.9.9). The exception is that of copper green, a colour made with verdigris. A pattern book of 1809 gives a recipe for this and it is found occasionally in patchworks of the 1820s and 1830s (see fig.9.23, p.207). The colour was not fast and its use was discontinued by the 1840s. Many attempts were made from early in the nineteenth century to find a 'single' green – that is, a green that could be achieved in one operation. None was a reliable fast colour and the breakthrough did not come till 1895 with the discovery of alizarin green. Another landmark dye, Caledon jade green, a 'vat' dye discovered in 1920, gave at last a very fast clear green on the turquoise side.

Purple This was an important colour in the madder style, made by printing an iron mordant, followed by dyeing in madder or, later, alizarin. It was used as a colour on cotton and linen from the second half of the eighteenth century well into the twentieth century, very often on its own in two tones, a dark and a light, as they could be easily produced by printing a stronger and a weaker mordant (see fig.9.10). Purples became brighter after the introduction of alizarin (synthetized in 1868), and in the late nineteenth century a practice developed of adding a small quantity of another synthetic dye to give an even brighter colour. However, this dye was not fast and the colour lost its brightness. During the documentation sessions a defect of iron purple was noticed in quilts from all periods. It tended to revert to a brown through oxidization (see fig. 9.10, where the change can be seen on part of the purple). A leading textile chemist was consulted and he warned that washing with modern washing powders could exacerbate this degradation.

Brown Warm and cool browns, buffs and drabs in the madder style were made from a mixture of mordants and a mixture of dyestuffs. Such browns were often printed and dyed to give backgrounds for furnishing designs and are often referred to as 'tea' grounds (see fig. 9.2, p.186). A mixture of strong iron and strong alum was usually referred to as chocolate.

Black Black was in the madder style based on a strong iron mordant, first used with madder, later alizarin and also with the bark dye logwood. But new blacks appear in the 1860s based on aniline – a most useful addition to the palette for cotton printing.

Fig. 9.9. (1815-35) A lapis print showing front and back of new fabric with, in the centre, the same fabric in the quilt, which, through use and exposure to light, has lost its yellow.

Fig. 9.10. (1855-80) Roller-printed dress fabrics. Note that the iron mordanted purples dyed in madder or alizarin are degrading to brown. Designs probably inspired by woven silk ribbons of the period, mimicking watered silk.

Special Colours and Colour Combinations

Because of the limitations and possibilities inherent in most dyes, certain combinations became standard. These were particularly noticeable from the 1820s to 1850s, when there was much experimentation and many attempts to create new effects. Pieced quilts are often the main repository of these fabrics.

Cochineal Pink Cochineal gives a wonderful red on wool and silk but only an inadequate bluish pink on the cellulosic fibres. On cotton it was used to give a pink that is quite easy to distinguish from the lighter shades of alum madder (see fig.9.19, p.206 and fig.9.22, p.207). But it was not a fast dye on cotton and is not found later.

Lapis Style This is produced by a clever combination of processes and gives a madder red exactly adjacent to an indigo blue (see fig.9.9, p.195). An alum mordant is included in the printed resist under the indigo dye, which then gives a red on a second dyeing with madder. It was introduced as early as 1808 but was found, surprisingly often, in quilts of the period 1815-35. Because of its complexity as a process it was not used much after this in Britain.

Turkey Red and Other Strong Reds The first Turkey Red dyeworks was established in Scotland in 1785 and continued there until the 1940s. Turkey Red is a much brighter and deeper red produced from alum and madder (and, later, alizarin) by a long and complicated specialist process. It was used to give plain red cloth that is found in many quilts (see Chap.3, fig.3.14 on p.47). Although Turkey Red is a very fast dye it is possible to take the colour out with a bleaching process, and in the 1820s an important style of Turkey Red 'discharge' prints became important (see fig.9.13, p.199). Here the cloth, already dyed red all over, has been replaced by white, yellow and blue, using Prussian blue and lead/chrome yellow. In the early years the imagery was of isolated sprigs but it became famous later for designs in the Paisley style (see fig.9.30, p.211). In the second half of the nineteenth century, quilts contained Turkey Red discharge prints, printed on cotton woven in a twill weave and also on thinner cloth in a plain weave. It seems the latter cloth was for export (see fig.9.34, p.211). The very strong red produced by the Turkey Red process was rivalled, after its discovery in 1889, by the Azo colour Paranitraniline red, which could also be discharged.

Manganese Bronze This is a mineral dye which gives a greenish brown of various strengths, first used on cloth in 1823. It was cheap and easily dischargeable to white or by replacing the colour with lead-chrome yellow or with Prussian blue (see fig.9.23, p.207). An unstable colour because it is so easy to discharge with a weak acid, it tends to rot the fabric. Its heyday was the 1830s and 1840s.

Note There are many, many printing styles and it is sufficient here to draw the notice of readers to some only. A style that appears only in the twentieth century is colour discharge. Here, as with Turkey Red discharges, coloured grounds are discharged and replaced by other colours. Those of this period seen during the Project were rather poor-quality colours, often with poor fastness.

Dyes for Wool and Silk

Wool and silk, protein fibres, are much easier to dye than the cellulosic fibres. Until 1856 all dyes were made from natural sources and most were mordant dyes – madder and cochineal for reds, various yellow plant dyes and wood dyes such as logwood for different browns and greys. Indigo was used for blue with the addition of Prussian blue. Some lichen dyes were also used.

Then, in 1856, the first synthetic dye from coal tar, the bright purple called 'mauve', was discovered by W. H. Perkin. This was followed in rapid succession by other colours, but it is important to realize that these aniline dyes were primarily suitable for wool and silk, as they needed extra treatment for cotton and produced fugitive colours. (There was no breakthrough for cotton dyes until the discovery of artificial alizarin in 1868.) The situation for wool and silk was quite different and there was a spate of new colours, several named after Queen Victoria and one after Bismarck. The wide range of bright colours is evident in pieced quilts of silk from the last quarter of the nineteenth century.

PRINTING TECHNIQUES

The ability to recognize different printing techniques is most helpful in 'reading' quilts, particularly as the imagery may often be similar at different periods but the printing techniques give different characteristics.

Block Printing using wooden blocks, lifted by hand, then 'charged' with a thickened dye paste from a saturated pad and stamped on the cloth, was the method most commonly used in pre-1815 fabrics examined by the Project (see fig.9.11). In the period 1815-35 roller printing came to rival blocks. In the next period, 1835-55, blocks were used for a few cotton dress fabrics only, but throughout our period (1780-1960) furnishings were block-printed, although in the later nineteenth and twentieth centuries only the best quality. Block printing for silk dress fabrics continued until the 1960s, but these were rarely seen in the quilts documented.

Fig. 9.11. (1780-1815) Large range of styles. Dark and light ground chintzes, some pinned backgrounds, geometrics and stripes. Mix of dress and furnishing fabrics, block prints except for the figurative plate print on right. (Full quilt shown in Chap.3, fig.3.7 on p.42)

Fig. 9.12. (1780-1815) Plate print, typically monochrome, engraved lines giving very fine crisp details and shading; see ribbon motif.

One indicator of a block print is the pitch pin marks used for registration. (Made by hooked pins on the corners of the printing block which produces spots in the design, these are used for accurate placing of the block to print the next repeat.) There is often not enough cloth for these to be visible in a pieced quilt. It is more helpful to try to get a sense of the quality of the mark on cloth made by a gouged-out piece of wood (see fig.9.19, p.206). In contrast to wood, however, metal was introduced into the wood blocks, first as short lengths of brass wire referred to as pins. Figure 9.20 on page 206 shows a dotted background made with a pinned block. In the early nineteenth century extended lozenges, crescent and wedge shapes were made in metal; later, the whole of the first block used in a design to give an outline was made in metal. In order to print a solid area of colour – for example, backgrounds, usually referred to as blotch grounds – pieces of very solid felt were introduced as infills within outlines of wood.

Plate Printing was important for large-scale furnishing fabrics in the second half of the eighteenth century and into the nineteenth century, but very few were found in quilts examined on documentation days. Exceptions are figure 9.11 and figure 9.12. These show the main characteristics of such prints, which are made from large engraved metal plates equivalent to those made for printing paper. In plate printing, the lines engraved in the metal are the positive lines on the cloth. Figure 9.12 shows the fine close lines that would be impossible with block printing. Crosshatching was also possible. Figure 9.11 shows a glimpse of a typical plate-print design, which is usually figurative and on a large scale, and normally in one colour only – red being common. The Project discovered very few plate-printed designs in quilts – probably because these were almost always used for expensive furnishings, which were not subject to such changes of fashion as were dresses; also, there would not have been offcuts available in the same way as there were with dress fabrics.

Roller Printing eventually ousted plate printing completely and also block printing, with the exceptions listed above. A patent by Thomas Bell in 1783 for an engraved copper roller machine is taken as the starting date for roller printing. However, it was many years before there was clear evidence of roller printing in quilts. The earliest roller prints are probably the rather monotonous small-scale monochrome dress prints found in some quilts in the early nineteenth century. The heyday of adventurous roller prints is 1815 to 1835, when there was a fever of excitement in the printing industry (see fig.9.1 on p.186, and fig. 9.13 on p.199 and fig.9.25 on p.207).

Like plate printing, roller printing can give very fine marks on cloth. Early on, the rollers were engraved painstakingly by hand but an important development in the 1820s introduced the engraving of the large roller by a small cylindrical 'mill'. This process encouraged designs of small repeats and very fine line imagery, seen often in dress fabrics. In the period up to 1835 these roller prints, however, were often used just for fine outlines in black, red or chocolate, and then the other colours were introduced by block, a favourite style being the printing of a white resist under a light indigo blue. Sometimes these beautiful floral stripes were printed on the diagonal (see fig.9.1, p.186). Another achievement of this period was the roller prints giving graded colour (see fig.9.13).

The interaction between roller and block printing is also seen in furnishing fabrics during this period. Figure 9.2 on page 186 is interesting because it shows a chinoiserie design with the main colour printed by a stippled roller, which enabled three-dimensional form to be indicated by the clustering of small dots. This was achieved by indenting the surface of the metal roller with a blunt tool. Additional colour was added by block or by a roller with a wooden printing surface used for areas of colour. This was usually known as a surface roller. In the 1840s furnishings with very fine backgrounds of geometric roller-printed patterns, often combined with block prints, became popular (see fig.9.14). From the second half of the nineteenth century, roller prints for dress fabrics became very clever but seemed to have less vitality. These were now the bread-and-butter prints of the trade. There was a new style in the 1880s: small, isolated, finely engraved motifs such as heads (see fig.9.18, p.203) or sporting motifs such as jockey caps and whips or musical instruments (see fig.9.8, p.194).

Screen Printing was first introduced into Britain in the 1920s. It had two main advantages. First, it made easy both the printing of large areas of flat colour and the reproduction of any painterly marks that could be made with a brush or a pen on paper. Thus it complemented the freer approach to design in the interwar years. Secondly, it made small runs of one design economical so experimentation was encouraged. Up to 1960, screen printing would have been done by hand on long flat tables. At first it was used for more expensive fabrics, especially silk and wool dress fabrics and 'modern' furnishing design.

A screen is a wooden frame covered with a fine cloth mesh through which dye paste can be pushed on to the fabric. The design was painted in a photographic opaque paint on transparent film. This was then placed tightly against the screen which had been coated with a light-sensitive emulsion and exposed to light to set. The emulsion protected by the opaque paint was washed out afterwards, allowing the dye paste to be passed through. One screen was used for each colour as with block printing.

Fig. 9.13. (1815-35) Milled roller prints giving fine small-scale dress prints, e.g. Prussian blue pattern at the top middle. Emphasis on colours shading one into another. Note sprigs on Turkey Red background discharged to yellow, blue and green.

Fig. 9.14. (1835-55) Furnishing. Traditional block-printed floral design, combined with a fine geometric 'net' background pattern which is roller-printed.

Historical Context and Motifs

During the documentation sessions two quilts appeared which were placed in the seventeenth century, one by style and subject and the other by the embroidered date. One wholecloth quilt of plain weave, self-coloured silk, is dealt with in Chapter 5 (see fig.5.3, p.66). The other, a silk embroidered quilt of cream cotton, is also in Chapter 5 (see fig.5.6, p.70). Apart from these, which were the earliest pieces, a few quilts were found to contain eighteenth-century fabrics in association with younger ones. As is to be expected, the proportion of quilts increased as 1960 was approached. Through various influences, the period 1780-1960, the time span covered by the Project, seemed to break down into six periods: 1780-1815, 1815-35, 1835-55, 1855-80, 1880-1920, 1920-60. The following paragraphs, under the different dates, describe the influences that dictated the cloths, colours, techniques and design motifs: also the political and social events that had some bearing.

1780-1815

Prior to this time, British textile printers had been taking inspiration from either the beautiful Indian chintzes that were luxury articles prized by the upper classes or from the woven silks of the time. The home textile trade of linen and wool had felt severely threatened, and in 1720 an Act of Parliament was passed banning the use and wearing of imported Indian chintz. This Act rendered those prestigious fabrics even more precious and the merest scraps were treasured. They were allowed into the country for immediate re-export and many did slip through the net. However, the British cotton industry developed rapidly and the dating of cottons of this period is helped by the Act of 1774 (repealed in 1811) which required three blue threads to be woven into the selvedge of the new British all-cotton cloth. This allowed the printer to claim the lower excise tax. Although these threads make such fabrics indisputably British woven and printed, their absence does not necessarily mean foreign printing, as some firms preferred to print on imported Indian calico. A quilt documented at Swavesey (see fig.2.11, p.26) has examples of printed cloth where these threads are visible because the selvedges have been joined edge to edge instead of making a seam.

This is also the period of the commemorative medallions, described earlier. Classical designs printed in the 'Pompeian' colours of yellow, terracotta and black were current and no doubt the inspiration for this style were the treasures that Sir William Hamilton acquired while he was British Ambassador living in Naples. Extensive excavations had taken place at Herculaneum and Pompeii prior to his term of office and the highly coloured wall decorations that had been recorded were something startlingly novel. Meanwhile, French archaeologists and students had been exploring Egypt, resulting in the excavation of Luxor and Karnak. This led to Egyptian motifs being used in designs and getting caught up in the classical idiom.

Previously, there had been two waves of chinoiserie. A third came at the turn of the century and was embraced vigorously by the Prince of Wales when he decorated the Royal Pavilion at Brighton in 1802. These fashions were not displayed in textiles alone, as wallpapers and furniture all reflected the 'design motif' of the time. Being aware of motifs displayed by these other media can be a very useful adjunct to dating fabrics.

Shawls were a fashionable item and small geometric designs often closely repeated were very popular in this period. These were referred to as shawl motifs. They would have appeared in the ground on shawls as a foil to the borders that would have been at each end (see fig.9.21, p.206).

Checks and stripes appear throughout all the periods, but vary in their representation. At this time they were simple, printed both vertically and diagonally in single colours or in combination, often coloured by overdyeing. As the weaving of check or stripes is the easiest form of design to achieve on a loom, it was a surprise how few of these weaves were encountered.

Ribbons, too, were a fashionable item, always made of silk and, at this early time, often made in single soft pale colours. As selvedges on ribbons are displayed, special attention was paid to these and looped edges were devised which are called purl selvedges. A single purl at regular intervals was called a 'picot'; two double picots close together were called a 'tuft' and graded picots were called a 'scallop'. This period was the great one for purl ribbons.

Britain's naval and military prowess was reflected in design motifs such as oak trees, and leaves or acorns, signifying 'ships of oak' and 'hearts of oak'.

1815-35

British textile printers showed a great confidence at this time, and by fully employing the dye effects and new roller-printing techniques they produced some extraordinarily skilful and beautiful cloths, especially for dress. The constraints imposed by the circumference of the roller meant that the images used were different. When wood blocks had been used there was no restriction on the size of the image, the only limitation being the printer's ability to manipulate the block. This meant that designs had a freedom and looseness which disappeared once the roller had been embraced. This led to the flowing floral trails being

Fig. 9.15. (1835-55) Roller-printed dress fabrics. The Chinese lantern design shows complex shaded colour. Four colourways of this design seen in this quilt.

Fig. 9.16. (1835-55) Block-printed furnishing, probably for a blind. Political references to Anti-Corn Law League founded in 1838 by Richard Cobden and John Bright. Colours are those of traditional chintz on tea ground.

replaced by formally arranged garlands, often printed diagonally to maintain the flowing feel of the former period. This technique was exploited for geometrics as well, with vertical stripes of one colour being crossed with a diagonal stripe of a second. The flowing feel was often enhanced by the diagonals being made to undulate and given a broken edge to make them less rigid. With the clever control of shading colours some very sophisticated effects could be achieved, and checks could be shaded within a rigid structure or checks could be suggested by shading. Instances of these can be seen in figures 9.13 on page 199 and 9.1 on page 186. The latter figure also illustrates the diagonal floral garlands, but shown here on a blue ground.

During the years 1827-38 Audubon published his *Birds of America* and these beautiful plates were adapted for use on furnishing fabrics, either in isolation or often in company with butterflies amongst exotic foliage.

Ribbons reflected the confidence felt throughout the textile industry, possibly throughout the country too, with the wealth that followed the conquests of the early 1800s. Stronger colours were used, such as shot colours, where the warp in one colour is crossed by a weft of a different colour. Selvedge warps were denser, giving a corded effect, but as the weft was more apparent there was a lovely emphasis of colour, often with very subtle effects. In 1822 George IV visited Scotland, the love affair with all things Scottish began, and tartan ribbons were produced in quantities.

1835-55

Production had developed to meet the ever-increasing demand for cotton cloth. It had become cheaper and consequently lost its prestige status. Industry, in its endeavour to produce greater variety at speed, lost its innovative design skills and relied on reworking previous images. This method of working had a static quality, having lost all spontaneity. Ready-made dresses for the working classes were now a possibility, creating the necessity for samples to be available. The trade increased with the coming of the first practical sewing machine in 1851. The diagonals, which must have given skirts such a lovely swirl, disappeared and there was great emphasis on the vertical. Checks were implied by the crossing of vertical imagery with an undulating one (see details in fig.9.26, p.210). Geometrics became very complex with some quite remarkable effects (see fig.9.15). Alongside this cleverness some traditional themes persisted. Stripes were still available and checks exhibiting the influence of the tartan appeared to be plentiful.

Commemorative themes moved into cloth sold by the yard and the medallion was abandoned. The example in figure 9.16 shows

Richard Cobden (English economist and politician) proclaiming his Anti-Corn Law League in 1838, a curious subject for a furnishing fabric. The fact that Cobden started his working life as a calico salesman, progressing to a calico printer with a printworks bearing his name, may offer an explanation. Whether his factory produced this cloth needs more research, but the probability is real. What this fabric illustrates is the uncomfortable scale of images, the figure against the arches and then the overlying flowers all resting very uneasily with one another.

A general deterioration of good taste was reached in this period culminating in the Great Exhibition of 1851 – thought by some to be a vulgar affair. In 1855 the rebuilding of Balmoral Castle was completed, thus rekindling the love of all things Scottish. Tartan was the rage, especially in the ribbon trade. In this industry all patterning was woven and checks and stripes reached a great sophistication.

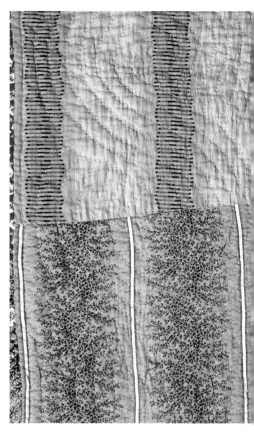

Fig. 9.17. (1855-80) Finely engraved roller printed dress fabric. Also probably inspired by woven silk ribbons. Note the printed 'selvedges'.

1855-80

By this time enormous mass-production had led to a deterioration of design skills, but growth of great specialized technical achievements led to an ability to mimic woven structures. Alongside the exuberant vulgarity of a lot of the cloths produced were some very beautiful executions of printed ribbons (see figs.9.10, p.195 and 9.17).

The shawl finally disappeared from the fashion scene. However, the Paisley-style designs from shawls were an enduring image (fig.9.34 on p.211 is a good example of the different scales of the design used). With the discovery of the new dyes, silk ribbons acquired a whole new palette with strong vibrant colours. They became more complex in their structure and black was a very popular colour.

1880-1920

Pendulums inevitably swing in the opposite direction and what had started as reactions to the over-complex designs seen at the Great Exhibition resulted in a new simplified, but rhythmical, decorative style. This ultimately was reinforced by the formation of the Arts & Crafts Society Exhibition in 1888 by William Morris and Edward Burne-Jones. In Germany, at much the same time, the Jugendstil movement arose and in France the Art Nouveau: both adopted very similar design styles. These movements used soft, flat colours, shading having disappeared. A few Art Nouveau-style fabrics were recorded, but it was surprising that no William Morris textiles appeared on documentation days. Dress cottons were cheap to purchase and of a very poor quality. Consistent with their price, manufacturers restricted their palette, and what they lacked in substance designers tried to replace with novelty. This was the era of small, isolated images taken from field sports, gambling games,

Fig. 9.18. (1880-1920) Roller-printed heads, typical of the very fine isolated motifs fashionable in the 1880s, contrasted with two roller-prints in the same colourway, being another example of the prints based on woven structures.

animals, anchors, bows, ribbons; anything that could be thought of was portrayed in this manner (see figs.9.8, p.194 and 9.18, p.203).

Alongside this comparative 'poverty' of printed cotton textiles ran the great era of the silk ribbon quilt. The ribbons had reached a great height of sophistication and the quiltmakers matched this with the designs they used. They manipulated the ribbons so that they created further textile designs, somewhat reminiscent of the planning demonstrated in the quilt of 1790-1805 used to illustrate this chapter (see fig.9.19, p.206).

Queen Victoria celebrated two Jubilees during this period: her Golden in 1887 and her Diamond in 1897. Both were inspiration to designers, but a more unusual print has been chosen to illustrate this point (see fig.9.38, p.214).

1920-60

A further revolution took place at the start of this period. Silkscreen printing by hand was put into commercial production. This allowed a great freedom of drawing and, influenced by the modern abstract movement, designers produced a more painterly and sketchily drawn image. Almost any colour was now available for any fabric.

Following on from the Arts & Crafts movement, this was the great time of the artist-craftsmen such as the block printers Barron and Larcher or the Omega Workshop set up by Roger Fry that employed artists such as Duncan Grant and Vanessa Bell. There were hand weavers, namely Ethel Mairet and Valentine Kilbride of Gospels Workshop at Ditchling, and many others. Being labour intensive their textiles were likely to be expensive and therefore exclusive, so it is not surprising that none was recorded in the Project.

Freed from the deprivations of World War I, British industry required promotion and the British Empire Exhibition was staged at Wembley in 1924. There was a strong Egyptian theme as the tomb of King Tutankhamun had been discovered two years previously. The following year, 1925, the Exposition des Arts Decoratifs et Industriels was staged in Paris, giving its name to the Art Deco movement; again 'Egyptiana' was the abiding style.

World war was to break out again in 1939 and to last for six years. Clothes rationing was introduced in Britain in 1941 and was not to be lifted until 1949. It was a lean time for quiltmakers.

Celebrating the end of the War and giving industry a boost, the Festival of Britain was held on the South Bank site in London in 1951. Science was breaking new ground and there was a spate of designs based on molecular imagery. None of these fabrics appeared at documentation sessions, but the fine linear drawing they employed was characteristic of textile design at this time.

1780 – 1815 DRESS FABRICS

Fibre Weaves & Finish	Design Motifs & Scale	Colours	Dye Effects	Print Techniques	Comments
Cotton: Plain weave as base cloth for printing. Dimities. Eighteenth-century cotton has a very substantial quality and irregular character owing to the spin of the yarn and the weave. Linen: Plain weave, often hand-spun and hand-woven. Cotton and linen mixed, in the cloth not the yarn. Finish: Early in this period cotton and linen were highly glazed; but glaze frequently disappeared through washing. Silk and wool would have been used for dress, but none was encountered in the pieced quilts.	Florals: Fine trailing stems with long repeat, reflecting contemporary woven silks. Geometrics: Checks, diamonds, ovals, shawl motifs, spots, stripes; also vertical stripes crossed with diagonals.	Grounds: White, tea, green, dark chocolate brown: plain or dotted textures. Prints: Full chintz with black outline, two tone blue, pink and black, pink and olive, yellow and black. *Note* deep, rich colours produced by overdyeing.	Paste resist under indigo. Two printed indigo particular to this period. Green achieved by overdyeing or pencilling yellow on blue. Yellow dyes fugitive at this period. They have often disappeared rendering greens blue. Overdyeing indigo on mordant printed and dyed cloth to produce several colours for spots and checks.	Wood block, block with metal pinning, blotch grounds. Pencilling giving smudged effect. Some roller printing towards end of period, but difficult to distinguish; probably monochrome; not used for furnishing.	Greater range of patterns than at later periods. Bell's patent for roller printing 1783. Much white, much space in both quilt and fabric design. More often in this period than later furnishing and dress cloth appears in the same quilt. Base cloth for printing very similar for both dress and furnishing. Printed cloth scarce, so patches are often pieced.

1780-1815 FURNISHING FABRICS

Fibre Weaves & Finish	Design Motifs & Scale	Colours	Dye Effects	Print Techniques	Comments
Cotton: Plain weave as base cloth for printing. Dimities. Linen: Plain weave, often hand-spun and hand-woven, used especially for plate prints.	Florals: Large scale; leaves, acanthus, oak. Flower sprays; roses, morning glory, pinks, cornflowers, auriculas. Geometrics: Simple and small scale; stars, spots, checks. Figurative: Chinoiserie scenes, swags and tails of drapery in both large and small scale, palm trees, islands, pheasants, Egyptian, classical. Units: Printed medallions, often commemorative; ovals, rectangles, irregular octagons, containing roses, thistles, shamrock, flowers listed under floral sprays.	Grounds: White, drab, tea, yellow, pale blue, dark chocolate brown. Prints: Full chintz with black outline, two-tone blue, Pompeian colours of yellow, terracotta and black.	Similar to dress.	Similar to dress with the addition of plate prints used for narrative scenes with characteristically large repeat size, usually in a single colour.	Similar to dress. Examples of only eight Indian chintzes and eight plate prints appeared, fewer than expected. 1798: Nelson's victory at Battle of the Nile. 1805: Nelson's victory at Trafalgar. 1810: George III Golden Jubilee. 1813: Wellington's victory at Vittoria. 1815: Wellington's victory at Waterloo. No botanical symbol for Wales.

Fig. 9.19. White important between pieces and within fabric designs. All block prints. The formality of the pieced design is a reflection of the formality of the printed motifs. Typical colour combinations of pink/black, yellow/black, printed blues.

Fig. 9.20. Full chintz, block-printed sprig with black outline. Pinned block used for dotted background producing negative spray images. Secondary motif seaweed type.

Fig. 9.21. White dimity diamonds giving textured stripes. Two versions of shawl motif – 4th from left, top row; 6th from left, 2nd row. All block prints.

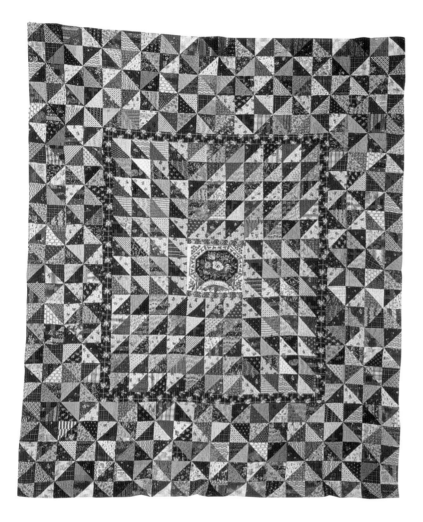

Fig. 9.22. Block-printed central Waterloo medallion 1815, other fabrics dated later, and almost all roller prints for dress. Quilt dated 1834 in the quilting. 844 triangles, 252 different fabrics, 216 pieced triangles.

Fig. 9.23. Detail of fig 9.22 shows changes in colours due to new dye effects, e.g. top row, manganese brown and yellow sometimes also with Prussian blue, also a triangle with copper green used for background. 2nd row, cochineal pink print and red/blue lapis print. Revival of dark ground prints, less formal, more open than in previous period, some on twills.

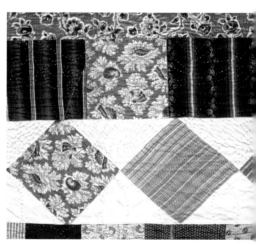

Fig. 9.25. Roller-printed dress fabrics. Some traditional colours, e.g. resist under dark and pale indigo. Typical twisting foliage stripe used for the Dorothy bag. (Full quilt shown in Chap.4, fig.4.5, p.54)

Fig. 9.24. Top border, block-printed furnishing. Roller-printed dress fabrics below; note fine engraving used for the seashells and seaweed.

1815-1835 DRESS FABRICS

Fibre Weaves & Finish	Design Motifs & Scale	Colours	Dye Effects	Print Techniques	Comments
Cotton: Plain weave as base cloth for printing, thinner and more even than before. Twills, especially for dark grounds. Linen: Very little. Finish: No longer glazed.	Florals: Smaller, tighter closer. Geometrics: Very small-scale, very clever, e.g. checks shaded, undulating stripes, some on the diagonal. Figurative: Fireworks, sea shells, seaweed.	Grounds: White, yellow pale blue, copper green, manganese brown, the last two newly introduced colours. Prints: Full chintz, two-tone blue, bright red. Prussian blue introduced, new yellows arrived, quercitron and chrome yellow. Different pinks with cochineal. Shaded colours. Colourways of same design becoming evident.	Light blue produced by resist under indigo. Turkey Red discharge. Note very complex prints invoving the dyeing of the cloth three timoc, e.g. for madder, indigo, and yellow dye. Possibility of red exactly adjacent to blue; lapis effect.	Roller prints now important, especially milled rollers. However, the more expensive chintzes were usually block-printed. Block printing continues, often used with roller printing in the same design. It is not always easy to distinguish roller and block prints as they influenced each other.	Great era of roller printing; many have designs diagonal to the weave of the cloth. Often same 'dye style', e.g. manganese and yellow, used for different designs. Deterioration; manganese browns rot. For these first two periods cotton is prestige fabric. Often seaming in quite a small patch, showing the value of the fabric, e.g. one quilt had 844 triangles, 252 different fabrics, 216 triangles pieced. 1822: George IV visited Scotland and the love affair with all things Scottish started, tartans proliferate, especially for ribbons.

1815-1835 FURNISHING FABRICS

Fibre Weaves & Finish	Design Motifs & Scale	Colours	Dye Effects	Print Techniques	Comments
Cotton: As base cloth, for printing same as dress. Finish: Highly glazed.	Florals: As previous period. Geometrics: Becoming more complex and tighter. Figurative: Early in the period, chinoiserie as borders and blinds.	Grounds: White, tea, yellow, pale blue. Prints: Full chintz, but generally fewer colours. Very strong yellow.	Light blue produced by resist under indigo.	Stippled roller prints giving 3D effect. Some use of surface rollers for printing areas of solid colour, often resulting in ill-fitting registration. Block print still. Plate-print designs adapted to rollers resulting in cramped, uncomfortable images, but none found in the documentation Project.	Great era of roller printing. Scales of designs have become larger and lend themselves less to use in quilts, consequently only occasionally found in the documentation Project. During the years 1827-38 *Audubon's Birds of America* published.

1835-1855 DRESS FABRICS

Fibre Weaves & Finish	Design Motifs & Scale	Colours	Dye Effects	Print Techniques	Comments
Same as previous period. Printed wools and silks are important, but rarely seen in the quilts.	Large scale designs (often with Prussian blue). Many designs were achieved by the crossing of vertical stripes by horizontal undulating imagery, giving the effect of checks. Graded colours employed in these complex designs. Alternate vertical stripes of different motifs.	Dominance of Prussian blue which is nearly always shaded, often used in conjunction with manganese brown. Traditional full chintz and madder styles continue.	Continuation of all traditional colourings.	Mainly roller, sometimes in combination with block prints.	Very great emphasis on the vertical and a reworking of previous designs. 1851: First practical sewing machine available.

1835-1855 FURNISHING FABRICS

Fibre Weaves & Finish	Design Motifs & Scale	Colours	Dye Effects	Print Techniques	Comments
Same as previous period. Highly glazed.	Floral: Two scales of flowers appear on the same cloth in stripes. Geometrics: Very small geometric roller backgrounds, sometimes produced on their own as linings . Figurative: Commemorative motifs move into fabric by yard and away from medallions. Use of animal skin motifs, giraffe etc.	Traditional full chintz colours. Great age of Prussian blue. Experiments with single greens at this time, none evident in documentation Project.	As for dress.	Roller prints. Block prints, sometimes with roller-printed grounds.	Uncomfortable juxtaposition of scale, e.g. tiny people or ruins with huge foliage. 1851: Great Exhibition. 1855: Rebuilding of Balmoral completed; rekindling of love affair with all things Scottish.

Fig. 9.26. Predominance of Prussian blue.
This large-scale design could be for dress
or furnishing in this period. In detail, note
crossing of vertical stripes by horizontal
undulating imagery giving effect of checks.
Probably a combination of block and roller
printing.

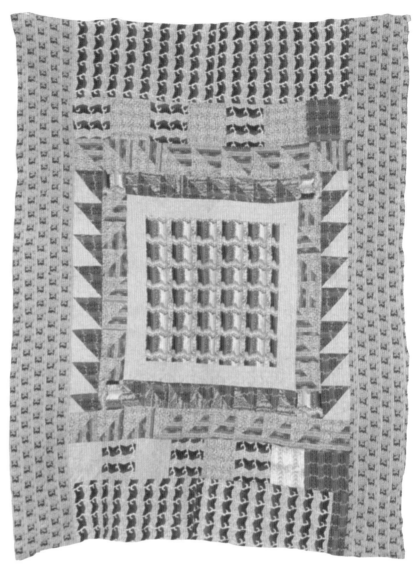

Fig. 9.27. Dark ground block-printed
furnishing (could be of an earlier date),
with traditional type roller-printed dress
fabrics. Note lapis still with its yellow giving
a brick red.

Fig. 9.28. Roller-printed dress fabrics
showing shading and complex association of
imagery. Manganese and cochineal still in
use.

Fig. 9.29. Typical redesigning of earlier
styles, using simplified individual motifs but
layering them to give a crammed effect.

Fig. 9.32. Roller-printed furnishing and dress fabrics. Note high glaze on pink-brown pieces. Traditional designs reworked, with cleverness, but no fresh impetus.

Fig. 9.33. Roller-printed dress fabrics. Note close diagonal stripes mimicking twill weave.

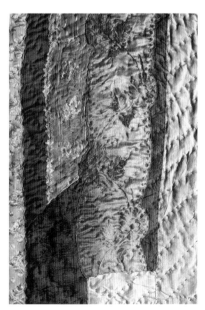

Fig. 9.30. Roller-printed dress fabrics in the Turkey Red discharge technique. The design derives from borders of European or Indian shawls.

Fig. 9.31. Detail from a quilt, the top of which is made entirely of silk ribbons. Shows a variety of selvedges including a purl edge to the cream ribbon on the extreme left-hand side.

Fig. 9.34. Roller-printed dress fabric produced on thin, loosely woven cotton, most probably for the export market. Turkey Red discharge prints are here reduced to red and white having largely lost their blue, and certainly all their yellow, through fading and washing.

1855-1880 DRESS FABRICS

Fibre Weaves & Finish	Design Motifs & Scale	Colours	Dye Effects	Print Techniques	Comments
Base cloth for printing as before, with the poorer quality cloth being produced for export. Quilts beginning to be made from silk ribbons.	Traditional print motifs redesigned, sometimes in complex combinations. New styles produced by mimicking of fine woven structures in fine roller prints, e.g. twill and watered silk. Exotic shawls inspired prints in Turkey Red discharge.	Cotton: Traditional palette expanded to create clarets and some new greens. Turkey Red discharge in combination with blue, green and yellow becomes prominent. Purple, usually in two tones or with black, now becomes a classic colour style. Silk: 1860 and onwards, black a very popular colour for ribbons. Many new colours including mauves.	1856: Revolution in dyes for silk and wool after the invention of Perkin's Mauve followed by many aniline dyes, but these were not appropriate for printed cotton fabric. 1868: Synthetic alizarin discovered. Mordants now include chrome for clarets. 1860: Artificial indigo synthetized in Germany.	Roller printing entirely for cotton fabrics. Block printing continues for silk and wool, but not evident in documention Project.	Enormous mass production leads to deterioration of design skills, but growth of great specialized technical achievements, e.g. fine engraving of rollers, Turkey Red discharge printing and control over purple mordants. 1870: Shawls finally go out of fashion after more than 100 years.

1855-1880 FURNISHING FABRICS

Fibre Weaves & Finish	Design Motifs & Scale	Colours	Dye Effects	Print Techniques	Comments
Printed furnishings continue as before. More fabrics with woven designs. Highly glazed.	Continuation of previous styles, including animal skin motifs.	Little change.	Not affected by changes.	Increased use of engraved and surface roller printing. Block printing only used for the more expensive fabrics.	Period of little change except for beginnings of reaction to the over-complex designs seen at the Great Exhibition. 1856: Publication of Owen Jones's *Grammar of Ornament*.

1880-1920 DRESS FABRICS

Fibre Weaves & Finish	Design Motifs & Scale	Colours	Dye Effects	Print Techniques	Comments
Base cloth for printing of a poor quality, a great contrast to the silks and woven fabrics often seen in quilts of this period. Taffetas now often 'weighted' with tin salts, which causes the silk to shatter.	Printed designs are repetition of tried-and-tested motifs, with rollers reused for years. Novelty figurative fabrics introduced in the 1880s with designs based on sporting and recreational themes. Silk ribbon designs show very skilled knowledge of woven structure and quality yarns.	Restricted palette on printed cotton, often only two colours on white. Red and white continues. Purple continues. A new synthetic blue. With the wide range of chemical dyes, almost any colour now available for silk, used with great skill and restraint, with black continuing to be popular.	Increasing mastery and control over widening range of synthetic dyes which nevertheless does not oust the alizarin madder style for cotton.	Entirely roller-printed cotton, but block printing for exclusive silks and wools.	Cotton no longer prestigious and has become a lowly fabric. Great contrast between quilts of cheap cotton roller prints and those made from beautiful silk ribbons. As the documentation Project progressed it became clearer that many silks were ribbons rather than dress silks. 1887: Queen Victoria's Golden Jubilee. 1897: Queen Victoria's Diamond Jubilee. 1914-18: World War I.

1880-1920 FURNISHING FABRICS

Fibre Weaves & Finish	Design Motifs & Scale	Colours	Dye Effects	Print Techniques	Comments
Cotton and linen union base cloth for printing. Wide range of woven furnishings in cotton, linen, silk, wool and mixtures. All furnishings have become denser and heavier. Velvets important in various modes, e.g. embossed, printed, voided.	Traditional florals parallel with Art Nouveau designs.	Traditional palette and the introduction of soft colours for Art Nouveau styles, blues, greens, pinks, beige and fawn.	Indigo discharge replaces indigo resist (a particular technique of William Morris). In general, similar for dress and furnishing.	Rollers, engraved and surface, for majority of furnishing, but block printing for high-class work using many colours.	New simplified but rhythmical decorative styles encouraged by the formation of Arts & Crafts Society exhibition in 1888. No William Morris fabrics encountered in the Project.

Fig. 9.35. Woven furnishings from the end of the nineteenth century, very 'heavy' in design, colour and structure. Velvets voided and prin ted and woven damasks. The detail shows the Art Nouveau style.

Fig. 9.36. Woven silk ribbons. Central hexagon a brocaded sprig, surrounded by diamonds of shaded red ribbed silk and taffetas, set in a cream ground of watered silk with three satin stripes. Additional ribbons of plain weave checks, stripes and damask.

Fig. 9.37. This detail shows the complexity of some woven ribbons, e.g. the multi-stripe ribbon. As with printed fabrics, ribbons were woven in colourways. See brocaded roses.

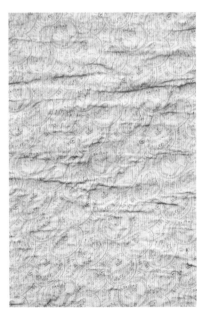

Fig. 9.38. Queen Victoria's Golden Jubilee, 1887, inspired many designs. This more unusual one is a roller print of coins of the British Empire.

Fig. 9.39. The early twentieth century saw a large number of wool quilts. The detail shows fine black and white check worsted, cream twill with pale mauve stripe and cheap woollen suitings. All woven for clothing. Note the 'tie' of mattress proportions.

Fig. 9.40. Woven and printed shirtings. These red, white and blue twill cotton fabrics are very substantial cloths, often found in quilts, but usually with faded colour. Probably produced for men's work shirts.

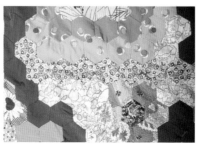

Fig. 9.43. 'Modern'-style dress fabrics (c.1920s-30s). Note these silks show a fluid quality through their woven structure, which often exploited the sheen of the silk. Crepe de chine, silk tweed, satins and ribbed. The printed fabrics with their freely drawn abstract designs are probably screen-printed.

Fig. 9.41. Good-quality cotton fabrics of the 1950s, all for dress except perhaps for the orange 'bud' (top middle). Good examples of the variety of current painting styles.

Fig. 9.42. Dress fabrics of the 1950s, including printed seersucker (bottom right). Colours and imagery typical of the period.

1920–1960 DRESS FABRICS

Fibre Weaves & Finish	Design Motifs & Scale	Colours	Dye Effects	Print Techniques	Comments
Cotton: Base cloth for printing, plain weave and textured weaves including seersucker. Cloths not printed: Ginghams, shirtings, seersuckers, pyjama cloth, winceyette, flour sacks. Linen: Cloths not printed, plain weave. Pseudo linens, e.g. Moygashel using rayon. Silk: Some used for printing, plain weave, crepe de chine, satins, tweeds, artificial silk, i.e. rayons, often very shiny. Wool: Woollen and worsted suitings. Twill weaves quite frequent. Flannels plain and printed, fine plain weave woollens printed. Trade mark fabrics, e.g. Moygashel and Tobralco.	Traditional designing now challenged by completely new approaches influenced by the modern abstract movements such as Art Deco and the technical possibilities of screen printing. Florals: Flat, painterly and sketchily drawn. Geometrics: Often including irregularly drawn rectangles.	Almost any colour now available for fabric.	New dyes continue to be discovered, e.g. Azoics and vat dyes, the latter giving Caledon green a very clear, fast, single green, from 1920. Discharge styles now include colour discharges on the other colours as well as Turkey Red.	As previous period. Early in this period silk-screen printing by hand put into commercial production.	Quilts contain a mixture of very traditional fabrics and modern designs. Great use made of sample books. 1922: Discovery of King Tutankhamun's Tomb. 1925: Exposition des Arts Décoratifs et Industriels held in Paris giving its name to the Art Deco style. 1939-45: World War II. 1941-49: Clothes rationing. 1951: Festival of Britain. *Note* no handmade artist-craftsmen fabrics seen in quilts so far.

1920-1960 FURNISHING FABRICS

Fibre Weaves & Finish	Design Motifs & Scale	Colours	Dye Effects	Print Techniques	Comments
Cotton: Base cloth for printing, plain weave and textured weave. Cloth not printed: Sateen for curtain lining. Linen union plain weave used for printing. Silk: Not encountered in quilts. Wool: Not encountered in quilts.	As for dress.	As for dress.	As for dress.	Mainly roller printing and block printing with some silk-screen printing.	Few modern furnishings seen in quilts during the Project. Important dates as for dress. *Note* no hand-made artist-craftsmen fabrics seen in quilts so far.

GLOSSARY

Aniline dyes Synthetic dyes which are more suitable for dyeing protein fibres such as silk and wool. They were developed after W. H. Perkin's Mauve in 1856.

Basting American term for tacking stitches.

Batting American term for filling or wadding.

Block patchwork Patchwork in which design is created on the basis of square units.

Block print Fabric which has been hand-printed with wooden blocks.

Broderie Perse Technique of cutting printed flowers, trees, etc. from one piece of fabric and applying them to another.

Butted quilt edge The most popular finishing technique in Britain. The raw edges of both the top and backing fabrics are turned inward and stitched together either by machine or by hand with a running stitch.

Calico Unbleached cotton cloth (called muslin in US).

Chinoiserie European adaptation of Chinese motifs in ornament and design.

'Comfy' quilt Commercial name of machine-made quilts manufactured in Britain from about 1920 to 1940.

Corded quilting Technique in which closely spaced parallel lines are stitched through two layers of cloth and the channels are filled with cotton or wool cord inserted from the back. *See* Italian quilting.

Coverlet Pieced, embroidered or appliquéd completed quilt top that has no wadding but may be backed.

Cut Chintz appliqué American term for Broderie Perse.

English patchwork *See* Mosaic patchwork.

Fent Remnant, damaged or mis-printed piece of cloth.

Filling or wadding Middle layer of a quilt. Can be carded cotton or wool, an old blanket, flannelette, an old quilt, cast-off clothing or household textiles. More recently the filling used is polyester.

Flat quilting Practice of quilting the top and bottom layers of a quilt which has no wadding.

Fold-and-cut appliqué Method of applying 'snowflake' patterns which have been created by folding and cutting either the fabric or a paper template. Similar in approach to American Hawaiian appliqué.

Frame quilt Term used to describe British patchwork layout in which central area is systematically surrounded by a series of borders.

Italian quilting *See* Corded quilting.

Knotted quilting *See* Tied quilting.

Marking Method of drawing a quilt pattern. This may be done with pencil, crayon, chalk, chinagraph pencil or a blunt needle. Also called stamping.

Medallion quilt American term for a patchwork layout where the central design is surrounded by a series of borders.

Mordants Chemicals such as alum or iron with which cotton cloth is printed or treated before dyeing with madder, logwood, quercitron, weld and other 'mordant dyes', thus improving the 'take-up' of the dyes.

Mosaic patchwork Sometimes called 'piecing over papers', 'paper template piecing' or 'English patchwork'. A hand-sewn construction technique using paper shapes (*see* below). Fabric is wrapped around the papers and tacked down before the shapes are oversewn together.

Oversewing Method used to sew mosaic patchwork pieces together A stitch which joins together the top edge of the folded fabric of two wrapped patchwork pieces. *See* whip stitch.

Papers Paper or thin card shapes used in mosaic patchwork The shapes are cut using a wooden or metal template or are taken from a drawn image which was subdivided into components. Simpler paper shapes are created by folding and then cutting paper.

Plate prints Fabric which has been printed using engraved metal plates.

Printed panel Octagonal, oval or circular printed design of flowers, fruits, birds, baskets etc., often with commemorative dates, which were frequently used in the centre of quilts.

Roller prints Fabric which has been printed from engraved rollers on a machine.

Rucken Name for ruched strips of fabric used in quiltmaking. Term associated with quilts made in Fraserburgh, Scotland.

Running stitch Most common quilting stitch where the complete stitch, down and back up through the fabric layers, is worked with the needle from the top layer.

Sashing Fabric strips (usually contrasting) that are sometimes used between patchwork blocks.

Soldiers' quilts *See* Uniform quilts.

Stab quilting Method of quilting by which the needle is passed from front to back and from back to front instead of in a running stitch.

Stampers Name for people who mark quilting patterns. *See* Marking.

Strippy Quilt made of alternating coloured strips running lengthwise. Generally quilted with patterns that follow the strips.

Stuffed quilting High-relief quilting technique in which designated areas of design are individually stuffed with wadding. *See* Trapunto.

Tacking Temporary stitches used to hold quilt layers in place or fix patchwork pieces to paper templates prior to sewing. *See* Basting.

Template Pattern, cut out in paper, card, wood or metal, used to cut patchwork shapes in fabric, mosaic patchwork papers or to help with marking quilting designs.

Tessellation Fitting together exactly, without spaces, of identical shapes – like a mosaic.

Tied quilting Quilt in which the layers are held together by knots tied at intervals. Also called knotting.

Trapunto *See* Stuffed quilting.

Turkey Red A dye-process incorporating madder dye which created the first non-bleeding, non-fading red, which arrived in Britain from the Continent towards the end of the eighteenth century.

Uniform quilts Since some of the so-called 'soldiers' quilts and coverlets were actually made by people such as tailors or were unconnected to the military, it is suggested that any quilt or coverlet incorporating thick wool cloth suitable for military or livery uniforms should be called a uniform quilt.

Wadding Synonym for filling/stuffing/batting.

Warp Thread stretched out lengthways in a loom to be crossed by the woven thread carried by the shuttle called a weft.

Weft Thread carried by the shuttle which is woven across the warp threads.

Whip stitch American term for oversewing.

Wholecloth quilt Quilt whose top is made with only one fabric (sometimes joined). The quilting may be ornate or utilitarian.

END NOTES

Chapter 1

1. Unpublished thesis by Tina Fenwick Smith: *Averil Colby, Patchworker and her Fabrics, 1900-1983*, p.2.

2. Ibid., p.7.

Chapter 5

1. Averil Colby, *Quilting* (London, 1972), p.90.

2. Ibid., p. 114.

3. Personal consultation with Textile Department, Victoria & Albert Museum, London.

4. Clare Rose, 'Corded Quilting and the World of Fashion', in Quilters' Review, *The Quilter*, Summer 1993, p.6.

5. Christine Stevens, *Quilts* (Cardiff, 1993), p.50.

6. Elizabeth Hake, *English Quilting Old and New* (London, 1937), figs.35 and 36.

7. Rosemary Allan, *Quilts and Coverlets from Beamish Museum* (Stanley, Co. Durham, 1987), p.15.

8. Averil Colby, op. cit., pp.51-2.

Chapter 6

1. Barrie Naylor, *Quakers in the Rhondda 1926-1986* (Chepstow, Gwent, 1986), pp.21-3.

2. Ibid., p.52.

3. Oral recording made in 1991. (Quilters' Guild Heritage Collection).

4. Ibid.

5. Susanna Gooden, *A History of Heal's* (London, Conran Associates, 1984).

Chapter 7

1. Documentary information from the archives of the Canadian Red Cross Society.

2. Personal communication to the author.

3. Communication from the British Red Cross Society to the author.

4. Wolfram Eberhard, *A Dictionary of Chinese Symbols* (London, Routledge and Kegan Paul, 1986).

5. Thomas K. Woodward and Blanche Greenstein, *Twentieth Century Quilts 1900-1950* (New York, E. P. Dutton, 1988).

6. T. Harry Williams, Richard N. Current and Frank Freidel, *A History of the United States Since 1865* (New York, Alfred A. Knopf, 1959).

7. Florence H. Pettit, *America's Indigo Blues: Resist Printed and Dyed Textiles of the 18th Century* (New York, Hastings House, 1974).

Chapter 8

1. Author's correspondence with Sally Marr, Abimelech Hainsworth, Spring Valley Mills, Stanningly, Pudsey, West Yorks.,15.7.94.

2. Martin Hardingham, *Illustrated Dictionary of Fabrics* (London, Cassell and Collier/ Macmillan, 1978).

3. W. Y. Carman, *Uniforms of the British Army – The Infantry Regiments* (Exeter, Webb & Bower, 1985).

4. Author's discussion with Mr Robert Gieves, Gieves & Hawkes, Civil and Military Tailors, 1 Savile Row, London, August 1994.

Allan, Rosemary. *Quilts and Coverlets from Beamish Museum* (North of England Open-Air Museum), Stanley, Co. Durham, 1987.

Allan, Rosemary. *Quilts and Coverlets:*

GUIDE TO APPRECIATION

Quilt owners who are curious about the age and composition of family heirlooms, or other old specimens of the patchwork and quilting craft, can, with a bit of guidance, undertake some of the investigation themselves. As well as assessing the textiles used (as discussed in Chap.9), they can size up other clues or evidence that life in the quilt's social history, sewing techniques, use of materials and patterns and quilting designs. Dating quilts is not a precise art (unless you have firm documentation) but much can be learned to increase knowledge and appreciation.

Family History
Most old quilts are not signed and dated and, even when they are, such information should be treated with caution. If, for example, a quilt has a centrepiece with initials and a date, this could indicate the time the quilt was started, not finished. Sometimes, in the nineteenth century, embroidery and crewelwork 'practice' pieces made by young girls were put aside when finished and then picked up later to be used as quilt centres. Anecdotal evidence is useful if dealing with a family quilt but it should be looked at very carefully. Without written documentation it may be difficult to establish precise details and there is often a tendency to 'mix' generations. Knowing when the quiltmaker was born and died helps establish useful guidelines, especially if this evidence is used in combination with other pointers.

Methods of Working
The 'mosaic patchwork method of sewing patchwork with papers can provide clues to dating, if the papers are still in the back of the quilt. Letters, newspapers and published announcements were often used as templates and, with a bit of luck, dates can sometimes be extracted. It is wise to remember, however, that in both the eighteenth and nineteenth centuries paper as well as fabric was in short supply and that quiltmakers squirrelled away both. Paper templates and patchwork pieces, once cut, could have lain in a workbox for some years before being used. Similarly, unquilted tops may have been pieced some years before they were quilted and finally finished. The backing fabric could, in this instance, provide the vital clue if it is patterned, since it would probably have been purchased specially for finishing. If a sewing machine was used to make the quilt – either to stitch the seams, put together the patches or finish the edges – then it is unlikely the quilt would have been made prior to 1860.

Edges
Statistical analysis of results from the Project indicate that wholecloth quilts from the North of England that date from about 1890 to the present tend to have butted and machined edges, while in Wales the tendency was for the butted edges to be hand-quilted. Quilts with bound edges appear to come from North America, while a wholecloth quilt with a frill would generally indicate a date between 1890 and 1910. Recent work has revealed that wholecloth and strippy quilts from the later nineteenth century and early twentieth century were frequently set up in the quilting frame after one side of both the top and backing fabrics were machined together. This pre-stitched edge was likely to be used as the leading edge in the frame. Once the quilt was completed the remaining edges were butted and stitched together. This stitching would continue along the pre-stitched edge as well.

Finding the Front

Look for the knots in the quilting thread if dealing with a wholecloth quilt. The side they are on should be the back, although a competent quilter should not leave any knots at all. Skipped stitches will also indicate that this is the back of the quilt, since a quilter working from the top sometimes missed needle passes. The colour of the quilting thread can provide a clue, since it was generally matched to the front fabric. It does not necessarily follow that the front of a quilt is the pieced or patchwork side. Sometimes experienced quilters laid out the quilting design and worked from the wholecloth side of the quilt instead of the pieced side. They might also have drawn the pattern on the plain side of a wholecloth quilt that is a mix of plain and print, even if they intended the print to be the top. The reason is obvious: it would have been easier to work from the plain side in both cases. Many of the older quilts are virtually reversible – a bonus to their owners.

Materials

A quilt can only be as old as the newest fabric it contains as long as this fabric was part of the original project and not a later addition to an unfinished piece or a later repair to worn fabric. Cotton sateen, a favourite fabric for wholecloth quilts, was available between 1880 and 1940. The first threads to be used for patchwork and quilting were of linen or silk. Machine-made thread first appeared about 1800 and six-ply thread suitable for machining came after 1840. Coloured cotton thread was not widely available before the middle of the nineteenth century. Although a test involving burning is often used to make a definite assessment of the type of thread used, a simpler method involves the 'twang test'. Pluck a largish quilting stitch with your fingernail and then let it go: if the resulting sound is a 'crack', then the thread is possibly linen. If there is no sound, the thread is more likely to be cotton. Not all quilts were wadded but, to decide what wadding may have been used, look for any small holes or broken edges of seam lines where the wadding may show through. The earliest quilts were wadded with wool and in some districts (particularly West Wales) it continued to be the preferred wadding. Generally, however, wool was superseded by cotton.

A quilt that is wadded with wool can be thicker and may therefore feel heavier and bouncier than one wadded with cotton. If you hold the quilt surface horizontally and level with your eye you may see the curly twists of wool fibres from the wadding which have worked through the top surface of the quilt. Cotton is also inclined to clump and bunch when washed and you can hold your quilt up to the light to see if this has happened. Look for the cotton seeds in this case – they will help confirm the type of wadding. Quilts were also filled with old and thinning woven blankets, and sometimes a collection of cut-up textile leftovers (old socks, shirts, etc.). If an old patchwork quilt has been used as the filling, blocks of brighter colours may show through the top fabric. Synthetic waddings were introduced in the 1950s.

Wholecloth quilts were marked with chalk or sometimes pencil. Often the pencil marks remain on old quilts. Elizabeth Sanderson used a blue pencil for marking her quilts and these often required several washings before the marks could be removed. Blue pencil was also in general use among other stampers. There is no evidence that blue pencil was used in Wales.

Quilting Patterns and Layout

It is possible, to some extent, to date quilting by layout and pattern. An all-over quilting pattern, where speed of completion was essential, can be found in every period. An overall pattern of clamshell or wineglass, however, would tend to be earlier – the first half of the nineteenth century. Crosshatching (also known as hanging diamond or chequer) was used throughout the years, as was patterning with parallel lines. The most obvious regional overall background pattern, the zigzag (or wave or chevron), was used in the Isle of Man and areas near the Irish Sea – in Ireland, north-west England and south-west Scotland. The 'delineated motif-and-borders' quilting layout was commonplace in Britain before 1820 and probably up until 1870, and quilting patterns were based on floral and leafy designs, with vases etc. The earliest strippy quilting layout dates from about 1820 and became very popular as time went on. The 'delineated motif-and-borders' layout continued to be preferred in Wales and the south-west of England, appearing everywhere except the north-east of England. Here the freer 'undefined motif-and-borders' layout typical of George Gardiner and Elizabeth Sanderson was developed.

The most popular quilting patterns used in Wales were the spiral (also called snail's trail, snail shell, twirl or whirl) and leaves presented in formalized variations of pointed ovals (straight, bent or elongated) or naturalistic shapes. Welsh quilts also can show a Welsh trail and church-window borders (the latter with a variety of fillings).

In north-of-England wholecloth quilts, leaves tend to be symmetrical. Feathers are a particular feature, having started about 1870-80. At about this same time, freehand floral designs or scrolling, used by George Gardiner and Elizabeth Sanderson, were introduced. International design styles such as Art Nouveau and Art Deco seem to have completely bypassed traditional quilters except in the making of cushions, tea cosies, etc. These were produced from commercially made transfers in corded (trapunto) quilting and reflected contemporary embroidery patterns. Aside from the influence of these movements, other corded quilting was popular between 1700 and 1800.

Patchwork Patterns

The geometric shape most often used in British quiltmaking was the square, followed by the hexagon and the diamond. Hexagons and diamonds were used frequently in all-over layouts and individual pieces were tacked over papers before being oversewn together. Recent work suggests that the most common patchwork shape from the eighteenth century is the half-square triangle and the equal-sided, equal-angled hexagon was not popular until later in that century.

Because of the tendency to work geometric shapes either in a frame or all-over pattern layout, the wide development of different block patterns with special names never developed in Britain as it did in the United States. Patterns, however, were simple: four-patch, nine-patch, Churn Dash (American term) or triangles. However, the Log Cabin block was used in Britain quite extensively – especially in Scotland and the Isle of Man – and some quilt historians, such as Averil Colby, have suggested that this form of strip patchwork can be traced back to the eighteenth century. Later historians have been unable to find examples before the second quarter of the nineteenth century however. In Wales, where block patchwork was sometimes used, colours tended to be dark because of the use of woollen fabrics

Crazy patchwork, with its embroidery and other embellishments, was at its heyday between 1860 and 1880 but continued into the early twentieth century.

'Manipulated' fabrics also appeared in British patchwork. Examples included the Suffolk puff in the late nineteenth century, the gathered patchwork pieces of the Edwardian era and folded patchwork pieces in the 1870s and 1880s. Fans appeared as a pattern about the same time but the Dresden Plate of the 1930s, with its sugar pink and pale green colours, is American in origin.

Turkey Red and Appliqué

The use of non-fading Turkey Red and white was a popular combination in British quilts, from about 1870 until about 1910. It appeared in piecing – in Irish chain and basket quilts – and was also used for wholecloth and strippy quilts. The appliqué of red on white was also popular, particularly the technique of folding and cutting patterns (snowflake style). The era of green and red appliqué on white began in the early 1900s in the north-east of England, and was influenced by appliqué styles in America.

Broderie Perse, a much older form of appliqué, was practised with a variety of embroidery stitches: invisible, buttonhole and herringbone. The herringbone stitch was most often used in Britain.

SELECTED READING

Allan, Rosemary. *Quilts and Coverlets from Beamish Museum* (North of England Open-Air Museum), Stanley, Co. Durham, 1987.

Allan, Rosemary. *Quilts and Coverlets: The Beamish Collections*. Stanley, Beamish Museum Co., 2007.

Bower, Helen. *Textiles at Temple Newsam*. Leeds, Leeds Museums and Galleries, 2000.

Brackman, Barbara. *Clues in the Calico: A Guide to Identifying and Dating Quilts*. McLean, Va., EMP Publications, Inc., 1989.

Caulfeild, S.F.A. and Saward, Blanche W. *The Dictionary of Needlework*. London, L. Upcott Gill, 1887.

Clabburn, Pamela. *The Needleworker's Dictionary*. New York, William Morrow & Co., 1976.

Colby, Averil. *Patchwork*. London, Batsford, 1958.

Colby, Averil. *Patchwork Quilts*. London, Batsford, 1965.

Colby, Averil. *Quilting*. London, Batsford, 1972.

Crill, Rosemary. *Chintz: Indian Textiles for the West*. London, V&A Publishing, 2008.

FitzRandolph, Mavis. *Traditional Quilting*. London, Batsford, 1954.

Garfield, Simon. *Mauve: How one man invented a colour that changed the world*. London, Faber and Faber, 2000.

Glazier, R. *Historic Textile Fabrics*. London, Batsford, 1923.

Hake, Elizabeth. *English Quilting Old and New*. London, Batsford, 1937.

Head, Carol. *Old Sewing Machines*. Aylesbury, Shire Publications, 1982.

Hefford, Wendy. *The Victoria and Albert Museum's Textile Collection Design for Printed Textiles in England from 1750-1850*. London, Victoria & Albert Museum, 1992.

Jenkins, M and Claridge C. *Making Welsh Quilts: The Textile Tradition that Inspired the Amish?* Newton Abbot, David & Charles Ltd., 2005.

Jones, Jen. *Welsh Quilts*. Towy Publishing, 1997.

Long, Bridget. *The Quilters' Guild Collection: Contemporary Quilts Heritage Inspiration.*

Newton Abbot, David & Charles Ltd., 2005.

Montgomery, Florence M. *Textiles in America 1650-1870*. New York and London, W.W. Norton & Co., 1984.

Montgomery, Florence M. *Printed Textiles: English and American Cottons and Linens 1700-1850*. London, Thames & Hudson, 1970.

Naylor, Barrie. *Quakers in the Rhondda 1926-1986*. Chepstow, Gwent, Maes-yr-Haf Educational Trust, 1986.

Notes on Applied Work and Patchwork. London, HMSO, 1949.

Notes on Quilting. London, HMSO, 1949.

O'Connor, Deryn, and Granger-Taylor, Hero. *Colour and the Calico Printer* (exhibition catalogue), Farnham, West Surrey College of Art & Design, 1982.

Osler, Dorothy. *Traditional British Quilts*. London, Batsford, 1987.

Osler, Dorothy. *North Country Quilts: Legend and Living Tradition*. Barnard Castle, Bowes Museum, 2000.

Parry, Linda. *A Practical Guide to Patchwork from the Victoria and Albert Collection*. London, Unwin, 1987.

Parry, Linda. *Textiles of the Arts and Crafts Movement*. London, Thames & Hudson, 1988.

Pettit, Florence. *American Indigo Blues: Resist Printed and Dyed Textiles of the 18th Century*. New York, Hastings House, 1974.

Prichard, Sue. *Quilts 1700-2010: Hidden Histories Untold Stories*. London, Victoria & Albert Museum, 2010.

Priestley, Ursula. *The Fabric of Stuffs: The Norwich Textile Industry from 1565*. Norwich, The Centre for East Anglian Studies, UEA, 1990.

Quilt Studies: The Journal of the British Quilt Study Group (The Quilters' Guild of the British Isles) Issues 1-11, 1999-2010.

Rae, Janet. *The Quilts of the British Isles*. London, Constable; New York, E. P. Dutton, 1987.

Rae, Janet and Travis, Dinah. *Making Connections: Around the World with Log Cabin*. Chartham, Kent, R T Publishing, 2004.

Robinson, Stuart. *A History of Printed Textiles.*

London, Studio Vista, 1969.

Robinson, Stuart. *A History of Dyed Textiles*. London, Studio Vista, 1969.

Rose, Clare. 'Corded Quilting and the World of Fashion' in Quilters' Review, *The Quilter*. The Quilters' Guild, Summer, 1993.

Rothstein, Natalie (ed.). *Barbara Johnson's Album of Fashions and Fabrics*. London, Victoria & Albert Museum and Thames & Hudson, 1987.

Schoeser, Mary, and Rufey, Celia. *English and American Textiles from 1790 to the Present*. London, Thames & Hudson, 1989.

Sheppard, Josie. *Through the Needle's Eye: The Patchwork and Quilt Collection at York Castle Museum (exhibition catalogue)*. York, York Museums Trust, 2004.

Silk and Rayon Users' Association Inc. *The Silk Book*. London, 1951.

Stevens, Christine. *Quilts*. Gomer Press in association with the National Museum of Wales. Llandysul, Dyfed, 1993.

Storey, Joyce. *Textile Printing*. London, Thames & Hudson, 1974.

Sykas, Philip. *The Secret Life of Textiles: Six Pattern Book Archives in North West England*, Bolton, Bolton Museums, 2005.

Tozer, Jane and Levitt, Sarah. *Fabric of Society: A Century of People and their Clothes 1770-1870*, Powys, Laura Ashley Ltd., 1983.

Turner, Mark, and Lesley Hoskins. *Silver Studio of Design*. London, Webb & Bower with Michael Joseph, 1988.

Thomas, Mary. *Dictionary of Embroidery Stitches*. London, Hodder & Stoughton, 1936.

Warner, Pamela. *Embroidery, a History*. London, Batsford, 1991.

The Victoria & Albert Museum. *Flowers in English Embroidery*. London, HMSO, 1947.

The Victoria & Albert Colour Books. Patterns for Textiles. Devon and London, Webb & Bower Ltd., The Trustees of the Victoria & Albert Museum, 1987.

The Victoria & Albert Colour Books. Rococo Silks. Devon and London, Webb & Bower Ltd., The Trustees of the Victoria & Albert Museum, 1985.

INDEX